"Albert H. Epp has given us an outstanding handbook on the greatest problem of the church today: making disciples of our children and our converts. The book shows how essential discipleship is for obedience to Christ and for the growth and maturity of the church. At once intensely practical as well as fascinating reading, this book shows how discipling ought to be done."

Kenneth S. Kantzer (Ph.D.), Deerfield, IL
Professor, Trinity Evangelical Divinity School
Senior Editor, *Christianity Today*

"This exciting book can revitalize any congregation. Its masterful challenge moves us to faith and fruit-bearing. Once working with men, Epp has successfully transferred his discipling methodology to working with women as well."

Jeanne Zook (R.N.) Portland, OR
Director of Nursing Education

"Epp's many years of experience in discipling and his wide reading in the field give him an extraordinary command of the subject. His tested principles are distinctly developed, succinctly stated, and richly resourced. They move a reader from theory to practice."

Levi Keidel (M.S., M.A.), Fort Wayne, IN
Author, veteran missionary, college instructor.

"Dr. Epp contends that conversion and church membership are the starting line, not the finish. He cites statistics on American church-goers and societal changes to document his thesis. Based completely in the Gospels, the book outlines 50 discipleship factors with practical applications every step of the way. Here are back-to-basics principles which can change lives."

Dr. David Mains
Radio director: The Chapel of the Air
Author: *8 Survival Skills for Changing Times* (Victor)

"I recommend this book for study and urge its use by congregations to engage the membership in a life together in the Spirit of Christ." (see the Foreword)

Myron S. Augsburger (Th.D.)
President: Christian College Coalition
Author: *The Christ-Shaped Conscience* (Victor)

"Albert Epp has given his vocational life to what the church needs: help in caring for converts. His biblical methodology has been 'tested in the trenches.' A well-crafted book: it's timely, it's usable, it's readable. Its twelve-topic division is geared to the quarterly rhythm of classes or groups, and excellent discussion questions conclude each chapter."

Donald R. Jacobs (Ph.D.), Landisville, PA
Director: Mennonite Christian Leadership Foundation
Author: *Pilgrimage in Mission* (Herald)

"Biblically, evangelism and discipleship fit together like two blades of a scissors. Albert Epp has presented a strong theological case for both. Well researched and well documented, this book is spiced with delightful anecdotes. Epp subtly scratches a lot of itches! I commend it to all believers who want to be true disciples."

Dr. Ted Engstrom, Monrovia, CA
President Emeritus, World Vision
Author: *The Fine Art of Friendship* (Nelson)

"As a seminary instructor and pastor, I found many resources centering on individual discipleship, but few which focused on leadership training within the context of the church. I see Epp's book as filling that void. Healthy discipleship is church-centered, a corporate process."

Larry Martens (Ph.D.), Fresno, CA
Past president, Mennonite Brethren Biblical Seminary
Author: *Life With Promise* (Kindred)

DISCIPLESHIP
THERAPY

Other books by author:

The Golden Stairway Discipleship Course (Revised-1990)
The Golden Stairway Discipleship Leader's Guide (Revised-1990)
How-To-Do-It Cassette (50 minutes)

Available from: Stairway Discipleship Inc.
                  P. O. Box D
                  Henderson, NE 68371

DISCIPLESHIP THERAPY

Healthy Christians — Healthy Churches

Albert H. Epp

Stairway Discipleship Inc.
Henderson, Nebraska 68371

Discipleship Therapy: Healthy Christians, Healthy Churches
Copyright © 1993 by Stairway Discipleship Inc.

Published by Stairway Discipleship Inc., Henderson, NE
Printed in the United States by Mennonite Press, Inc., Newton, KS

Library of Congress Cataloging-in-Publication Data

Catalog No. 93-85797

Epp, Albert H., 1931- Discipleship Therapy: Healthy Christians, Healthy
    Churches / Albert H. Epp

      p.   cm.

ISBN 0-9638185-7-0

1. Pastoral Theology. 2. Discipling (Christianity).
3. Christian Life-Mennonite Authors I. Title

CONTENTS

Foreword by Myron Augsburger XI
Author's Preface XIII

1. The Crippled Church 1
2. Following the Master 10
3. Counting the Cost 34
4. Born For Eternity 58
5. Fishing For People 82
6. Showing Good Works 106
7. Living By Prayer 130
8. Forgiving Without Limits 154
9. Giving With Generosity 178
10. Building Reconciling Relationships 202
11. The Healthy Church 226
12. The Committed Christian 252

Guide for Discussion Leaders 264
Notes 266
Name Index 275

50 Discipleship Factors

1. The Crippled Church
2. Following the Master   Page
    No. 1 Relational 12
        No. 2 Self-Denial 17
            No. 3 Loyalty 21
                No. 4 Obedience 24
3. Counting the Cost   No. 5 Reward 28
    No. 6 Opposition 36
        No. 7 Family-Loyalty 40
            No. 8 Paying-the-Price 44
                No. 9 Planning-Ahead 48
4. Born For Eternity   No. 10 Consecration 51
    No. 11 Estrangement 60
        No. 12 Supernatural 64
            No. 13 Incarnation 67
                No. 14 Belief 71
5. Fishing For People   No. 15 Conversion 75
    No. 16 Fishing 84
        No. 17 Acceptance 88
            No. 18 Commission 92
                No. 19 Sensitivity 96
6. Showing Good Works   No. 20 Banquet 100
    No. 21 Salt 108
        No. 22 Light 111
            No. 23 Love 115
                No. 24 Child 119
7. Living By Prayer   No. 25 Servant 123
    No. 26 Model 132
        No. 27 Intercessory 136
            No. 28 Power 140
                No. 29 Guidelines 144
8. Forgiving Without Limits   No. 30 Transmitting 147
    No. 31 Love-One-Another 156
        No. 32 Turned-Cheek/Second-Mile 160
            No. 33 Forgive 70-X-7 164
                No. 34 Love-Your-Enemy 168
9. Giving With Generosity   No. 35 The Process. 172
    No. 36 Management 180
        No. 37 Firstfruits 184
            No. 38 Emulation 188
                No. 39 Motivation 192
10. Reconciling Relationships   No. 40 Reciprocal 196
    No. 41 Golden Rule 204
        No. 42 Christlike-Spirit 208
            No. 43 Hostility-Control 211
                No. 44 Reconciliation 215
11. The Healthy Church   No. 45 Transformed 219
    No. 46 Accountability 228
        No. 47 Strategy 232
            No. 48 Educational 236
                No. 49 Hands-On Training 240
12. The Committed Christian   No. 50 Liberation 245

FOREWORD

"**N**o one knows Christ truly unless he follows him daily in life, and no one can follow him in life unless he knows him truly." This sixteenth century position statement is at the heart of this book. We are called by God in grace, called into relationship, and in this solidarity with Christ, we live out the new life.

The author's emphasis on the new life in Christ is a witness to a deep faith in God's transforming grace. This is a relevant word in times in which our acculturated religion is expressed in what Dietrich Bonhoeffer called "cheap grace." We need to recognize that God not only has forgiving grace but also transforming grace. When one is "in Christ" that person is a new creation.

Theologically, this book is built on a high Christology. Discipleship is always a matter of being disciples of Christ. And Jesus does not graduate his disciples. This Christology also answers the old, outmoded doctrinal questions of how we relate faith and obedience in our lifestyles. As disciples, we relate ethics to Christology in the same way in which we relate salvation to Christology. To put it another way, we are saved in relation to Jesus, and we "behave" our relation to Jesus!

This also overcomes the unfortunate separation made between evangelism and social responsibility. Discipleship not only prepares one for evangelism; discipleship is evangelistic. From my perspective of over forty years of pastoral/evangelistic/educational/urban ministry, I have found that evangelism is everything which makes faith in Christ a possibility for a person. Authentic evangelism is very demanding intellectually. It is not mediocre communication, but it is even more demanding in living out the life of love.

In a practical, down-to-earth way, Albert Epp has written for the congregation. His many quotes and anecdotes make it both interesting and insightful. He calls us to ministry. We find in these pages an elaboration on Paul's words to the Ephesians, that our ascended Lord has given gifts to his followers "for the perfecting of the saints for the work of ministry" (Ephesians 4:12).

I recommend this book for study and the disciplines of discipleship in the community of faith. I would urge its use by the congregation to engage the membership in a life together in the Spirit of Christ. In our increasingly pluralistic society, we need to understand more clearly the core of our own faith, but we also need to understand how to listen, relate to, and present Jesus to others. We are not called to judgmentally put others down in this form of religion, rather we are called to lift Jesus higher. As John wrote succinctly, "The one who has the Son has life, and the one who has not the Son has not life" (1 John 5:12).

Myron S. Augsburger (Th.D.)
President: Christian College Coalition
Washington D.C.
May, 1993

AUTHOR'S PREFACE

Churches in America often resemble hospitals—with only maternity wards—and no subsequent care. "Getting people in" gets the big push; but spiritual formation or convert-care is sadly neglected. Discipleship on the Jesus-Pathway is costly, time-consuming and requires commitment. But its rewards are many.

Mainline churches view Christian education as a children's enterprise, while evangelical churches don't assume adequate spiritual-parenthood for their converts. There is all too much hit-and-run evangelism. Again, Jesus is a pattern—he "discipled" his converts! Jesus was the Master-Discipler.

In my brotherhood, fifty years ago H. S. Bender reduced his "Anabaptist Vision" to three key ideas (Christianity as discipleship, church in community, love is nonresistant). In the decades that followed, we have had a stronger emphasis on human behavior (on doing) than on divine transformation (on being). Stephen Dintaman of Eastern Mennonite College, in a published essay entitled, "The Spiritual Poverty of the Anabaptist Vision" has observed that Bender himself, nonetheless, was drawing on a reservoir of basic evangelical doctrines pertaining to the cross, resurrection and Pentecost which we often overlook. So at times we fail to appropriate fully the forgiveness of the cross, or the formative power of the Holy Spirit—both essential to a supernatural ethic or to any effective evangelism. Simply put: our lack of empathy and patience in dealing with persons struggling with sin may reflect too much self-reliance. Basically, salvation is by God's iniative and requires his enabling grace.

No formal bibliography is included in this book. However, a hundred books helped shape this book. A perusal of the endnotes gets the reader in touch with a wealth of reading resources. Many of these I highly recommend. This book includes many true stories; but in many cases, actual names are changed to conceal the identity of persons.

A special word of thanks goes to a corp of friends who read certain chapters early on and gave valuable feedback: Myron Augsburger, Levi Keidel, Donald Jacobs, John Drescher, Angela and Erwin Rempel, David Garber, Raymond Frey, Daniel Kauffman, Larry Martens, Sylvia Epp, Linda Goertzen, Doris Kroeker, Donald Wall, Harold W. Kroeker and David Quiring. In the long run no one gave more editorial assistance than did Levi Keidel.

The book endorsements, given by ten persons who had access to the whole manuscript, were humbly and gratefully received. My heart was indeed warmed by this outpouring of affirmation by these Christian brothers and sisters!

The Board of Directors for Stairway Discipleship Inc. stood by with prayers and every conceivable form of assistance—while this book was being written. The encouragement and help this board gave cannot be overstated. Without their support this endeavor would have failed.

But no one stood by more faithfully—unwavering in confidence—than my wife, Susan Joann. From day one, she believed that our development of discipleship resources for the churches of America was our most significant God-given task. All of my preaching, teaching and counseling over the years, never compared to the impact we made on lives as we discipled 128 men at our house during the decade of the 80s. Following the example of the Master-Discipler, we discipled persons by twelves, and in the process stumbled into a technique that's 2000 years old; yet one that is relevant, effective and powerful.

— Albert H. Epp

Chapter

1

The Crippled Church

Perhaps 98 percent of American churches would welcome you as member—warmly and enthusiastically—if you fulfilled this fourfold caricature. You might even be eligible for any office in the church or any position of ministry.

Take a Stand, Shake a Hand,
Say a Prayer, Sign Right There.

Don't misunderstand me. Once, as a teenager in my home congregation on the prairies of Kansas, I took a stand in a moving act of dedication; it shaped the rest of my life. A pastor's handshake can be warmly affirming. A true penitent's prayer rings the bells of heaven (Luke 15:7); it is an admission pass at that celestial gate. And, signing a name is a truly accountable act. But speaking bluntly, church entrance standards show an all-time low. This infirmity is widespread. In fact, some churches require nothing beyond a handshake or a signature.This is only symptomatic of a whole array of concerns. We will enumerate six.

Concern No. 1 Graduation or Induction?

In daily life when a widespread disorder strikes children, we finally check the conditions under which they were born. Take the entry-point into a church: (1) a Lutheran girl expresses faith by fulfilling her church's requirements for Confirmation; (2) a Baptist teen requests baptism after accepting Christ in response to an altar call; (3) a Mennonite young person, after a year of catechism, professes his or her faith in Christ and follows him in baptism; or (4) an adult might affiliate with a Methodist church (or, Presbyterian, or some other) after an orientation session. Always, the event is seen as something to "celebrate."

Whenever ardent denominationalists view that ceremony as a "graduation," and member-families heave a sigh of relief that their loved ones are "now in the fold;" the church is defeated. The Early Church viewed this experience as an **INDUCTION** (Acts 2:42). It was the grand beginning of learning and sharing and serving. It was the starting line, not the finish.

Symbols of religious orientation are not without significance, but they can become substitutes for the real. People's answers to the question, "Are you a Christian?" quickly separate the authentic from the ostensible. Here are examples of the latter: (1) Well-uh, I was catechized and baptized by Pastor Pete; or (2) When at Grandpa's in Iowa I was confirmed; or (3) I got a perfect Sunday School attendance certificate; or (4) I went to the altar when Evangelist Eddie was here; or (5) I joined the church on Easter Sunday.

A superficial religious inoculation can actually immunize one against genuine faith. Have we really met Jesus Christ? Have we trusted his atoning sacrifice for our forgiveness? Have we surrendered our core of selfishness to his Lordship? Have we handed over our control-panels of living? Have we pondered the price for contemporary discipleship—the price of true faithfulness?

The bottom line: did that Sunday worship experience really "take?" Am I a different person on Monday and Tuesday—one who wants to read the Bible, feels like praying, has a new desire to help others, desires to serve Jesus, enjoys fellowship with Christians, whose life counts for God? Jesus once said, "Why do you call me, 'Lord, Lord,' and do not what I say" (Luke 6:46)? Salvation, beyond forgiveness, means walking in newness.

Concern No. 2 Crippled by Poor Health

Christianity in North America lacks good health. It can be called anemic, asthmatic, arthritic, or worse. Many churches are debilitated by diseases. According to Lyle Schaller, eight North American congregations die each day. He suggests that "...if the death rate due to curable diseases could be cut in half, and new life could be breathed into these sick churches, the saving would amount to at least $70 million annually."[1] (Remember that starting a new church costs between $50,000 and $250,000.) Churches of the USA and Canada never needed the Great Physician more than now.

Authorities are addressing the problem. Schools and denominations are training persons to diagnose the health of churches, and to prescribe the needed correctives. In the book, *Your Church Can Be Healthy,* C. Peter Wagner lists seven vital signs. Heading the list are good pastoral leadership and, secondly, a well-mobilized laity where spiritual gifts are discerned, developed and deployed.

This book is easy to read. Its uniqueness lies in the author's attempt to explain church pathology and actually label eight specific illnesses.[2] Two are terminal: Ethnikitis and Old Age. Ethnikitis is the urban case where the church becomes an island encircled by people of other ethnic backgrounds. "Old Age" is often a rural case where people move away, and the church dwindles to nothing. To me this book is valuable for the case studies of churches that creatively overcame unspeakable odds—churches that changed the seemingly impossible.

According to Wagner, six church sicknesses are curable. We will mention three: (1) Fellowship-Sickness. This is such an overdose of enjoying each other's company that the circle of friendship excludes new people. So church growth is inhibited. (2) Strangulation-Sickness. Such churches grow so rapidly that people must compete for a spot in the parking lot or for a seat in the sanctuary. (3) Arrested Spiritual Development. This creeping disease leaves churches introverted, self-seeking, and stagnant. Causes vary. One is that many members are not "born again." It is difficult to nurture a life that has never been born.

The Barna Research Group discovered that over half (52%) of those who attend church do not claim to be born again.[3] (In the United States four out of ten adults attend on any given Sunday. Of the 40% who attend, half attend every week, while one-fourth attend at least once a month, and the rest less.)[4]

Why don't more purport to be born again? To this writer, two plausible ideas flash into mind. First, some may never have accepted Jesus Christ as Lord and Savior (using evangelical terminology), and simply lack salvation-assurance. So these become a vast mission field within the church—persons that need to be evangelized. Secondly, others may be confused in their theological thinking. Those biblically illiterate may be unaware that the Bible uses terms like believer, born-again-one, disciple, or follower synonymously to designate the normal Christian.

Concern No. 3 Education: Low Dosage Exposure

With women entering the work force in unprecedented numbers, the pool from which churches draw their volunteers is shrinking rapidly. This not only affects the service areas of the church; it powerfully impacts the staff available for educational services. In many churches, people recruiting Sunday School or Christian education teachers are harried, discouraged and exhausted.

However, few perceive the depth of the crisis. Search Institute conducted a 3-year study on "Effective Christian Education." The project, unprecedented in size, compared 20 million members in five "mainline" denominations with 15 million members of the Southern Baptist Convention. The findings are startling, even appalling! "...Christian education ends for most Protestants at the 9th grade...."[5] In general, educational work at churches is viewed as an enterprise designed to benefit children.

According to the study, Christian education gave adults and adolescents a "low dosage exposure" of about 30-40 hours **per YEAR,** at best. Where adults asked for more, churches likely could not deliver. Research directors Peter Benson and Carolyn

Eklin gave their impression: "Christian education matters much more than we expected. Of all the areas of congregational life we examined, involvement in an effective Christian education program has the strongest tie to a person's growth in faith and loyalty to one's congregation and denomination. While other congregational factors also matter, nothing matters more than effective Christian education."[6] These findings are published precisely as Sunday School work lags everywhere.

Concern No. 4 Men Need Special Assistance

The Search Institute found that many more women than men displayed a mature integrated faith. Men need special attention by those shaping church strategy and programs. In my pastoral experience I found the same to be true. In the church, men more often than women are dysfunctional in faith and practice. They especially lack opportunity for peer group growth, sharing or involvement.

While the general population is about 53 percent female and 47 percent male, the male participation in many churches is declining. Often the attendance ratio is 60 percent female and 40 percent male. Some even have a 65-35 ratio. Observes the noted parish consultant, Lyle Schaller—the recent consideration of some Methodists, Lutherans and Presbyterians "...to place a legal ceiling on male participation may not turn out to be an effective means of reversing this trend."[7] Schaller's book is worth reading. He lists eighteen qualities which attract men to churches. He gives observations which the average church needs to heed!

Concern No. 5 Hush! Don't Mention Money

Because we believe our country bulges with affluence, statistics by the Social Security Administration startle us. Some 85 out of 100 Americans have less than $250 in savings when they reach age 65.[8] By world standards, we are wealthy. By biblical standards, we have a crisis in money-management. Anabaptist sociologists, J. Howard Kauffman and Leo Driedger, notice a negative correlation between urbanization (also education) and giving. Their conclusion is on target, "...an emphasis on tithing, or other emphases on giving will be necessary to prevent further decline in proportional giving."[9]

In my first parish, missionary J. Arthur Mouw held our congregation spellbound as he told of pioneer work among the Dyaks of Borneo. He taught them until late at night—by candle-light. Hundreds accepted the Gospel. One day God urged him to teach tithing, and about the "windows of heaven" (Malachi 3:10). He balked, "Lord, these people are too poor!" The Holy Spirit persisted. As Mouw taught, people brought eggs, chickens, ears of corn and rice. These were traded for materials to build a church. As hundreds of Dyaks began tithing, immeasurable blessings descended, both spiritually and economically.

At times, tithing is seen as (1) strictly Old Testament, (2) theologically fundamentalistic, and (3) psychologically damaging to family harmony. After all, why add a burden to an already-stressed family budget. So in Borneo, people looked too poor to tithe; in North America they appear too rich (or too debt-encumbered) to tithe! This book will illustrate that our family (from my grandfather to my sons) has "tested" God, as the scriptures suggest. As a consequence, we believe in firstfruits tithing, and are committed for life, out of love for Christ.

Concern No. 6 Watering Down Discipleship

Finally, I come to my prime concern—biblical discipleship. My farm roots make the words of Joe Aldrich picturesque: "I guess I'm tired of watching human rodeos—people herded into corrals, dehorned, vaccinated, branded, and put out to pasture. High-speed, short-term, results-oriented: we have turned the mechanics of ministry into the ministry itself."[10] I, too, weary of seeing "cultural Christianity" water down discipleship ideas into a blurred assembly line process.

Earlier in the Twentieth Century, God raised up voices to call the church to discipleship: Episcopalian Samuel Shoemaker,

Quaker Elton Trueblood, Methodist E. Stanley Jones, Catholic Bishop Fulton Sheen, Lutheran Dietrich Bonhoeffer, Christian and Missionary Alliance A. W. Tozer, and Mennonite Harold S. Bender, to name a few.

In our day, no one states the case more succinctly than the Southern Baptist professor, Dallas Willard. While critics cite many reasons why churches do not more effectively impact societal problems, Willard insists that liberals and conservatives have one big thing in common. "For different reasons, and with different emphases, they have agreed that discipleship to Christ is optional to membership in the Christian church. Thus the very type of life that could change the course of human society—and upon occasion has done so—is excluded from the essential message of the church."[11] Willard uses the metaphor of car buying.

A car buyer chooses from options: stereo, air bag, white-wall tires, painted pin-stripes, rear defogger, sun-roof and a score of other items. First, there is the basic car, then the extras. "The disciple of Jesus is not the deluxe or heavy-duty model of the Christian—especially padded, textured, streamlined, and empowered for the fast lane on the straight and narrow way. He stands on the pages of the New Testament as the first level of basic transportation in the Kingdom of God."[12] New Testament discipleship is the basic irreducible model. Its kind of Christianity and current religious models are, at times, far apart.

Herein then resides the primary concern of this book—discipleship with a capital "D." Costly as commitment is, it alone will lead the church to greater effectiveness and fruitfulness. We do not seek successfulness, in the modern sense, but faithfulness in the biblical sense.

This study limits itself to the life and teachings of Jesus as found in the Gospels. At the core, this book has ten chapters which contain fifty discipleship factors, and these are by no means exhaustive. (Vast important areas remain untouched.) These 50 themes draw on scripture, highlighted by the caption: Light on the Pathway. This composite offers a glimpse of God's heartbeat in his eternal kingdom. In turn, we get a clearer view of the Jesus-Pathway of discipleship.

Much good material has been written in our day. However, an avalanche of books may be needed before the urgency of renewal dawns on a beleaguered church. I am humbly grateful to God for this opportunity to add my voice in this crisis hour of need in God's kingdom.

Questions for Discussion:

1. What do you think is the number one problem in the church?
2. This chapter lists 6 concerns. To you, which 2 are the most important?
3. What other concerns would you add to this list?
4. Who are most neglected in your church—youth, women or men?

PRACTICING HIS PRESENCE: DEVOTIONAL PAUSE FOR BUSY DISCIPLES
Theme of the week — The Crippled Church

	Monday	Tuesday	Wednesday	Thursday	Friday
Light on the pathway	Matthew 11:28-30	Mark 2:15-17	Luke 6:39-40	Matthew 6:31-34	John 15:14-17
Lesson for this day	Concern #1 Inducted	Concern #2 Crippled	Concern #3/4 Educated	Concern #5 Assisted	Concern #6 Discipled
Life in Jesus' way	Take time to pray	Take time to pray	Take time to pray	Take time to pray	Take time to pray

PRACTICE HIS PRESENCE IN CHURCH ON SUNDAY

Chapter

2

Following the Master

1. Relational
2. Self-Denial
3. Loyalty
4. Obedience
5. Reward

Introduction

If European Christianity gave the American church birth, European history may now be writing the American church's epitaph. A Methodist tourist from Kansas, visiting the quaint old Swedish church of his ancestors, found only ten of the 850 members at Sunday worship.

Church planters in France, like my nephew, speak the language fluently, but find a meager response. John Duerksen, a social worker, spent his junior high years in Germany. His father was a church pastoral relief worker there. While living in Mainz they attended an "evangelical" house church. John's classmate remarked, "You go to church each week. We only go when we feel the need." Actually, many Europeans attend church only on high holidays. One comic has joked: people go to church thrice in a lifetime, once they walk in and twice they're carried in—at their baptism, wedding and funeral!

As in Europe, so in America, a church can boast 850 members (or, 8500)! But are members active? Chuck Mylander, helping four Friends churches in California, invented a term: "Composite Membership"—adding membership roster, worship attendees, and Sunday School attendees, divided by three—thus involvement is tested.

The uniqueness of the American scenario (1750-1950), as regards religion, is spelled out by Franklin H. Littell in *From State Church To Pluralism*. It's unprecedented—the influx of members, the giving of dollars, and the deployment of missionaries. Revivalism swept millions into the churches; however, adequate catechetical instruction was missing. America's hope of escaping the religious blight of Europe hinges on a single requisite: discipling **WITHIN** the church!

I recall my Nebraska parish—one of the largest of our denomination. The women clearly excelled in their zeal, prayer, service and spiritual concern. Many men, however, were varyingly dysfunctional: (1) unable to communicate spiritual truths to spouse and children, (2) insecure in their commitment to Jesus, (3) uneducated on stewardship, (4) fearful of praying in front of others, and (5) lacking enthusiasm for the work of their church.

In my tradition, Harold S. Bender articulated our faith and saw Christianity as discipleship, a "following" as Jesus stated, "Whoever serves me must follow me" (John 12:26). It is a voluntary following, to be sure, but very deliberate. Church vitality is never accidental "by hook or by crook." Hans Denck, a Swiss Brethren (1527) said, "No one may truly know Christ except he follow him in life." Sound discipleship is intentional, it claims ownership to one's behavior.

First, we look at Jesus and the way he recruited his disciples for his work in the Kingdom of God. The relationships he built were intense; he demanded (1) a surrender of self, (2) a loyalty that supersedes all loyalties, and (3) an unconditional obedience. And finally, we pinpoint the rewards which Jesus promised to those who would thus follow him.

01. the **RELATIONAL** *factor*

How did Jesus enlist his followers? He placed a volunteer sign up sheet in the synagogue of Nazareth, right? No, a thousand times—NO. He busied himself with personal recruitment in the flow of everyday life. Jesus modeled how to build relationships for God and the church: befriending and winning. Jesus taught, touched, healed, prayed, cared, wept, and sympathized. By so doing, he won 120 disciples who eventually gathered at Pentecost (Acts 1:15).

RECRUITMENT MODEL NO. 1 (JOHN 1:29-51)
Light on the Pathway (John 1:38-39)

...Jesus...asked, "What do you want?" They said..."where are you staying?" "Come...and you will see." So they went and...spent that day with him....

In John chapter one Jesus enlisted his first five followers. John the Baptist encouraged two of his followers to switch to Jesus. They did, and Jesus took them home for the rest of the day. Then Andrew got Peter, Jesus recruited Philip, and Philip in turn brought Nathaniel.

What a striking corrective for the hit-and-run evangelism of our era. We rush into people's lives, win a commitment, and rush out without assuming any responsibility. We sneak nervous glances at the clock when persons stay 30 minutes. We protect our schedules. How refreshing, then, to see Jesus hosting at home his first two followers. Jesus modeled healthy convert-care.

A second lesson—Andrew and Philip each brought a friend to Jesus. It is easily demonstrated that converts who anchor into a typical church have less and less contact with non-Christian people. All Christians are to have the role of being witnesses; nonetheless, Church Growth experts surmise that only ten percent of Christians have the gift of evangelism. Therefore it is crucial for new Christians to use old relationships for immediate evangelism.

Peter Wagner, in a class lecture, told of the conversion of a 32-year-old Albuquerque barmaid. First, she changed jobs, but sent special cards of invitation to former bar friends to attend her church baptismal service. They came and filled two pews. They attended the reception following at the house of a friend. In the first year eight of these accepted Christ. This lady matured and busied herself in the church; but her outreach slowly dwindled to almost nothing.

RECRUITMENT MODEL NO. 2 (MATTHEW 4:18-22)
Light on the Pathway (Matthew 4:19)

"Come follow me," Jesus said, "and I will make you fishers of men."

Three of the fishermen were part of the previous disciple enlistment, six to eight months earlier. So this call to evangelism and training was a confirmation, a kind of encouragement (See "Fishing Factor," Chapter Five).

Jesus went to places of employment. His recruitment was relational and he left nothing to chance. He made things happen as all good leaders do! When I recruited 12 people for a Professional Discipleship Group I visited a bank, a school, professional offices and some homes. I met people where they were. A United Brethren pastor (Flint, Michigan) had a clever idea. From his discipleship group, he chose one person per week, for a lunch at work. His disciples loved it.

RECRUITMENT MODEL NO. 3 (LUKE 6:12-16)
Light on the Pathway (Luke 6:12-13)

...Jesus...spent the night praying to God. When morning came, he called his disciples to him and chose twelve of them, whom he...designated apostles....

At first, a reader supposes this to be the initial contact. Careful study reveals otherwise. This is one and a half years (or more) into Jesus' ministry. He chose his Twelve from a whole band of followers. According to Mark, "He appointed twelve...that they might be with him and that he might send them out to preach and to have authority to drive out demons" (3:14-15). In hopes of delegating his earthly ministry to this little bunch, he spent quality time in teaching, training and nurturing. Basic to discipleship are long-term relationships.

A Sunday School teacher with less prayer, less planning, and less patience than Jesus, once suggested we lop off the names of the irregulars in her class! She thought their absence proved disinterest. Just think: we might have dropped a Martin Luther or a Menno Simons, a Billy Graham or a Mother Teresa, a Rebecca Pippert or a Donald McGavran. That teacher made no home visits.

The biblical concept of the priesthood of all believers was revived during the Protestant Reformation. In my lifetime, books like: *A Theology of the Laity* by Hendrik Kraemer, triggered off voluminous writings on equipping laypersons. Since then, thousands of sermons have expounded from Ephesians 4, placing the work of ministry in the lap of Mr. and Mrs. Church Member.

Some parachurch groups excel in mobilizing laypersons for small-group leading, one-on-one evangelism, and discipleship training. We cite three examples: (1) Serendipity has published, *The Serendipity New Testament For Groups,* with superb group exercises. (2) InterVarsity sponsors "Urbana," challenging thousands of youth with international service options, and (3) NavPress is maturing, having published the Colson Discussion Series on Justice, Political Action, and Transforming Society. These are A-1 quality—resources any church can utilize.

Discipling Within the Church

Recently, I visited with Hal Jensen, Director of Discipleship at the Saddleback Valley Church in Mission Viejo, California. They have 4000 members, and rent a public school facility. Hal uses his "Navigator" expertise to train 160 lay ministers to lead the 1200 persons enrolled in their small-group network. This is refreshing. Here is "intentional" discipling, all within the church structure.

As old structures collapse, some predict a wave of lay ministers (with no seminary stint) doing church work. First, I favor equipping the saints: that is biblical. My years of discipleship training suggest that proper preparation in disciple-making will in fact produce a wave of lay ministers doing the work of the church. However, since so many parishioners are college graduates, we still need thousands of seminary trained persons in the ministry.

In my third parish I developed the Golden Stairway Discipleship Course and eventually published it. At first, I discipled men in their 30s and 40s (in groups of 12). A few years later, a laywoman, Vernelle, began discipling women in groups of 7 to 12. Eventually, two of my disciples and four of hers also began discipling, until 300 were discipled. The worship in God's house, and the Bible study in Sunday School were thus augmented with a small-group network, where lay people ministered to each other via remarkable group dynamics. The sharing and caring was powerful in changing lives. Christ's church came alive!

Pastors and Discipling

I'm convinced that senior pastors have no higher calling than to disciple people. Jesus is our example. Granted—on rare occasions a pastor may be limited to the gift of prophesy/proclamation/preaching and should delegate discipling to others. Notwithstanding, delegating can be a convenient ploy for shirking a duty. Normally, a pastor with gifts of leading, pastoring, or teaching (in any size church) should set discipling as a priority item. In nine years Susan Joann and I discipled 128 men at our house. We're convinced it was the most productive thing we ever did in the Kingdom of God. It's the nuts and bolts of evangelism.

At the St. Louis Airport I met a pastor reading *The Disciple Making Pastor*. Recently, I bought this superb book. Author Bill Hull resonates the discipling mandate and holds the job description of American pastors against the grindstone of the Great Commission. The sparks fly! "Not much will change...until pastors start reproducing themselves through others...until congregations allow pastors to spend most of their time on...training the spiritually well minority, rather than servicing...the unmotivated and disobedient majority."[1]

Dr. John R. Martin notes that Anabaptists, 400 years ago, showed discipling accountability.[2] Today, few churches of any tradition have discipling patterns in place. Again, Jesus shows us how, as he leads the way.

02. the SELF-DENIAL factor

Jesus gave some exacting requirements for following him, like denying ourselves. It meant forsaking all human culs-de-sac and embarking on the Jesus-Way.

Light on the Pathway (Matthew 16:24-28)

Then Jesus said to his disciples, "If anyone would come after me, he must deny himself, and take up his cross, and follow me. For whoever wants to save his life will lose it, but whoever loses his life for me will find it...."

Our age glorifies the superman macho image in sports, the sensual free spirit in pleasure, the self-indulgent lifestyle in materialism, and the liberated free thought in intellectualism. Each of these philosophies is self-gratifying, godless, and human to the core.

A Christ-shaped mentality reverses the expectations of our age. So the big lotto winners, and the much-envied success-primed multimillionaires are really eternal losers. And this life's apparent losers, he declares, may in reality be heaven's heroes. "What good will it be for a man," says Jesus, "if he gains the whole world, yet forfeits his soul" (Matthew 16:26)?

Here is the accountant's balance sheet from heaven's point of view: the assets: gaining all the world's wealth; the liabilities: selling one's own soul to get it; the bottom line/net worth—zero. Based on Jesus, the eternal winner is not the arrogant self-achiever nor the driven do-gooder. Absolutely not! Jesus calls for total surrender—the denying of oneself.

Search Institute of Minneapolis (1990) has sounded an alarm about the seductive nature of our North American culture. After studying 561 congregations (Methodist, Presbyterian, Lutheran, Baptist, and several Christian denominations) it urges all

Christian education departments of churches to ask, "To what extent are we able to combat the effects of the secular culture, which constantly 'scripts' us to adopt an individualist, consumerist, militarist set of values? How can we effectively inspire in members a desire to formulate a Christian world view and adopt an accompanying set of values and behaviors?"[3]

The Current Crisis

Charles Colson also blows the whistle on American society. He calls it a crisis of immense proportions! He rules out our headline crises: trade deficits, nuclear holocaust, stock market collapse or the greenhouse effect. He says: "The crisis is in the character of our culture, where the values that restrain inner vices and develop inner virtues are eroding. Unprincipled men and women, disdainful of their moral heritage...are destroying our civilization...."[4]

When Jesus demands denial of self, he calls us to break free from our dependence on the secular, the sinful, and the selfish. Jesus expected all followers to enter the Kingdom on their knees: (1) as humbly as a penitent sinner pleading for pardon, (2) as teachable as a curious child walking by faith, and (3) as desperately as a drowning victim clutching a rope. Jesus was not jesting when he claimed: "I am the way...the truth...the life..." (John 14:6).

Self-denial is sometimes reduced to giving up candy, dessert, or cigarettes during Lent. Its real meaning lies in giving up basic selfishness, in dying to self. The poet views us as stripped of all self-righteousness, and clothed in the righteousness of Christ: "Nothing in my hand I bring, simply to your cross I cling!" In "justification" we are accepted, not by our attainment, but by his atonement.

Who can forget that scene in *Pilgrim's Progress*, where Pilgrim left family behind in the city of sin. Arriving at the cross he fell prostrate, and the burden of sin rolled off his back into the empty tomb. Three shining ones appeared. One said, "Your sins are forgiven!" Another gave him a robe of white. The other placed a mark on his forehead, "When you reach that celestial gate, here is proof you have been at the cross."

There is a paradox of the gospel: you must lose your life to find it (Matthew 16:25). Two options are: (1) losing oneself in service, forsaking selfish ambition, being wholly sold out to God, or (2) dying as a martyr. As a teenager I feared I would be unwilling to die for Jesus. As an adult I know that living for Jesus may be harder than dying.

In his study on economics, E. Calvin Beisner asserts that Jesus made self-denial the core of maturity. The proper progression is: "deny self, serve others, and follow Him. Serving others is the point of taking up the cross. As Jesus came...to serve by giving himself as a ransom for many (Matthew 20:28), so the Christian's cross is his or her work of service to those in need."[5]

Robert E. Coleman finds references to suffering or self-denial totally absent in American Church Growth literature. Churches in the Two-Thirds World often show great vitality, though not necessarily, even when suffering oppression or poverty. He writes that in the Western world, "...where affluence abounds and church affiliation is a mark of social acceptance, if not good politics...prosperity and success are more cherished than radical obedience."[6]

The Wycliffe Series of Christian Classics brought to my generation John Bunyon's famous allegory, *The Holy War*. King Shaddai and son, Emmanuel, lose and recapture the world and the human body/soul in particular. It is war against Diabolus, the devil himself. Two features pinpoint the relevance of denying oneself and cross-bearing. The first comes at a Christian's entry level. The forces of King Shaddai plan to conquer the town of Mansoul via the Ear-gate and Eye-gate. King Diabolus sends Mr. Loathe-To-Stoop with eight compromise proposals to avert war. They range from retaining half the town to maintaining friendship contacts and keeping consultation privileges. All offers are declined.

As Emmanuel's forces attack, Diabolus makes a last-ditch offer to stay in town as Shaddai's deputy. He makes grandiose promises to cease hostility, bring reforms and give lectures at his own expense! Emmanuel's reply is classic: "In Mansoul, I will be the sole Lord and possessor of all, or of none at all." He adds—Shaddai would be grieved if Diabolus remained to hatch and plot treason.[7]

A second insight clarifies "sanctification." As Diabolus was imprisoned, Emmanuel got control. Small diabolonians still lurked at the edges, hard to catch and hard to kill. Mr. Evil-Questioning and wife Lady No-Hope bore children: Unbelief, Live-by-Feeling, Self-Love, Wrong-Thoughts-of-Christ, and many others! Not one diabolonian wanted to die. Secretary of Mansoul (Holy Spirit) helped crucify the deeds of the flesh. Yes, dying to self is an all-out battle![8]

Self-denial and Self-esteem

How does self-denial relate to self-esteem? A certain degree of assertiveness is essential to healthy mental development. Christian therapists continually wrestle with the issue of wholeness, and how healthy self-esteem is distinguished from sinful pride and selfishness.

Christian psychologist F. Franklin Wise of the Wesleyan tradition believes that "The losing of self in the act of complete self-denial and self-submerging seems to create either a 'worm-in-the-dust' or a 'holier-than-thou' syndrome." Many "holiness" people, he says, fall victim to false humility and are abjectly self-effacing. But they are not as obnoxious as those whose superior religiosity breeds exclusiveness. Both kinds of saints misread things. Sanctification—Wesleyan style—enhances true selfhood, never negating one's humanity with natural drives and urges, enabling one to accept them and to bring them under consistent control of God's will.[9]

Short and simple—Jesus asks for the complete surrender of self. This denying of self sounds negative; but it really isn't; it is positive and healthy. It places one unreservedly under the Lordship of Jesus Christ, becoming what God created us to be!

03. the LOYALTY factor

A Jesus-style discipleship is multifaceted. First, it is relational. Secondly, it is radical with a denying of self. Thirdly, it is loyal. Jesus demands loyalty. This is poignantly dramatized in Luke 9.

Loyalty Case Number One
Light on the Pathway (Luke 9:57-58)

...a man said to him, "I will follow you wherever you go." Jesus replied, "Foxes have holes and birds of the air have nests, but the Son of Man has no place to lay his head."

Jesus did not know from day to day where he might lodge that night. No doubt, he wanted to warn this person of such uncertainty. No special luxury is promised, not even the normal convenience of a secure home. The stark truth is that one could be homeless and penniless and still possess radiant faith in Christ. One man told me that when he became a refugee—fleeing with all his belongings tied to his back, he actually made his deepest commitment to Christ and felt God the nearest. Stripped of everything, he still had the most important thing in life!

The would-be disciple needs to consider what he or she is getting into. It is a known fact—two church members exit the back door for every new member coming in the front door. Kenneth Chafin, while in the Billy Graham Chair of Evangelism at Louisville, asserted that half of all people who confess Christ will eventually drop out of church. They quit because they have not counted the cost of loyalty. They make member retention an enduring problem of the church.

Jesus' response to this querying candidate suggests the man understood neither the cost of following nor the nature of commitment. Some converts may drop out because they are mishandled at birth. Some may leave from neglect, when the "spiritual pediatrics" of a church fails to provide adequate care. It is imperative for all churches to heed the questions: Do your prospective members know what is expected of them? And secondly, when members drop out, do you know why?

Loyalty Case Number Two
Light on the Pathway (Luke 9:59-60)

He said to another man, "Follow me." But the man replied, "Lord, first let me go and bury my father." Jesus said to him, "Let the dead bury their own dead, but you go and proclaim the Kingdom of God."

Some feel this man wanted to await the death of his father before committing himself. In Judaism, even the burial of strangers was deemed meritorious, and the burial of parents was viewed as very obligatory based on the fifth command—to honor parents. Jesus categorically asserted that the Kingdom of God took precedence over the burial of the dead.

F. F. Bruce tells the fascinating story of a Scottish preacher named John McNeill. He was advertised to preach at an evangelistic gathering in central England. He got word of his father's funeral scheduled for the same day. He pondered the idea of cancelling out. But Jesus, standing by him, seemed to say, "Go preach the gospel. Would you rather raise the dead or bury the dead?" So he went to preach.[10]

Loyalty Case Number Three
Light on the Pathway (Luke 9:61-62)

Still another said, "I will follow you, Lord; but first let me go back and say good-by to my family." Jesus replied, "No one who puts his hand to the plow and looks back is fit for service in the kingdom of God."

There was a biblical precedent for such a request 800 years earlier (I Kings 19:19-21). Elisha, son of a wealthy family, was plowing with twelve yoke of oxen—he was driving the 12th pair. Elijah, the noted prophet, threw his mantle on him. Elisha understood. "Let me kiss my father and mother good-by," he said, "and then I will come with you." Getting approval, Elisha went home. He butchered his two oxen, cooked the meat over a fire fueled by the wood of his plowing apparatus and threw a big farewell party. After that he followed Elijah.

Jesus' call is more demanding than that of Elijah. His kingdom work is urgent. No delays are permitted. Family ties take second place to the kingdom of God. Loyalty to Christ supersedes love for family! Woe to parents who obstruct the kingdom's progress.

This loyalty to God is tested in our day as well. In a pastoral role, as I enrolled 12 men for discipling classes throughout the past decade, I often asked 15 or 20 before I got twelve who said, "Yes." A father of three, in his mid-thirties, said, "I'll first ask my dad." Dad's verdict: "No Way!" Another fellow gave this response, "My dad warned me to stay away from small-groups at church; but I'll accept. After all, I'm 30 and must make my own decisions."

The Vision of Fathers

By contrast, one Christmas a man in his fifties brought a cake to my house. "Pastor," he said, "I hear you are discipling young men. How about asking one of my sons to join your next group?" I included a son of his in each of my next three groups. Later I notified him that he owed me two more cakes. He agreed! It is always a thrill to see parents coveting spiritual growth for children.

Nowhere is this yearning to see family members enfolded into the church more markedly illustrated than in the life of Psychologist, James Dobson. Biographer Rolf Zettersten tells of Dobson's great-grandfather, George McCluskey, who prayed many hours over the years for the spiritual welfare of his family. Before death George was assured that everyone in four generations would serve Christ.

Imagine the excitement as that promise was realized! One Sunday night Nazarene Pastor, James Dobson Sr., invited people to come to the prayer altar. James Jr., three years old, left his mother's pew and joined twenty persons up front. (I use this illustration not to suggest that preschool conversions are normative, but rather to highlight the power of family prayers and parental covenants.)

Fifty years later Dr. Dobson wrote, "...I joined them spontaneously. I recall crying and asking Jesus to forgive my sins. I know that sounds strange, but that's the way it occurred. It is overwhelming for me to think about....Imagine the King of the universe...caring about an insignificant kid barely out of toddlerhood!" The Dobson family affirmed Jim's commitment with a special celebration. It was viewed as fulfillment of Grandpa's prayer covenant.[11]

Putting the Hand to the Plow

Jesus' plowman-reference (9:62) holds another lesson. All farmers know that plowing a straight furrow is impossible while looking back. As a boy I learned to plow on a Model D John Deere tractor. It was simple—push the throttle, engage the hand clutch and control the steering wheel.

Dad placed a flag on yonder end of the field, "Keep the flag in view but drive toward an intermediate goal—a clod or sunflower, and never look back!" The lesson: God's kingdom requires undivided, single-hearted concentration. When you understand God's goal for your life, go for it, as though pleasing him means more to you than anything else. That's kingdom loyalty.

04. the OBEDIENCE factor
Light on the Pathway (Matthew 28:18-20)

Then Jesus came...and said..."Therefore go...make disciples of all nations,...baptizing...teaching them to obey everything I have commanded you...."

This obedience-phrase, our fourth concern, is the "great omission" of the Great Commission. The Greek text has one imperative, "make disciples," and three participles: going, baptizing and teaching. In reality, it may be hard to discern which is actually more neglected—going worldwide or teaching obedience to Jesus.

Children in a permissive society hardly find obedience a

popular subject. Neither do comfortable affluent flabby-fleshed churches tolerate much obedience-talk! Church cartoonists love to sketch a preacher, flanked by his sign-waving deacons, each with a "taboo" sermon topic. Nonetheless, Jesus placed obedience in his commission. Christians ever since, are obligated to comply.

Small wonder then that Jesus' command to put up a "for sale" sign baffled the rich young ruler of his day—and every old scholar of our day (Matthew 19:16-26). In a chapter, "Luxurious poverty," Donald B. Kraybill compares the rich ruler with the rich tax collector (Luke 18-19). In one case Jesus invited himself to dinner. The rich man volunteered half of his wealth to feed the poor (with 4-fold restitution to boot). The details are sketchy but the verdict of Jesus is clear—Zacchaeus has salvation.

In the other case, the wealthy man ran to Jesus, and quizzed him. The verdict of Jesus: sell out, give to the poor and follow me. Why dispose of his riches? "Wealth has captured his heart," writes Kraybill in *The Upside-Down Kingdom*, "Selling all will refocus his attention on the heavenly kingdom. Jesus...also invites him to 'come, follow me.' We should accent the follow rather than the sell."[12] In teaching, Jesus often tightened-the-screws on the idea of obedience. It is not the "talkers" but the "doers" that help the kingdom. In the Sermon on the Mount Jesus said, "Not everyone who says to me, 'Lord, Lord,' will enter the Kingdom of heaven, but only he who does the will of my Father who is in heaven" (Matthew 7:21-23).

A Heritage of Obedience

Most church bodies can point back to some era in their religious history where faith was held at the risk of death. So can we. A few decades ago, John C. Wenger (Goshen Biblical Seminary) was a prolific writer on Anabaptism. His 115-page book, *Even Unto Death* (printed by a Presbyterian press), ranked among the best of the popular-style summaries of our heritage. In my decade of discipling men, 93 disciples in eight groups (age 24-66) read my one and only copy [and the book still survives]! Person after person was moved by this gripping account of Sixteenth-Century Anabaptists and their heroic witness.

John Knox Press gives this tribute: "The sufferings of the Anabaptists have borne rich fruit...their belief in the separation of church and state is a firm principle of American democracy, their doctrine of believer's baptism is widely held, and their emphasis on total discipleship is an integral part of the church's message. Protestantism owes them a great debt of gratitude!"[13]

Looking at Obedience Today

The issue of obedience looms large in conservative circles today. People ask, "Can we accept Jesus as Savior and not as Lord?" The prominent Los Angeles pastor, John MacArthur Jr., insists that receiving salvation requires obedience to Christ. There is no salvation without bowing to his Lordship.[14] Meanwhile, Zane Hodges of Dallas, and others, write vigorously to uphold "nonLordship salvation." While scholars split theological hairs, pollsters find that evangelical church members have an ethic almost identical to that of society. Clearly, the common theology, "forgiven and scot-free" is unhealthy. A dose of medicine called "obedience" might help. Declaring Christ as Lord is essential.

The obedience question, "Why do you call me 'Lord' and do not what I say?" is applied by one scholar to the national scene in *The Priestly Kingdom.* In a critique on "civil religion" he insists that "the religious undergirding of national interests at the expense of the wider righteousness...is idolatry!"[15] The issue is: do we merely invoke God's help, or will we truly be God's servants?

He probes once more: "We call a nonviolent man 'Lord' and in his name rekindle the arms race. We call a poor man 'Lord' and with his name on our lips deepen the ditch between rich and poor. We call 'Lord' a man who told us to love our enemies and we polarize the globe in the name of Christian values, approving of 'moderate repression' as long as it is done by our friends."[16] Yoder admits to a bit of ambivalence here; but he believes that if our goal is the application of care in a Christian way to public life, then the word to our nation is the same as to a person: repent, recognize God's sovereignty and seek to serve others.

Interview with a Church Statesman

Recently, I visited J. B. Toews, retired church leader. Dr. Toews had told me that discipleship work in America was often self-serving, using God only as a convenience. I coveted this interview. He was in touch with both Anabaptists and Evangelicals. His denomination was spawned in a revival movement (Russia-1860) and is today a voting member in The National Association of Evangelicals.

Nowadays, he said, Evangelicalism is all too often "convenient pietism" using God as a resource but not capitulating to his sovereignty and authority. There is a pietistic emphasis, and rightly so, on witnessing, sharing, giving, and growing through small-groups. But this piety falls short of real biblical discipleship as demanded in the Gospels—a following that abandons the self-life.

Gray-haired, in his mid 80's, a pillar in his brotherhood, Toews became more animated. Even evangelism is defined as "finding God," as though it is by human initiative. This affects our concept of conversion. Coming alive with emotion Toews said: "I know some church members who participate in evangelism, even disciple some converts, and at the same time build themselves million-dollar homes! What stewardship of the gospel is this?" Next, Brother Toews laid bare the issue. "Absent," he said, "are the concepts of obedience, self-denial, cross-bearing, restricted lifestyle, and kingdom-priorities as taught in Matthew 10, Luke 14 and John 12. I reviewed 20 discipleship courses and each missed the heart of my concern: obedience to the absolute authority of Jesus Christ."

Recalling that interview, I wondered—was he too harsh? Is it possible to manufacture spirituality? Do we cook up renewal at will, like baking a batch of cookies: selecting the right ingredients, mixing them, and turning up the heat? On second thought, I have seen spiritual fervor in churches visibly heightened through the vision of leadership, faithful teaching, compassion for the needy, sharing the gospel worldwide and intercessory prayer. Obedience pays!

Conclusion. Why did the early followers of Jesus suffer joyfully? They understood the cosmic conflict between the Kingdom of God and the Kingdom of Satan. They accepted the fact that obeying Jesus as "Lord" could cost them the same price as Jesus paid in obeying his Father. For the believer, cross-bearing, self-denial, obedience and loyalty are all integral to discipleship. Christ's call "to follow" is anchored in his costly atonement and glorious resurrection!

05. the REWARD factor

Another aspect of following Jesus is that of reward. Christians today are bombarded with graphic explicit sensual media appeals—to gratify lusts for sex, violence and greed. Are the old-fashioned virtues of honesty, morality, and integrity still tenable? Does it still pay to serve the King of Kings and the Lord of Lords? What about Kingdom-compensation?

Light on the Pathway (Matthew 19:27-30)

Peter answered him, "We have left everything to follow you! What then will there be for us?..."

Simon Peter's inquiry was most practical—what's in it for me? Jesus gave a direct 3-fold answer: (1) you will rule, (2) you will have a 100-fold reward, and (3) you will inherit eternal life.

The Reward of Ruling

First, we will rule and reign with Christ in the Age to Come. In majestic imagery, the Prophet Daniel pictured the Ancient of Days and the Son of Man controlling the reins of history (Daniel 7:9-27). At his trial before the Sanhedrin, Jesus applied this vision to himself (Mark 14:62). And here in Matthew 19 Jesus promises thrones of glory to his disciples as well. Myron Augsburger explains: "The symbolism of the twelve tribes of Israel is to emphasize God's covenant people, and this new Israel will sit in judgment upon those whose unbelief and legalism kept them from entering the covenant."[17] So here is our first promise.

The 100-Fold Reward

Secondly, Jesus promised a 100-fold reward for leaving the comforts of home, the fellowship of family and the security of owning land. What did this fantastic promise to Peter really mean? In what ways are the disciples of Jesus really compensated? The reward-motif of Jesus is real; yet it is often misconstrued. The evangelists of the health-and-wealth gospel teach explicitly that every Christian has "name-it-and-claim-it" rights, as though each is entitled to be healthy and wealthy. Let me clarify this.

Of course, a wholesome Christian lifestyle will be good for one's health, and in addition, many will experience divine healing in direct answer to prayer. Nonetheless, many godly people will encounter sickness or death just as all other people in society. And regarding the wealth issue, certainly a lifestyle under the Lordship of Christ will bring economic gains as the old-life of drunkenness, gambling, and carousing drops off. Church Growth theorists label this phenomenon (the rising of the economic level among believers) "redemption lift." In no way does Jesus promise all disciples riches. Many of our rewards are nonmaterial, and many await the Age to Come.

A further caution is in order. Applying scripture literally without understanding its intent can lead to bizarre behavior. Obviously Jesus is saying that love for the Kingdom of God takes precedence over love for family. But this is no defense of child abuse or spouse neglect. Peter, the apostle to whom Jesus promised rewards for forsaking family, never forsook his own wife. Twenty-five years later he was still faithful, enjoying her companionship (see I Corinthians 9:5).

What is then the meaning of "100-fold" rewards? Probably the simplest answer is the best and most natural. As disciples respond to the call of Christ and leave their biological families,

God provides hundreds of "spiritual fathers-mothers-brothers-sisters" in all the districts, provinces and countries to which they are called. The spiritual ties in strange countries can be more precious than family reunions at home. Our bond in Christ is marvelous. Furthermore, we may forsake jobs and possessions; yet the tithes of a hundred people may support us in a lifetime of service.

The Reward of Eternal Life

The third item Jesus promised Peter was the inheritance of eternal life. Ralph Earl (NIV Study Bible) asserts that the three terms used in Matthew 19: (1) having eternal life (v. 16), (2) entering the kingdom of heaven (v. 23), and (3) being saved (v. 25), are generally synonymous and also appear in Luke and Mark. They refer to a disciple's entry point into that realm of eternal reward.

According to George Ladd, the rich young ruler, whose question precipitated this whole discourse (19:16), was thinking of the eschatological life as taught in Daniel 12:2—an entrance into the Age to Come.[18] The verse reads, "Multitudes who sleep in the dust of the earth will awake: some to everlasting life, others to shame and everlasting contempt." (This Old Testament verse is the first clear reference in the Bible to the dual nature of eternal reward.)

Christians are "pie in the sky" visionaries, so the caricature goes. Indeed, Jesus used this future reward factor as a motivational tool. Heaven in all its glory is certainly our kingdom-compensation. By means of "Christ-honoring" deeds we store up treasures in heaven for enjoyment in the Age to Come.

On a mountaintop Jesus gave his inner circle of three a sneak preview—a glimpse of glory (Matthew 17:1-13). In a flash Moses and Elijah appeared. Moses was a superb model of temporary self-denial on the way to an "Eternal Land." As a palace kid he chose maltreatment over the fleeting pleasures of sin; his eyes focused on future rewards (Hebrews 11:24-28). Peter was enthralled—he wanted to have it all, right now! Jesus said in effect, "There has to be suffering first, the rewards come later."

My In-laws Inspired Me

The reward-theme of Jesus has permeated the consciousness of God's people down through the years of history. Take my father-in-law, Joe M. Walter. This Dakota farmer was converted at age 28. He once lost his farm, but not his faith. He counted his wealth each morning—not by balancing his checkbook—but by naming each family member in prayer. He praised God with special joy for each child and grandchild in Christian service. He was known to sing: "...When I wake with the blest in the mansions of rest, Will there be any stars in my crown?"

Grandpa was devout. The desire to please God through witness was etched deeply in his soul. He retired early to give ten years to Christian service. His prayers had a home-spun originality, like: "God, put your guardian angel in front of the car, behind and on both sides." At age 88 his last prayer was, "O, God, take care of Grandma and send an angel to take me home." In ten minutes he was gone. The funeral sermon centered on rendezvous, rest and reward. The text read, "...Blessed are the dead who die in the Lord...they rest...their deeds...follow them" (Revelation 14:13).

I invited Grandma to our home in Nebraska. She moved in: wheelchair, pottychair, Bible and all. For six years we cared for this saintly invalid! Her faith was great, disposition sweet, and mind clear. She loved the old hymns. After her 90th birthday she weakened. Finally we prayed that God would send his chariot. On April 18, 1990 Grandma was sitting in her wheelchair at the kitchen table. Susan Joann was feeding her supper and she went limp. The doctor said, "What a blessed way to go!" I put her into bed and kissed her warm cheek good-bye. She had gone to claim her "inheritance of eternal life" as promised by her Lord.

In the final chapter of the Revelation, Jesus Christ the Lord says, "Behold, I am coming soon! My reward is with me, and I will give to everyone according to what he has done" (22:12). The blessings of the kingdom (and the joys of heaven) are never merited or earned by our efforts; they are given by the sheer grace of God. However, once we repent and trust in the merits of Christ, our faithfulness as disciples is richly rewarded. It pays to serve the King of Kings!

Conclusion

We have covered a few of the basics in following Jesus as Lord. Disciples harness all relationships for kingdom-use. They surrender their personal self-serving agendas. They live intensely loyal to the Lover of their soul and cling to every word of his instructions. And the Kingdom of Jesus has a profit sharing plan. There is kingdom-compensation.

The Risen Christ gives a penetrating diagnosis of seven churches (Revelation 2:1-3:22). He delights in each good sign of health, but is alarmed at their malignancies: cold love, divided loyalties, lukewarmness, and halfheartedness. The Great Physician appeals to all churches with terminal illnesses to repent, to return and to accept their divine healing. "Here I am! I stand at the door and knock..." (3:20).

Walter Elwell calls the scene tragic, "...Christ must humbly seek entrance into the church he purchased with his own blood."[19] But notice the touch of tenderness; it should melt us. The victorious Lord, with no display of power, knocks gently at the door. He offers fellowship as blessed as a shared meal. This is a standing invitation to every church and every disciple.

The punch line (3:21), we dare not miss it. Jesus promises to those who will give him his rightful place as Lord—who will overcome as faithful to the end—the honor of sitting with him on his throne. If we allow him to rule our hearts in this life, he will share with us his rule in the Age to Come!

Questions for Discussion

1. What can we learn from the Jesus-Way of building relationships?

2. Do you agree with Charles Colson's assessment of American society?

3. In what way do our families help or hinder our walk with Christ?

4. Is obedience to God a crucial issue today?

5. Name the threefold reward Jesus promised his followers. Explain.

PRACTICING HIS PRESENCE: DEVOTIONAL PAUSE FOR BUSY DISCIPLES
Theme of the week — Following the Master

	Monday	**Tuesday**	**Wednesday**	**Thursday**	**Friday**
Light on the pathway	John 1:29-51	Matthew 16:24-28	Luke 9:57-62	Matthew 19:16-26	Matthew 19:27-30
Lesson for this day	Factor #01 Relationship	Factor #02 Self-denial	Factor #03 Loyalty	Factor #04 Obedience	Factor #05 Rewards
Life in Jesus' way	Take time to pray	Take time to pray	Take time to pray	Take time to pray	Take time to pray

PRACTICE HIS PRESENCE IN CHURCH ON SUNDAY

Chapter

3

Counting the Cost

6. Opposition
7. Family Loyalty
8. Paying the Price
9. Planning Ahead
10. Consecration

Introduction

A football receiver runs full speed into enemy territory, then turns to catch the pass. His eye scans the opposition. If he leaps to grab the ball, he'll get hit, and hard. For a moment he wavers, counting the cost. Then with determination he leaps, brings down the ball, and gets clobbered. For the joy of advancing his team 20 yards, he gladly pays the price.

Many Christians on the road of life seek to advance their spiritual team, the church. The stakes are high: life is short and each person has one opportunity. And the team looks dejected, discouraged, and depressed. So brave parishioners tackle some heroic deeds. For example, a lady in my first charge asked for membership by way of Believer's Baptism. We had not mandated this; but she was determined, "I'm 50 and have just accepted Christ. I've wasted too much of my life at another church, I want to make up for lost time."

She volunteered to work with Junior High kids. Being courageous and innovative, she soon got blasted: "How can we build spiritual lives around beach parties?" or "We have never done it like this before."—like the hymn: "As it was in the beginning, Tis now, And ever shall be." Oh, how the kids loved her! The group kept growing, and a beautiful togetherness developed. Well, for the joy of seeing her team advance ten yards, she hung in there—

with a 10-year stint of youth ministries. Praise God for disciples who have tough hides and tender hearts—who count the cost, pay the price and make things happen.

Again in football imagery—each disciple, each church, and each denomination that runs special plays of "faithfulness" will get pummeled by criticism. Only one question matters, "Is Coach Jesus pleased?"

This chapter (1) probes the sources of opposition that make discipleship costly, and (2) pinpoints the antagonism one's own family can express. At the center (3), the chapter discusses cost— the price we pay. Finally, (4) the need of planning and (5) the role of personal consecration finish up the chapter.

06. the OPPOSITION factor

When people are won to Christ and recruited for church membership, adequate discipling-formation is necessary, lest the commitment be short-lived. If persons are not taught the conflict-nature of the church (Kingdom of God versus Kingdom of Satan) trials may seem overwhelming.

On the other hand, if converts profess faith in Christ with a full awareness of the price to be paid, and realize that the whole church is their support team, they feel strongly affirmed. Resuming the football analogy, they appreciate each brother or sister who is running, blocking, passing, receiving, punting, or kicking. They understand—the whole church is in this jointly. A feeling of comradeship protects fledgling believers from spiritual discouragement and burnout.

In the gospels, only Luke tells of Jesus sending out the 72 (traditionally, called The Seventy). This was the wider circle—other than the 12, whom Jesus recruited to go ahead of him to towns where he would come (Luke 10:1-23). The orders reflect an urgency. Travel light. Accept hospitality. Omit the chitchat. Here's the job: teach and heal the receptive; but warn the unreceptive.

Opposition: Wolves in the World
Light on the Pathway (Luke 10:1-7)

...He told them, "The harvest is plentiful, but the workers are few. Ask the Lord of the harvest, therefore, to send out workers into his harvest field. Go! I am sending you out like lambs among wolves...."

Three times Jesus refers to opposition. This mission is dangerous and the seventy are defenseless—totally dependent on God. Thus being properly forewarned of potential hostility, they were mentally prepared. They could always fall back on the assurance that Jesus had commissioned them.

As 20-year-old college kids, two of us talked our dads out of 7 weeks of farm work one summer. (How we got permission still surprises me!) We went to the back hills of the Ozarks under a local mission to teach VBS and conduct some preaching missions. I still chuckle. We stayed in schoolhouses, eating and sleeping in the same rooms where we taught VBS and preached in the evenings. We were roughing it. To heat soup, we had a tin contraption with orders: "Unfold, place soup on top, put pill underneath, light a match to it, and heat soup."

Our Ozark mentors, veteran missionaries, must have detected a bit of fear. At any rate they assured us with this story: In a remote area two ladies stayed overnight in a school—to teach Bible the next day. The front door had such a gaping hole the ladies shoved their suitcases through without opening it. In the dark of night they heard men circling the school, trying every window and door. The ladies fell to their knees praying. At the same moment one of their mothers (300 miles away) was jolted out of sleep with a deep burden!—so she prayed. One prowler said, "This place is locked, we can't get in, let's go." Amazing.

The Receptive and The Unreceptive
Light on the Pathway (Luke 10:8-16)

"When you enter a town and are welcomed, eat what is set before you. Heal the sick who are there and tell them, 'The kingdom of God is near you....'"

Again, a second naming of opposition. Jesus gave precise orders, one set for towns friendly, one set for those unfriendly. This information shielded these disciples from discouragement; and aided them in planning strategy. The unreceptive hosts were to be warned—to be reminded of Sodom. But the emphasis is positive, on finding the receptive. Stay there. Eat the food. Enjoy hospitality. Bless them. Pray for the sick. Teach that God's kingdom is near.

What a lesson. A seminary professor once advised me, "Al, watch for the cream that comes to the top. Work especially with people responsive to your kind of ministry." That is food for thought. Why focus your eyes on the grumpy and disgruntled? They'll spoil your day and derail your priorities.

Church growth theorists remind us that "receptivity" to the Gospel—worldwide—is providential. At times, missionaries should concentrate on the hearts God has prepared. An agrarian analogy might help. If a farmer has two combines and two fields, he doesn't send one to the ripe field and one to the green field. Donald McGavran claims that people—the Yorubas—were once "receptive." However, Christians generally were too preoccupied with perfecting their saints. So Muslims stepped in and won three million converts without even providing education, medicine, or the emancipation of women. It's simply a case of people being winnable at a given time and someone responding to their search for truth.[1]

Satanic Opposition is For Real
Light on the Pathway (Luke 10:17-24)

The seventy-two returned with joy and said, "Lord, even the demons submit to us in your name." He replied, "I saw Satan fall like lightning from heaven. I have given you authority to trample on snakes and scorpions and to overcome all the power of the enemy; nothing will harm you...."

The third opposition-idea came in Jesus' phrase that he saw Satan falling (10:18). In his ministry of exorcism, Jesus often spoke of the Kingdom of Satan being diametrically opposed to the Kingdom of Heaven. Certainly, Christian workers who understand Satanic opposition are most likely to weather the storms in Christian service. The 70 were ecstatic that demons submitted to Jesus' name.

For centuries commentaries referred this to Satan's cosmic fall from heaven in the remote past (Isaiah 14). Scholars today insist that Jesus saw Satan being defeated right as they were ministering. In his monumental work—the sum of his life's study on the Kingdom of God—George Ladd suggests that the "falling-from-the-sky" phrase is metaphorical language. The successful mission of the 70 was decisive, a clear defeat of Satan; but his final destruction awaits the end of the age. The inclusion of this event by Luke, according to Ladd, is most important in theology because it shows that the 70 had the same kingdom-power as the Twelve. And secondly, the real enemies were not hostile nations as in the Old Testament, but spiritual powers of evil.[2]

Witch Doctor and His Magic

A foreign missionary spotted a witch doctor performing a miracle in public: he levitated a man horizontally three feet above the ground. The mission worker ridiculed the whole matter: "Sir, this must be a trick of some kind!" Suddenly, an invisible power grabbed the missionary by the throat; he gasped for air. Then he understood! He went home to pray. Returning, he witnessed the same feat. "In the name of Jesus," he commanded, "let this power be broken." The man dropped to the ground. Of course, the witch doctor was furious that this "Jesus-Power" had broken his spell. The general public took notice that the Christians were not intimidated by the magic of the witch doctors (see also Revelation 12:11).

The book of Revelation, asserts George Ladd, depicts the unrelenting enmity of Satan against the people of God which often finds historical expression. He says, "The modern evangelical fear of suffering in the great tribulation has forgotten the biblical teaching that the church in her fundamental character is always a martyr church (Acts 14:22). The true victory consists in conquering the Beast by loyalty to Christ to death" (Revelation 15:2).[3]

Despite all worldwide advances in education, tolerance, and the protection of human rights—even today, somewhere in the world the church of Jesus Christ suffers severe opposition, often martyrdom. Thousands die for Christ every year. The Upper Room Discourse of Jesus gives perspective to discipleship and suffering: "Remember the words I spoke to you—No servant is greater than his master. If they persecuted me, they will persecute you also" (John 15:20).

07. the FAMILY-LOYALTY factor

In this chapter on discipleship-costs we continue our theme of "opposition," but broaden our scope to include some family-oriented "Hard Sayings" of Jesus. Our families are friends—or foes—to faith. Our closest kin can oppose us.

Faith and Family Tensions
Light on the Pathway (Mark 3:31-35)

....they told him, "Your mother and brothers are outside looking for you." "Who are my mother and brother?" he asked. Then he looked at those seated...and said, "....Whoever does God's will is my brother and sister and mother."

Was Jesus rude to his family, or profoundly spiritual? This incident reminds us of the day Jesus was in the temple at age twelve. His parents looked for him three days. "Son, why have you treated us like this? Your father and I have been anxiously searching for you" (Luke 2:48). The text says that Jesus went home "obediently," while Mary treasured or pondered the matter (2:51).

Tension can be expected when a visitor from outer space (or eternity) comes to live on planet earth. "In some real sense God's Kingdom came into history in the person and mission of Jesus."[4] In kingdom talk, the blessings of the Age to Come broke in on This Age. The two ages overlap in the Church Age. The church is sandwiched between Christ's Resurrection and Christ's Parousia.

Hate Parents. Love Enemies. Really?

Jesus dramatized heaven's ideal versus earth's reality in radical hyperbole! A classical passage is Luke 14:26-35. We study it throughout this chapter.

Light on the Pathway (Luke 14:26)

"If anyone comes to me and does not hate his father and mother, his wife and children, his brothers and sisters—yes, even his own life—he cannot be my disciple."

Right off, we're startled—even shocked. Any reference to hatred for parent, spouse or child seems absolutely contradictory to our Sunday School memory of Jesus—the meek and mild. But lest we get all bent out of shape, we take another look: "If anyone...does not hate...even his own life...!" That's clue enough. We better search for deeper meanings.

Few express our perplexity as succinctly as F. F. Bruce. This hard saying is difficult to reconcile with the general teachings of Jesus. "...it...goes against the law of love to one's neighbor which Jesus emphasized and radicalized. If the meaning of 'neighbor' must be extended so as to include one's enemy, it must not be restricted so as to exclude one's nearest and dearest."[5] Well put.

In Semitic language, the use of contrasts (love/hate, darkness/light etc.) was normal. When Jesus called for a drastic costly commitment for each would-be disciple, he was using acceptable terminology. And it was strikingly realistic. Nowhere was the love/hate tension more keenly felt than in family relationships—as people contemplated following Jesus.

This love/hate contrast was already used in Old Testament times and came as no shock to the Jews. There was a biblical precedence for such imagery. It was normal: "...I have loved Jacob, but Esau I have hated..." (Malachi 1:2-3). "When Scripture talks about God's hatred," says Walter Kaiser, Jr., "it uses a distinctly biblical idiom which does not imply that Yahweh exhibits disgust, disdain and a desire for revenge...there is a specialized meaning." The same idea is found in Jacob's case. The hated one is the one loved less (cf. Genesis 29:30-33, Matthew 10:37).[6] (We will return to Luke 14 after a bit.)

Light on the Pathway (Matthew 10:34-37)

"Do not suppose that I have come to bring peace to the earth...I have come to turn a man against his father, a daughter against her mother, a daughter-in-law against her mother-in-law—a man's enemies will be the members of his own household. Anyone who loves his father or mother more than me is not worthy of me; anyone who loves his son or daughter more than me is not worthy of me."

Jesus challenges all loyalties. Loving allegiance is first learned from the gleam of a mother's eye, an affectionate squeeze, the soothing sounds of comfort. As we absorb love in childhood, it appears, we become equipped to bestow love in adulthood. The home, by design, is a spawning ground for learning, loving and loyalty. But the Kingdom of God demands a fidelity that overrules all others.

A Caution to Christian Youth

Jesus confronts loyalties in courtship and marriage. David Swartz is the author of *The Magnificent Obsession*. As a Baptist pastor he offers a most poignant caution against mixing kingdom loyalties and non-Christian marriages. "...I gave up a relationship in college because the girl wouldn't commit herself to Christ. Today I could go back and show you where I sat on the curb and watched her walk out of my life. It was hard then and it hurt....In over twenty years of being a Christian, I've never seen one person lead a vibrant Christian life who voluntarily, knowingly married a non-Christian. All have known heartache and compromise; some have encountered shipwreck."[7] Those contemplating marriage need to make the decision with extreme care.

Candidly, I must admit, my counseling experience fairly well parallels that of Swartz. I recall an incident—many years ago— where a teenager attended my yearlong catechetical instruction, professed faith and requested baptism. Later in courtship this youth fell in love with a non-Christian, a blatant nonchurch-attender. All counsel fell on deaf ears. Finally the ultimate rationalization: "Pastor, maybe I'm really not a Christian after all!" The marriage seemed a deliberate closing-of-the-door on Christ and his church.

The kingdom of God—how decisive. Moses once demanded "....Love the Lord your God with all your heart..." (Deuteronomy 6:4-8). Jesus, the Son of God, asks no less. No love for person, nor for possession, dare supersede our love for him. Such devotion often divides: estranging sisters, disconnecting brothers, alienating children from parents, and fragmenting families. Radical discipleship, given the conflict-nature of two Kingdoms (God versus Satan) is often divisive.

Lessons From Asian Evangelism

Evangelism in Asia uniquely tests a person's loyalty to Christ. Non-Christian people often have deep religious roots—reaching back centuries. Their zeal can be fanatical. In many cases, families disinherit their members who convert to Christianity. One father tried to poison his Christian son. So members often bolt from family-held religions at the risk of their lives. A child becoming a Christian, is not so much an embarrassment as a traitor, so the perception goes. Many a pagan father prefers a dead son, over an alive-Christian son.

One college youth in Japan accepted Christ at a preaching service. He went home and told Dad. "No, you can't," yelled Father, "How do you hate us like that?" "I love you, Father," insisted the son, "but I believe Jesus was really the Son of God who died on the Cross for my sins. I have accepted his salvation. I have assurance I'm bound for heaven." "No—No—You don't!" screamed Father hysterically, "Renounce Jesus, or walk out of that door!" He walked out—out of his family and out of his religion—into the arms of a Heavenly Father, into the care of a Christian church, into the love of Christian brothers and sisters.

From Hong Kong comes a heartwarming story told by David Morken. A lady embraced Christ through a Bible study. She couldn't tell her husband; he was Moslem. He would divorce and disown her!—she was positive. Day by day, she prayed for her "beloved" and his conversion. One day, two years later, he came home from a business trip to a foreign country. He said, "Wife, I have news for you. You may be very disappointed; I have become a Christian." She shouted, "Wonderful!" and fell into his embrace. The pair followed Christ in baptism, and finally, in affiliation with a local church.

08. the PAYING-THE-PRICE factor

In the game of football, as I stated, a receiver expects a hard hit, if he jumps to catch a pass. He pays that price. In addition, there is the cost of training—lots of sweat and hard work. Victory likely goes to the team that excels in self-discipline and determination. Here is the heart of this chapter: the cost of discipleship. Of course, this issue has confronted the church all through history. Dare we ask?—does today's church have the moral fiber, the heart, and the toughness that is required? Or, does it take the easy road?

The theology of the cross and the theology of cross-bearing in discipleship are intertwined. "On the cross of Calvary, our Lord Jesus guaranteed to us all the spiritual blessings we will ever need. At the point of saving faith we get acquittal, acceptance and sonship. At Christ's return, we enjoy perfection, glorification and eternal joy in heaven. In between, in the here and now, there is untold wealth for our taking: deliverance, victory, fruitfulness, growth, and the filling of the Holy Spirit, to name a few. These are ours if we really want them, insist on having them, and wholeheartedly go after them. It is up to us."[8]

First, a comment on the gospels. Phrases like "taking up your cross" or "following Jesus" are the epitome of cost-talk. Jesus was preparing disciples for life-and-death service. Luke's eleven verses (14:25-35) are very basic to our subject. At the center are twin parables (28-33), unique to Luke. (These we will discuss in the rest of this chapter.) The verses before and after are somewhat analogous to teachings in Matthew (10:37-39 and 16:24-28).

When the Romans crucified a criminal, the victim was compelled to carry the cross. John A. Martin writes: "Carrying his cross through the heart of the city was supposed to be a tacit admission that the Roman Empire was correct in the sentence of death imposed on him...So when Jesus enjoined His followers to carry their crosses and follow Him, He was referring to a public display before others that Jesus was right and that the disciples were following Him even to their deaths. This is exactly what the religious leaders refused to do."[9]

The Exacting Cost in the Great Reformation

Next, a glimpse of history. Menno Simons was a carefree, pleasure-loving Roman Catholic priest in Holland. When his brother was swept up in the revolutionary Muensterite uprising— and was killed—Menno was jarred out of his complacency. (Until his dying day he blamed himself for failing his brother.) At age 40 (30 January 1536), he renounced his Roman priesthood and joined the Anabaptist movement. He had one desire: to glorify Jesus Christ regardless of the cost.

Becoming the key leader, he worked 25 years in Holland and Germany, giving Mennonites their name. His book, *Admonition on the Suffering, Cross, and Persecution of the Saints,* (ca 1554) protested the persecution endured from Catholics and Protestants alike: "How many have they betrayed?...Some they have hanged... Some they have roasted and burned alive....hated by all men, abused, mocked, slandered, defamed, trampled upon, styled 'heretics.' Their names are read from pulpits and town halls; they are kept from their livelihood, driven out into the cold winter, bereft of bread, [and] pointed at with fingers...."[10]

Persecution was intense. Saints were hunted and hounded. About 5000 Anabaptists died in the immediate decades following that memorable Saturday night at Zurich, Switzerland (21 January 1525) when a small Bible Study group (among the Swiss Brethren) quite spontaneously baptized and ordained each other. George Blaurock and Conrad Grebel were leading participants.

Leenaert Bouwens, a dynamic speaker, was ordained by Menno as bishop in Holland (1551). Leenaert's wife objected—the risk looked too big. In a letter of loving tenderness, Menno recited the urgency of the work, pleading with her to trust God's care. Leenaert kept a name list of those he baptized—all 10,252. He died in Hoorn, Holland in 1582—amazingly—of natural causes![11]

The Church of the 21st Century

Now a glance at today's world. As history approaches and passes the year 2000, ominous signs appear. The church, like a battered ship at sea, hopes to reach port. Jesus once queried, "...when the Son of Man comes, will he find faith on the earth" (Luke 18:8)? What wrenching anxiety must grip our Savior! The crowd of the religious is multitudinous, the "company of committed" is not.

The soft easy lifestyle of average Mr./Mrs. North American Church Member, pumped up with the helium of affluence, of convenience and of expedience, hardly responds to discipleship talk. Words like sacrifice, cost and discipline sound as scary, adverse and negative as pain, death and taxes!

A Survey: Mainline Churches

Six mainline denominations (35 million people) held an epochal 3-year study, led by Search Institute and summarized in Christian Century: "Follow some church members through the week. Few will show any signs that they are Christians. They won't read their Bibles or pray. They won't work in a soup kitchen or homeless shelter. They won't participate in rallies to fight injustice or discrimination. People in mainline churches live lives unaffected by their faith."[12]

In an analysis of the above study, a list was made of pivotal qualities one finds in parishioners who have a "mature-integrated-faith." At the apex of the list was "family religiousness." "Christian education" rated a close second. Take the family aspect. In this television-saturated age, building Christian families costs busy households a heap of commitment: in time, energy, and relationships!

We often talk of things being as American as Grandma and apple pie. Peter Benson discovered that old-fashioned Kingdom-virtues still impact lives better than anything else: (1) families reading the Bible and praying together, (2) children aged 5-12 conversing with a parent (especially mother) about God, and (3) families uniting in a service project, e.g. Dad, Mom and the kids making a meal and taking it to a sick or needy family.[13]

A Debate: Conservative Churches

So much for mainline churches. On the opposite end of the theological spectrum, Fundamentalism acts squeamish over "the cost of discipleship." The concept smacks of works-salvation rather than "by faith alone, by grace alone, by scripture alone." To top it off, some conservatives defend a dispensationalism that sees not-one-trace-of-the-gospel in the Sermon on the Mount!

Now from the bastion of Fundamentalism rises a book to challenge such assumptions. Not surprisingly—it reignites an old debate—says *Christianity Today*. The book, *The Gospel According to Jesus* by John MacArthur Jr., California pastor from Sun Valley, calls the Sermon on the Mount "pure" gospel (see Matthew 7:13-23) and teaches that people who accept Jesus only as Saviour and not as Lord aren't really Christian.[14] Opponents quickly label this "lordship salvation."

The Foreword by James Boice, Presbyterian pastor in Philadelphia, laments a weakness in American evangelicalism: "that one can be a Christian without being a follower of the Lord Jesus!" Absurd—thinks Boice—a reductionist Christianity. This reduces the gospel to mere facts about Christ's death for sinners, asking persons only the barest intellectual assent, and promising them eternal security! Boice claims that this gives false hope to many not truly in God's family.[15]

Today's church work tends to be superficial, often lacking cross-bearing. Of course, would-be followers need "space" to count the cost. "Cost-effectiveness" studies, however, prove that family religiousness at home makes the strongest impact on spiritual lives; and dynamic church Christian education comes a close second. Christianity—vital and vigorous—exacts a costly price from any church, from any family and from any disciples who pledge faithfulness to Jesus Christ!

09. the PLANNING-AHEAD factor

Our son Greg, a Certified Public Accountant, works as a controller for an oil firm in a nearby city. All investments, according to Greg, have "opportunity costs" rated according to yield potentials. Rewards on investments should be commensurate with their risk-factor. Recently, Greg ran a break-even analysis on one of their convenience stores to determine whether the store should remain open.

Planning For Successful Results

Light on the Pathway (Luke 14:28-30)

"Suppose one of you wants to build a tower. Will he not first sit down and estimate the cost to see if he has enough money to complete it?..."

Jesus borrowed cost-effectiveness ideas from the business world to bring home a discipleship lesson. Builders of towers calculate cost. Planning is linked to job-completion, asserts Jesus, and protects the builder from public ridicule.

A fascinating example of counting the cost while planning a Christian lifestyle—comes from a university law student in Brazil. He belonged to a family of industrialists that had no reputation for integrity. Jim Petersen, a Navigator worker of dogged persistence, met each week with Sergio for Bible study at a lovely spot overlooking the city. Gradually Sergio moved from agnosticism to faith, and by graduation time was quite mature as a Christian disciple.

In graduation week Sergio made two decisions and reported them to Jim: to put God first and to be honest! Back in his hometown, he opened a law office. One day he went to an auction. A farm was being sold to collect taxes. Sergio bought the farm. All saw him as a wealthy opportunist; but this Christian lawyer shocked his town! He gave the land deed back to the farmer, and suggested the farmer repay as he could. Sergio acted out grace to the farmer, just as God had once acted out of grace to him, while a law student.[16]

The Need For Faith Maturity

The aforementioned study by Search Institute of mainline churches, views faith maturity as "...a vibrant, life-changing faith, the kind of faith that shapes one's way of being, thinking and acting."[17] The bottom line—this 3-year investigation unveils an acute and urgent need for churches to beef up their Christian education departments. The situation is critical!

Let's spot-check a few findings: (1) 36% of adults have undeveloped faith, (2) in ages above 30, women show greater faith maturity than men, (3) half of the men in their 40s have an undeveloped faith, and (4) most youth and adults have an obvious bias against participating in Christian education at their church.[18]

In a penetrating chapter on redefining maturity, Penelope J. Stokes, draws a pithy contrast between sun-ripened tomatos and the unsightly, tasteless, fastgrown kind: "The church today is full of hothouse tomatos—people whose lives are marked by fast-forward maturity. Unwilling to take the time...necessary for... growth, we pump ourselves full of spiritual vitamins, load up with teaching...and drop from the vine green. When...we look as if we have it all together, we are declared 'mature' and sent forth to plant the seed of our unripe faith in someone else's garden."[19] How accurate!—churches thrive on fast-forward procedures.

Uppermost, churches must plan-to-rehone educational tools. People ask for better programs, avers Peter Benson, but few can deliver. "Christian education in a majority of congregations is a tired enterprise in need of reform. Often out-of-touch with adult and adolescent needs, it experiences increasing difficulty in finding and motivating volunteers, faces general disinterest among its 'clients,' and employs...procedures that have changed little over time."[20]

Valuable Mid-Course Corrections
Light on the Pathway (Luke 14:31-32)

"Or suppose a king is about to go to war against another king. Will he not first sit down and consider whether he is able with ten thousand men to oppose the one coming against him with twenty thousand?..."

In the previous portion of our text a builder risks ridicule. Here a warrior-king risks annihilation: it is either do or die. The king ponders the option of compromise: negotiating some "terms of peace."

Christ's stories are as current as the daily news! In fact, during Super Bowl—91 on January 27, a Newsbreak announced that Desert Storm would cost about fifty billion dollars.[21] President Bush was counting on allies to kick in big bucks. Time and again Jesus skillfully illustrated spiritual truths, drawing on the rough and tumble events of world affairs. Jesus used everyday things to portray discipleship as a carefully calculated commitment—no blind naive following.

If the builder's analogy teaches the function of planning; if the king/war analogy teaches how to engineer mid-course corrections; what lesson then must the church learn? Does today's church face a crisis hour, an emergency hour, the zero hour? What changes must churches negotiate? What compromises are necessary? What corrections can revitalize burdened, beleaguered and battered churches?

Planning For Dynamic Ministry

Someone astutely said that dynamic churches have three things in common: leadership, leadership, leadership. When starting a church from scratch in the inner city of Washington, D.C., Myron and Esther Augsburger got the chance of a lifetime to plan creatively for Jesus! Myron loves to model his faith via small-group participation and empathetic preaching. Each Thursday evening the Augsburgers meet with their covenant-group of thirteen, and draw immeasurable strength and guidance from fellow Christians.[22]

The Washington Community Fellowship adopted a ten-point membership covenant as a basis for life together. Potential ministries—food pantry, learning center, credit union, dentistry clinic, or whatever—are not adopted by the elders unless an adequate vision or will-to-work rises out of the congregation itself. Goal-ownership is the word.[23] In the inner city, Augsburger and his wife try to minister via deliberate Christlike "identification."

How to revitalize a church encrusted by a 100-year tradition is quite another matter! My wife and I accepted this charge: 1600 persons including children, amid the lush irrigated corn fields of rural USA. By our denomination's standards, a large church with a good track record of giving and serving.

Susan Joann and I initiated a strategy in our home that became the joy of our lifetime—that of small-group discipling. (I'll share more about this in Chapter Eleven.) Over at church I huddled with leadership to pray and brainstorm about the 15-year decline in Sunday School. The upshot: shore up all classes and start a new large intergenerational class in the balcony. We followed proper channels; all boards approved.

The Business Board built a platform for a teacher and a blackboard. Many people wondered whether a class of this nature could be successfully assembled? Leaders drafted me, as Senior Pastor, to teach "The Life of Christ" as a way to launch the class. We mailed flyers to 400 people not enrolled in Sunday School.

We took no chances—we made personal contacts until we counted 50 yeses. The class enrollment totaled 100. One enrollee was a fellow named, Don. He and his wife became increasingly more active in our church. Soon I recruited Don for discipleship training. Later this stockbroker, at about age 40, taught this vibrant Faith & Life Class. He served with effectiveness and enthusiasm. So I reiterate: leadership, courage and long-range planning can shape destiny!

10. the PERSONAL-CONSECRATION factor

Light on the Pathway (Luke 14:26 & 33)

"If anyone comes to me and does not hate...even his own life—he cannot be my disciple....In the same way, any of you who does not give up everything he has cannot be my disciple."

We come to the disciple's heart of hearts, the inner core. George Ladd lays it bare: "Denial of self...means the renunciation of one's own will that the Kingdom of God may become the all-important concern of life...the cross means the death of self, of personal ambition, and self-centered purpose...one is to desire alone the rule of God."[24] In brief, our one and only passion is, to please God.

Here is discipleship in radical form—surrendering what one is and what one has. This is the acid test of the kingdom. It spells out beyond doubt, who is Lord! We surrender our right to lord it over others, our right to rule as lord over ourselves, and we pledge our obedience to him.

How does such radical submission impact our inner selves?—our health and wholeness. Psychologist Archibald Hart states: "We must not deny that part of the self called the ego, the 'I' or 'me.' This part of the self is who I am. It is the 'I' that lives in Christ and Christ lives in the 'me.' It makes no sense to speak of denying this part of me. It was worthy enough for Christ to die for and save, so it must be given liberty to become what he wants it to be."

Hart explains: "Selfish preoccupation with my own self-aggrandizement on the one hand and self-derogation or disparagement on the other are two extremes of dealing with myself that will only produce unhappiness." He goes on to say that a full yielding of our lower nature to the control of Jesus, a claiming of our heritage as his heir, and assertively doing his will, frees us to live a fulfilled life![25] In the yielding, and unselfish living, wholeness will blossom.

A Dramatic Visit By Christ

Few have dramatized this relinquishment to Jesus of all that is near and dear more effectively than Presbyterian educator, Robert Boyd Munger. His sermon: "My Heart—Christ's Home" was put into booklet form and reprinted time and again by InterVarsity. It was based on a verse (Ephesians 3:16) sometimes translated: "That Christ may settle down and be at home in your hearts by faith." The book illustrated Jesus' coming into Bob's heart, and replacing the emptiness with wonderful light, warmth and music (Revelation 3:20).

Bob gave Jesus a royal tour of the house: Library, Dining Room, Drawing Room, Workshop and all. In each room the Savior made alterations. One day Jesus said, "There is a peculiar odor in the house...something dead...upstairs...in the hall closet." Bob's self-talk was full of anger: "I gave him the run of the whole house and now he wants that tiny closet. True, those personal things are dead and rotten but I love them; I wanted no one to know about them." As the odor got worse, Jesus threatened to sleep on the back porch. Only then did Bob surrender the closet key. In a moment Jesus had the rotten putrefying filth cleared out and the closet repainted. What victory and release!

Bob wearied of housecleaning. Rooms dirtied as fast as he cleaned them. Trying to maintain a clean heart and obedient life exhausted him. "Lord," ventured Bob, "is there any chance of you taking responsibility for the whole house, like you did for the closet?" Bob saw Jesus' face light up. "Certainly," he said, "you can't be victorious as a Christian in your own strength."

"But remember," said Jesus, "I'm only a guest. I have no authority to take over since the property is not mine!" Bob saw the light. He fell on his knees and declared Jesus Lord of his house. Next he ran to the security box and grabbed the deed of title and signed it over to Jesus. "Here," Bob said, "here it is, all that I am and have forever. You run the house, I'll remain as a houseboy and a friend."[26] That's FULL CONSECRATION— Lordship in graphic style!

Light on the Pathway (Luke 14:34-35)

"Salt is good, but if it loses its saltiness, how can it be made salty again? It is fit neither for the soil nor for the manure pile..."

Jesus clinched his discipleship lesson with an analogy to salt. Already in the Sermon on the Mount, he had labeled his followers—Salt of the Earth. In kingdom-talk, in the cosmic struggle between good and evil, disciples not radically committed are like leached out salt—tasteless, useless, and worthless.

An Interview With Leonard Ravenhill

In the USA and Canada, what are churchgoers really like at heart? What basic motivation drives them? Leonard Ravenhill recalls preaching at a church. The sanctuary was swank and three thousand people waited for worship. At that sacred moment when pastors and deacons meet before entering the worship service, one deacon blurted out: "What kind of score do you think our football team will rack up today?" Ravenhill observed, "America has one king—it's SPORTS, and one queen—it's ENTERTAINMENT." Where is that prime devotion to Jesus Christ?

On radio, in The Chapel of the Air, David and Karen Mains enriched their talks on the Prophet Amos with three broadcast interviews with Leonard Ravenhill. The consultation was taped in Texas due to the health of the aging revivalist. His fiery passion for the standards of holiness and his weeping compassion for the welfare of souls was not one bit diminished.[27]

Mains had painted the desperate state of our nation, where the average 17-year-old (via TV) has vicariously experienced 18,000 murders! Ravenhill finished the portrait: America puts Sodom and Gomorrah to shame in devising evil. In Texas alone, the number of people venting violent anger in child abuse and spouse abuse is shocking. Think of legalized abortions, the massive adultery, and the divorce parade. How can God tolerate this? America—the only nation on earth to barbecue a whole city of people in a couple of minutes! Violence and corruption are epidemic, even demonic.

In the Old Testament prophet-style, Ravenhill made a caricature of evangelistic efforts. The city wide crusade might cost two million, but the message is watered-down, benign, and harmless: "Get happy and go to heaven!" or "Relax and get raptured." But who is really "pulling down the strongholds?" Who devotes the prayer time necessary to harvest the four billion people of earth outside the church of Jesus Christ? Where are the tears of brokenness?

David Mains and Renewal

At one point Mains creatively illustrated the origin of church-renewal via a quiz. (Can you fill in the blanks?) It is bacon and ? (yes—eggs); Salt and ?, Bread and ?, Knife and ?, Hammer and ?, Shoes and ?, Table and ?, Pencil and ?, Crackers and ?, Boy and ?, Ball and ?, Revival and ?. [Answers: pepper, butter, fork, nails, socks, chairs, paper, cheese, girl, bat, prayer.] Yes, that's it—Revival and Prayer—the inseparable twins.

As David Mains kept probing Ravenhill about the crisis in churches of our day, the aging evangelist finally said: "The number one defect is prayerlessness. No, on second thought, the greatest deficiency is worship. The woman with the alabaster, silent in his presence, giving Jesus total devotion, that's the greatest need!"

My heart of hearts resonates an "Amen." Mains and Ravenhill have their fingers on the pulse of the crisis. Our discipleship requires a full surrender to Jesus Christ—that's consecration. And it requires keeping our vows and our promises made to Christ and to his church—that's integrity. And it requires all of our witness, service, and worship to surge forth from the overflow of a Spirit-filled life—that's Pentecost. Discipleship is costly, but so rewarding. It is time for every church and every believer to declare Jesus LORD, and to bask in the joy and inspiration of his "Presence."

Conclusion

I close this chapter on the cost of discipleship with a tribute to a peaceful Dutch watchmaker family. On the fateful day of February 28, 1944, the German Gestapo stormed their home, accusing them of sheltering Jews. (Yes—they had a secret hideout!) Betsy, Father and Corrie ten Boom were trucked, with others, 200 miles to The Hague, the Gestapo Dutch headquarters—at the federal penitentiary.

One by one, prisoners were questioned. Abruptly, the head-interrogator noticed Father: "That old man....Did he have to be arrested?" They led Father to his desk. The Gestapo chief said: "I'd like to send you home, old fellow...I'll take your word—promise to cause no more trouble?" Father stood erect and answered calmly, "If I go home today, tomorrow I will open my door to any man in need who knocks!" The kindness drained from the Nazi's face. He yelled, "Get back in line—Schnell!"[28] That's "cross-bearing" in purest form—serving Jesus as Lord, and humans as brothers and sisters with a total disregard for one's life and safety for the sake of the gospel. (Father soon died in prison.)

Like a receiver—dressed in his football uniform—counts the cost, so the church—dressed in her service overalls—calculates the price. All too often the brand of discipleship is an economy variety: cheap, domesticated, cut-rate, and bargain-basement! This evokes a tinge of embarrassment, especially since the church is bulging with successful business persons—people who know about cost analysis and mid-course correction, and who, by the way, live in plush homes with the latest of gadgetry. Counting the cost in discipleship implies that we give more attention and priority to God, the church and its worldwide mission than we do to our personal comforts, livelihood and family pursuits.

Questions for Discussion

1. Discuss your sources of opposition—self, family, church peers, society?
2. What ways does Satan use to weaken your church?
3. Where does your church need more planning and goal-setting?
4. Is Ravenhill correct: sports is king and entertainment is queen?
5. Discuss the words of Corrie ten Boom's father—spoken to Gestapo leaders.

PRACTICING HIS PRESENCE: DEVOTIONAL PAUSE FOR BUSY DISCIPLES
Theme of the week — Counting the Cost

	Monday	**Tuesday**	**Wednesday**	**Thursday**	**Friday**
Light on the pathway	Luke 10:1-23	Luke 12:49-53	John 15:18-27	Luke 14:25-35	Mark 3:31-35
Lesson for this day	Factor #6 Opposition	Factor #7 Family	Factor #8 Cost-analysis	Factor #9 Planning	Factor #10 Surrender
Life in Jesus' way	Take time to pray	Take time to pray	Take time to pray	Take time to pray	Take time to pray

PRACTICE HIS PRESENCE IN CHURCH ON SUNDAY

Chapter

4

Born for Eternity

11. Estrangement
12. Supernatural
13. Incarnation
14. Belief
15. Conversion

Introduction

People's estrangement from God makes divine intervention expedient. This is illustrated by a story Newscaster Paul Harvey has told and retold at Christmas time. A man declined his wife's invitation to attend the Christmas Eve Service. After all, this hustle and bustle of Christmas seemed meaningless. Staying home, he settled into his easy chair to read. A thud against the window startled him. He noticed birds huddled in the cold snowy outdoors. Apparently one had tried to fly into the warmth of the well-lit house.

Moved with pity, he grabbed his coat and went outside to the barn. He opened the doors and turned on the lights; maybe the birds would come find shelter—but they didn't. So he waved his arms and made noises hoping to shoo them in. Finally, he made a trail of bread crumbs to the barn. Still the birds squatted amid the snow drifts—shivering in the cold, neither trusting him nor understanding his well-intentioned activities. In his desperation a thought occurred to him, "I would almost have to become a bird to communicate with them and give them help." Just then the bell rang in the tower of the village church and the man fell to his knees.

This chapter centers on soteriology—themes of salvation. God's unlimited grace has not left people stranded. The

Incarnation is God's answer to humankind's alienation. What a marvel—the Christ of glory becomes the Jesus of the manger. He shoulders our living and dying; we share his rising and reigning. And Jesus unveiled a secret: God is delighted to give us his kingdom (Luke 12:32)!

Five salvation factors comprise this chapter. The central one is the Incarnation (Christ assuming human form). Leading to it we examine the estrangement of humankind from God, and the supernatural dimension of conversion. Leading from the Incarnation we will explore the nature of saving faith, and changes ensuing from conversion. The brief conclusion offers tips on how the small-group setting can help facilitate the teaching of salvation-assurance.

11. the ESTRANGEMENT factor

Jesus graphically illustrated people's lostness. Luke records the triple parables of lost things. This teaching was prompted by the "muttering" of the Pharisees that Jesus was socializing with the unclean riffraff of society—like tax collectors, prostitutes and who-not-all (15:2). While the religious elite shuddered at this blatant disregard for Jewish purity-laws, Jesus demonstrated that he was part of God's great "rescue-operation," and that all people were potential benefactors of God's kingdom (cf. Luke 19:1-10).

Light on the Pathway (Luke 15:1-32)

1. Parable—The Lost Sheep. *...Jesus told them this parable: "Suppose one of you has a hundred sheep and loses one of them. Does he not leave the ninety-nine in the open country and go after the lost sheep until he finds it?..."*

2. Parable—The Lost Coin. *"Or suppose a woman has ten silver coins and loses one. Does she not light a lamp, sweep the house, and search carefully until she finds it?..."*

3. Parable—The Lost Son. *Jesus continued, "There was a man who had two sons. The younger one said to his father, 'Father, give me my share of the estate.' So he divided his property between them. Not long after that, the younger son got together all he had, set off for a dis-*

tant country and there squandered his wealth in wild living. After he had spent everything, there was a severe famine in that whole country, and he began to be in need. So he went and hired himself out to a citizen of that country, who sent him to his field to feed pigs. He longed to fill his stomach with the pods that the pigs were eating, but no one gave him anything. When he came to his senses, he said, 'How many of my father's hired men have food to spare, and here I am starving to death! I will set out and go back to my father'..."

If all the teachings of Jesus have the Kingdom of God as a backdrop, then function and fulfillment are important. A lost sheep is aimless and belongs with the flock. A lost coin is useless and belongs in the owner's purse. A runaway boy is homeless and belongs with his family. The ministry of Jesus actually touched the aimless-useless-homeless pockets of society. Jesus was recruiting for God's great kingdom—the place where all estranged people belong—to fulfill the purpose for which they were created.

Note the accelerating intensity. The shepherd searching for a wandering sheep—one out of a hundred—would hardly be as frantic as the woman who through negligence loses a precious coin—one out of ten—and lights every corner and sweeps every inch. Yet neither the shepherd nor the woman feel the emotional pathos of the father who lost a son—one out of two—to the wild life of sin and sex in the far country. A sheep can stray, a coin can be mislaid, but this son deliberately defied his father's love, his father's ethics and any obligation to his father's estate.

As people listened to the sheep story, Jesus was, in a sense, answering his critics: "...there is more rejoicing in heaven over one sinner who repents than over ninety-nine righteous persons who do not need to repent" (15:7). Minutes later Jesus repeated the same punch line in his coin story: "there is rejoicing in the presence of the angels of God over one sinner who repents" (15:10). Nowhere is this rejoicing more dramatized than in the father's response when the son returns home (15:20-24). The listening audience soon caught on—these parables carry potent lessons about God, heaven, salvation and repentance.

The Threesome and the Lesson

The central truth in these three parables, insists George E. Ladd, is that God yearns for the lost. God, as it were, is seeking a sheep, a coin, and a son. Of the three, the last parable gives the fullest portrait of God—the father who loves, waits, forgives, and celebrates. This is more a parable of a waiting father, than of an erring son. However, it does not teach a universal Fatherhood of God, where all are saved in the end.[1] Notice: the father restores a penitent son who seeks reconciliation, "Father, I have sinned against heaven and against you. I am no longer worthy to be called your son" (15:18).

The father's acceptance of his ragged, hungry, hurting son was spontaneous. His open-armed embrace and his loving kiss affirmed uninterrupted sonship! This nixed the prodigal's planned speech. Back in the pigpen, when the son "came to him-self" he planned to volunteer for a hired-servant status. However, before he could drop to his knees like a slave to kiss his father's feet, or kneel to kiss his father's hand, his father embraced him and kissed him.[2]

The prodigal blurted out his confession of unworthiness— his sin against God and family (15:21). Surprisingly, the father called for special items reserved for honored guests: the best robe, the ring, the sandals and the fattened calf. As in the other two parables, the "finder of the lost" calls friends together, "For this son of mine...was lost and is found," and they began to celebrate.

They're Lost and Who Cares?

But the older brother (like the Pharisees and scribes) is unhappy, unmoved, and unappreciative (15:25-32). "This kid is a good-for-nothing rascal: a money-waster, home-hater, and prostitute-lover. He hits bottom and comes home for a handout. Why under God's heaven does Father throw him a party?" This is akin to that "holier-than-thou" feeling: "Let the wicked stew in hell—they deserve it." But Jesus, in effect, is saying, "Listen, I came to seek the lost. Every time your good-for-nothing brothers or sisters repent and come home to God, the bells of heaven will ring again!"

These stories of Jesus entertain, but deep down they reveal the eternal import of evangelizing "sinners." In context Jesus explains "lostness." A rich man ignoring God's revelation (Moses/the Prophets) lands in hell (Luke 16:19-31). Myron Augsburger exposits (cf. Matthew 18:6-9), "...Hell is the end of a Christless life! It is to go out into eternity without God, to be lost and alone in the darkness of separation, where there is no light, no love, no fellowship, no hope, no God."[3] All the while the Heavenly Father waits with open arms, not willing that any should perish but that all should come to repentance.

In the past 200 years, countless missionaries were motivated by a conviction that people were lost and needed the Gospel. (Love, justice, and humanitarian caring are also key motives.) For one, Adoniram Judson lay sleepless "thinking of the teeming millions beyond the sea sinking into Christless graves."[4]

Barna: America and Heaven

Our alienation from God is also a relevant issue in North America, today. The Barna Research Group, in an annual nationwide telephone survey, found that only 35% of Americans agreed to the statement, "When you die, you will go to Heaven because you have confessed your sins and accepted Jesus Christ as your Savior." A full 16% chose one of three other options on why they expected to reach heaven: (1) they kept the Ten Commandments, (2) they were basically good, or (3) they trusted God to be loving. And another 7% were not certain what would happen when they died.[5]

Belief in the alienation of humankind from God is on the decline. For example, a survey covering Anabaptist churches asked: Do you agree: "Accept Christ as Savior or you'll suffer eternal punishment?" The Brethren in Christ and the Mennonite Brethren scored high marks—75% and 78%, respectively.

However, the tally-average of all groups indicated that 68% agreed, a nine percent decline in seventeen years.[6]

How do we explain this trend? In an era of pluralism, some may doubt that Jesus is the "Only Way." Others may be swayed by the appeal of universalism—that all will be saved. Certain ones may question whether hell implies everlasting conscious punishment, and with Clark Pinnock may opt for a hell that is, in essence, annihilation—an ultimate disappearance of those who are unable to enter into life.[7] In my view, the Incarnation was fraudulently costly, if in fact humankind is not estranged from God. I contend that heaven will become exceedingly precious when we recognize what God has saved us from.

12. the SUPERNATURAL factor

Since people's repentance and restoration activate the angelic choirs, conversions should never become commonplace. But it appears that the salvation of self-perceived "religious" people often requires a demonstrative supernatural encounter. In our experiences, few equaled what we saw in Los Angeles. My wife and I got word that the elderly minister of the nearby South Gate Chapel had experienced a "conversion." Some months later (17 July 1966), on a Sunday night, Dr. Ray Jarman shared dinner with us and told his life-story to our church.

The Conversion of Dr. Ray Charles Jarman

Ray Jarman was born in 1896 in Kansas City. His parents were faithful to the Disciples of Christ (Christian Church). He was taught that regeneration came at one's baptism. His parents were delighted at his interest in becoming a pastor. He attended the denominational university in Missouri, where professors taught a new "enlightened" theology coming from the University of Chicago.

In the "Life of Christ" class, the teacher said the Virgin Birth, unmentioned in Mark, was contrived later by Matthew and Luke. Ray inquired, "If you don't believe one part of the Bible how can you believe any of it?" The prof threatened to expel him. By year's end Ray endorsed "Higher Criticism,"—a denial of Jesus' divinity, miracles, rising or ascending—and scored second in the class.

Ray started preaching in 1914 at age 18. In 1920 he graduated from the University of Kansas; married Grace, his childhood sweetheart; and took his first full-time pastorate at Bowling Green, Missouri. His parents were proud of his achievements, though secretly he had strayed far from their beliefs.

A dying woman said, "Pastor, tell me about heaven." Concealing his own disbelief, he read from John 14. His "self-talk" responded: "You're deceiving her. You should leave the ministry." In Kansas City he tested the idea with a church leader. "No, my son," the man said, "soon nobody will believe the Bible. We need you. Find something you can believe—without violating integrity—and preach it." Jarman determined to heed that advice.

When a Michigan church (Benton Harbor) called Jarman, he jumped at the chance; it opened doors to graduate studies at the University of Chicago under a world-renowned faculty. They taught that angels and demons are human creations to explain good and evil; that only verifiable truth is believable; that Modernism takes the best from all world religions (Christianity, Judaism, Islam, Hinduism, etc.) and formulates a beautiful syncretistic philosophy—the wave of the future.

During the Great Depression Jarman served Ohio parishes. In 1942 he moved to California to the Huntington Park Christian Church. Here, again he drew followers rapidly. He could communicate well—quoting long Bible passages from memory and holding audiences spellbound. His radio talks enhanced his popularity, as did also his Shriner and Rotarian memberships. Conducting weddings and funerals gave him a hefty income. Yet he was strictly humanist, believing nothing supernatural.

Over the years his wife, Grace, remained true to her Disciples of Christ upbringing. She read the Bible and prayed daily. She radiated a lifelong genuine faith. She frequently expressed her uneasiness over Ray's philosophical leanings. While she busied herself raising their two children, Jarman busied himself with his counseling ministry. After the children left home Grace's health gradually failed. She died, leaving her husband unchanged.

Over the years, Jarman noticed that his "re-make yourself" theology was powerless to change people. He kept searching "in dangerous water" as he later called it. From a smorgasbord of religious ideas he dabbled in Yoga, astrology, spiritualism, Christian Science, hypnotism, and even reincarnation. But nothing compared to his Menlo Park experiment! He paid doctors $500 for a religious-LSD experience. He saw God at the top of a jewel-studded ladder, but he himself kept helplessly sliding downwards towards Hell, where the devil was tormenting people familiar to him. It was horrifying! A psychologist escorted him home, 400 miles. It took him days to recover.

One day Shannon, a 14-year member, asked about the deity of Christ. "Jesus was no more divine than we are," quipped Jarman. "History has mountaintop figures like Lincoln, Shakespeare and Jesus. Some seize upon that quality." Shannon was shocked! At a Full Gospel Businessmen's rally in Phoenix, Shannon was converted to Christ and baptized in the Holy Spirit. Back home he began carrying his Bible.

Jarman despised Bible toters. So when Shannon tried to dialogue on Christianity, his pastor responded with a knee-jerk defense. Soon, Jarman noticed that his own sermons were becoming an apologetic to counteract Shannon's ideas!

Miracles persisted. Carmen Benson, Jarman's secretary had a dream. Her local Metaphysician was baffled. Accidentally, on Gospel Radio, she heard a story: a hen died to protect her chicks. Instantly Carmen understood—the pure white bird in her dream was a symbol of Christ's death—washing sins white as snow. On her knees, she felt great love as she wept, worshiped, and accepted her Christ.

What a shock—Jarman's closest aid began flashing a Bible! This spawned lively dialogue. One lunch Carmen heard sophisticated arguments against biblical doctrines. Gently she replied, "If you don't believe one part of the Bible, how can you believe the rest?" Jarman's mealtime was ruined!

One spring, Dr. Jarman told his secretary, "Carmen, I wish I had what you have. I wish I could be born-again. It's no use, I'm too old and set in my ways." On March 28, 1966, Shannon appeared at Jarman's apartment. "Ray," he said, "you are seeking God in wrong ways—by your own wisdom. You must approach God as a helpless child comes to a mother. Just accept Jesus." "Shannon, I want Him," said Jarman. As Jarman kneeled God showed him the load of his sin: having deceived thousands of people during 52 years of preaching. An avalanche of agony crushed him. Suddenly he felt a glorious peace. A terrible weight was lifted. In a vision he saw double doors open—Christ entered and touched him. "I was overwhelmingly aware that I was born-again in Jesus Christ....I was changed in the twinkling of an eye— spiritually, morally, philosophically, socially, theologically—in all ways...a new creature in Christ."[8] He said, "I had assumed that Bible-believing Christians were...unenlightened. Yet when I got up from my knees that night...suddenly I knew the Bible was true!"[9]

13. the JESUS-INCARNATION factor

Central to our theology is this unique birth. Jesus was more than a great teacher; he was the Son of God, fully divine and fully human.

His Miraculous Birth
Light on the Pathway (Matthew 1:18-25, Luke 1:26-38)

...an angel of the Lord appeared to him in a dream and said, "Joseph son of David, do not be afraid to take Mary home as your wife, because what is conceived in her is from the Holy Spirit..." ..."How will this be," Mary asked the angel, "since I am a virgin?" The angel answered, "The Holy Spirit will come upon you, and the power of the Most High will overshadow you..."

According to T. M. Dorman, "textual evidence" finds these infancy narratives flawless.[10] The whole incarnation event is, of course, awe-inspiring, profound and mysterious. As evangelicals, we simply affirm the witness of scripture—this is how it happened. "The doctrine of the Virgin Birth has most often been used to argue that this Jesus so born must have been divine and sinless. Actually, it is more proper to think of the Virgin Birth as the declaration that the Word actually became flesh!"[11] Using this supernatural event as a starting point is called "doing Christology from above."

Today the Virgin Birth is too lightly dismissed. That it appears in only two gospels is no argument. On those grounds the Sermon on the Mount can also be nullified. The view that Christians copied pagan-hero ideas is also untenable. Central to pagan thought is the idea that mythical gods lusted sexually after mortal women.[12] This text has a rare dignity and mystique, devoid of any immoral lust. Since Christians in the Early Church were obligated to add what they knew to the Oral Tradition, physician Luke may well have consulted Mary personally to validate his account.

His Marvelous Life and Teachings
Light on the Pathway (John 6:66-69)

From this time many of his disciples turned back and no longer followed him. "You do not want to leave too, do you?" Jesus asked the Twelve. Simon Peter answered him, "Lord, to whom shall we go? You have the words of eternal life. We believe and know that you are the Holy One of God."

The Apostles' Creed, a powerful affirmation of the great truths of Christianity, jumps from the birth of Jesus to the trial and crucifixion, bypassing the life and teachings of Jesus. (The creed first appeared under that title in about A. D. 390 and was used only in the Western churches.) Since some churches today quote this creed in their weekly liturgy, this omission is unfortunate.

The Incarnation, seen from a discipleship point of view, needs to accent the life and teachings of Jesus, as well as his birth, death, and resurrection. Jesus emphasized disciple-making (Matthew 28) with instructions to go worldwide, to baptize publicly in the name of the triune God, and to implement sound educational methods, "...teaching them to obey everything I have commanded you." This is called "practicing Christology from below," where the church uses the life and teachings of Jesus for instructions regarding crucial kingdom issues in our day. Discerning and dispensing these ideas is highly important in Christian education.

The Jesus-way-of-life as reflected in the Gospels is part of God's unfolding revelation of himself. Jesus Christ is the climax to a progressive kind of revelation beginning in the Old Testament. The Jesus-Event is a watershed. Everything in the Bible points forward to him, or back to him. As an evangelical I believe in the inspiration of the scriptures. I do not mean to say that the Gospels are more authoritative than the Epistles. Both were written by the followers of Jesus. (Remember, Jesus wrote no book!) While the total lifestyle and teachings of Jesus are important, some of the fullest interpretations of Christ come in the epistles of Romans and Hebrews, where all is placed in theological perspective.

His Vicarious Death
Light on the Pathway (John 3:16-18)

"For God so loved the world that he gave his one and only Son, that whoever believes in him shall not perish but have eternal life. For God did not send his son into the world to condemn the world, but to save the world through him..."

At times Jesus spoke of the gracious lovingkindness of his Heavenly Father. Under the Fatherhood of God, by virtue of creation, rain and sunshine comes on both the just and unjust (Matthew 5:45). How bighearted our God is! Blessings come undeserved. In Reformed theology, this is called God's "Common Grace."

Moreover, there is also "Special Grace." It also reveals the incomprehensible love of God. Under the Fatherhood of God, by virtue of redemption, Jesus died for every person ever to set foot on this earth. Since people are sinners by choice, as well as sinners by nature, it is required that persons respond to the Good News: repenting, believing, accepting. To grant heaven to those who spurn God's gift of salvation mocks every universal standard of righteousness.

The splendor of redemption radiates from the cross and contrasts with the hopeless dilemma of humankind, like bright colors of a rainbow contrast with dark clouds in foreboding skies. I see four refractive rays in redemption's prism.

** **LOVE.** The death of Jesus on the cross was the supreme act of love, because the sinless Son of God died unselfishly for a world of sinners (John 3:16).

** **DELIVERANCE.** Jesus told his disciples that his work of casting out demons proved that the Kingdom of God had come (Matthew 12:28). The Bible sees Jesus' death as delivering people from Satan's reign. The Apostle John later wrote that Jesus appeared to destroy the devil's work (I John 3:8).

** **SUBSTITUTION.** The Communion Table is a constant reminder of the body broken for us and the blood shed for us. The Prophet foresaw us straying and God's Messiah as a substitute bearing our sins and our sorrows (Isaiah 53:4-6).

** **RECONCILIATION.** John's gospel portrays Jesus as "lifted up" in death, drawing people to himself (3:14-15, 12:32). The Epistles portray his atonement as removing the barriers between God and humankind (Ephesians 2:13-18). It was God—in Christ—reconciling the world to himself (II Corinthians 5:18).

His Victorious Resurrection
Light on the Pathway (John 10:1-18)

"...I am the gate; whoever enters through me will be saved....I have come that they may have life, and have it to the full. I am the good shepherd. The good shepherd lays down his life for the sheep....No one takes it from me, but I lay it down of my own accord. I have authority to lay it down and authority to take it up again..."

The Resurrection is the capstone of the Gospel. At first,

Jewish leaders squelched the news with hush money and the alibi that Jesus' disciples stole his body while the guards slept (Matthew 28:11-15). As for the disciples they saw, touched and handled the Risen Lord. Actually, the word "resurrection" implies that the same body that was flogged, crucified and speared was raised from the dead. Thus Jesus as a person was transformed bodily into a spiritual form already fitted for heaven—apparently not subject anymore to earth's time and space continuum. The reality of this resurrection event was so convincing that the Early Church risked life and limb to propagate the Good News.

In one sense, the Apostles spiritualized the Resurrection, and used it to symbolize Jesus' promise of the "abundant life" (John 10:10). Paul wrote "...like as Christ was raised up from the dead by the glory of the Father, even so we also should walk in newness of life" (Romans 6:4 KJV). The Radical Reformers of the 16th Century reclaimed the motto: "We Walk in Newness of Life."[13] They knew salvation required transformed living, and that the mighty power of God which raised up Jesus, offered to Christians anytime anywhere everything they needed.

Paul averred that Christians were as much saved by Christ's life as by his death (Romans 5:8-10). Nonetheless, it can be documented that after eyewitnesses of the living Jesus died, a gradual shift—over centuries—occurred. Eventually, Jesus' vicarious death on the cross got prime recognition; and the understanding of "salvation" narrowed down to the idea of "sins forgiven." The Early Church saw salvation as a life. They elevated the Resurrection into prominence, and consequently emphasized "walking in newness." They viewed forgiveness as one part—important certainly—of the new victorious life in the Kingdom of God.[14]

14. the BELIEF factor

From God's perspective, people's alienation from him, renders them useless. However, God took the initiative in Christ, and drew people back to himself—to replace uselessness with a task, aimlessness with a purpose, and estrangement with a sense of belonging. In essence, God out of lovingkindness provided the remedy. Our faith-surrender to him activates it.

Light on the Pathway (John 20:30-31)

Jesus did many other miraculous signs in the presence of his disciples, which are not recorded in this book. But these are written that you may believe that Jesus is the Christ, the Son of God, and that by believing you may have life in his name.

These verses as well as John 3:16 accent belief or "saving faith." This is no rare quality of faith, but a simple trust, where we take God at his word via the Bible. Salvation is received by faith (unearned—given as God's gift) and by grace (undeserved—flowing from God's mercy). The Apostle John declares that such belief provides our basis for the assurance of salvation (I John 5:11-15).

Saving faith has four aspects, wrote one theologian: (1) a confident trust in God and his Word, (2) a continuing self-surrender to God, (3) a longing to please God, and (4) a willingness to obey Christ regardless of consequences.[15] The last two, in a sense, are also forms of surrender. Jesus' disciple, Peter, later clarified—we are saved by faith and kept by faith (I Peter 1:3-5). In our growth towards becoming Christlike, good works do not enhance the value of our faith; rather, they validate the authenticity of our faith. Eternal life is ultimately a gift—unmerited—accepted by faith.

This idea of total surrender and trust was dramatized at Niagara Falls in 1859 as the "Great Blondin" carried a man across the Niagara River gorge on a tightrope. Blondin, trained as a stuntman in the European circus tradition, came to America at age 31 under the sponsorship of P. T. Barnum. On June 30, he held a huge crowd in the grip-of-suspense, for 18 minutes, as he crossed the gorge for the first time. As a showman with a 40-foot balancing pole, his hesitations, swayings and somersaults petrified the crowd. Once ashore on the Canadian side his delirious well-wishers gave him a champagne reception. Thus fortified he returned to the rope; then danced, skipped and frolicked back across it in 7 minutes, to thunderous applause.

The Blondin Escapades at Niagara

That summer he crossed the rope blindfolded, rode a bicycle, pushed a wheelbarrow, and finally announced that on August 19, he would carry across on his back his manager, Harry Colcord. Over 100,000 visitors watched this supreme test of Blondin's skill and stamina. It was a nightmare. Once the rope swayed alarmingly; and Blondin ran to the next guy rope. "...Blondin gasped for Colcord to get down. The terrified manager slithered down the sweat-soaked back to rest one foot on the swinging rope. This relieved Blondin of his weight sufficiently so the great acrobat could rest for the uphill climb. Soon they were off again. Six times in all Colcord had to dismount..."[16] So again Blondin had succeeded!

Colcord demonstrated total trust. Jesus Christ, the Risen Savior and Coming King, carries helpless fearful people across the chasm of sin and despair to the Promised Land of Eternal Life. When disciples place their faith in Jesus Christ, they stake their entire destiny on him. "...I am the way, the truth, and the life," Jesus said, "No one comes to the Father except through me" (John 14:6).

The Good Shepherd promises endurance—holding and keeping power: "I give to them eternal life, and they shall never perish; no one can snatch them out of my hand" (John 10:28). This is not written about people who live for the devil. These are sheep of a specific character (10:27): (1) they listen to the shepherd, (2) they are known by him, and (3) they follow him. Those who follow responsively and obediently are promised eternal life. It's a guarantee made good by Christ and honored by God—because Son and Father are one (10:30).

This is not something cheap, something superficial, something we unfurl on Sunday and hide on Monday. One man said, "...faith can be defined as confidence in God's love as revealed in Jesus which is expressed in following him."[17]

How Faith Impinges on Conduct

We insist that salvation is by the Word, by faith, by grace—always a gift. Notwithstanding, we contend repeatedly: Salvation besides forgiveness infers walking in newness. Disciples do not walk away from conversion scot-free. They are obligated. In Church history a degree of tension has existed between personal faith in Christ, and how that faith impinges upon conduct. This tension has manifested itself in a variety of ways. Following are four examples.

*** **An example with early Christians.** In the Early Church the Judaizers insisted on imposing certain legalistic demands on new converts, such as circumcision (Acts 15:1). When Paul wrote the letter of Ephesians he counteracted such legalism, "For it is by grace you have been saved, through faith...it is the gift of God—not by works....For we are God's workmanship, created in Christ Jesus to do good works..." (2:8-10). Paul upheld the grace-idea, gift-idea and faith-idea. God's grace transforms us; our new lifestyle and good works authenticate it.

*** **An example in the Sixteenth Century.** The major reformers rejected the Catholic merit-system of salvation (like buying indulgences, doing penance, and suffering in Purgatory), and heralded a new freedom based on justification by faith. Yet, tension arose between Martin Luther, exponent of salvation by grace alone, and the Anabaptists who (building on that grace) emphasized "imitating Christ"[18] and "living transformed lives"—as flowing from conversion.[19]

Consequently, the personal lives of Anabaptists, at times called Radical Reformers, were exemplary. One critic who viewed them as heretics, nonetheless, conceded that "...they are irreproachable. No lying, deception, swearing, strife, harsh language, no intemperate eating and drinking, no outward personal display is found among them, but humility, patience, uprightness, neatness, honesty, temperance, straightforwardness in such measure that one would suppose that they had the Holy Spirit of God."[20]

*** **An example in the Eighteenth Century.** John Wesley owed his experience of saving faith to a Moravian meeting at Aldersgate (24 May 1738), and among the Moravians he witnessed firsthand the Christian model of life-in-community. He learned the value of structures in society (and smaller bands) for nurturing faith. The two concerns that led Wesley to separate from the Moravians in 1740 were: (1) their view of the sacraments, and (2) their devaluation of the ethical side of Christianity (e.g. disciplined living, good works, and preaching the gospel to the poor). Wesley understood—good works never attained salvation. Like Radical Protestantism, he held that works were the evidence of regeneration.[21]

*** An example in the Twentieth Century. As we have stated, in conservative circles a debate rages over the minimum requirements for being a Christian. Zane Hodges promotes a view of salvation first spawned by Lewis Sperry Chafer, that accepts Jesus as Savior, but not as Lord. The meaning is that faith alone is required—neither faithfulness nor discipleship. Hodges and other very sincere people have the overriding fear of teaching a nonbiblical "works-salvation."

A forceful rebuttal, from the pen of the Los Angeles Pastor, John F. MacArthur, Jr. (who is also President of Master's Seminary), states: "The message of Jesus cannot be made to accommodate any kind of cheap grace or easy-believism. The kingdom is not for people who want Jesus without any change in their living. It is only for those who seek it with all their heart, those who agonize to enter. Many who approach the gate turn away upon finding out the cost."[22] As always, a balance in theology is imperative. To use a rancher's metaphor, some are in danger of falling off the horse on one side, and some on the other!

15. the CONVERSION factor

Our Lord portrayed people as needing conversion—a change of allegiance—from the Kingdom of Satan to the Kingdom of God. Like lost straying sheep, people move in the wrong direction—walking as it were, with their backs toward God. This calls for a threefold turnabout: in one's attitude, in one's nature and in one's sphere of living.

A Change of Attitude
Light on the Pathway (Mark 1:14-15)

...Jesus went into Galilee, proclaiming the good news of God. "The time has come," he said, "The kingdom of God is near. Repent and believe..."

In changing attitudes, faith and repentance go together. We have discussed the former (see Belief Factor), here we turn to the latter. "Repentance," says George Brunk III, "is the principal word in the New Testament to express the human decision to leave the old sinful life and to embrace the way of Jesus."[23] Repentance includes three aspects: a mental acknowledgment of one's sinfulness, an emotional feeling of godly grief (not ungodly despair) for one's unbecoming deeds and attitudes, and a volitional turning to Christ for salvation.[24]

In one of my pastorates, a deacon and his wife befriended their neighbors, Ann and Dave. Eventually, they had the joy of leading Ann to faith in Christ. Baptismal Sunday brought great rejoicing to our church. Dave, however, showed no interest. One Sunday after a sermon on prayer, 50 people volunteered to accept prayer-lists for daily use. Each list had ten names of unreached people in our neighborhood. Dave's name, however, appeared on no less than twenty lists!

One day Dave was hospitalized. I found him friendly and talkative. "Have you ever thought of accepting Christ and becoming a Christian as your wife has?" I asked softly. "Pastor," Dave responded, "do you think I should if I don't feel like it?" "No, surely not," I said, "but our feelings can mislead us!" We persisted in prayer. Then one Easter Sunday, in response to the sermon, Dave in true repentance and faith accepted Christ. The whole church was ecstatic!

In his interview before baptism, Dave told the Board of Deacons, "God spoke to me through the Easter sermon. While I had often entertained the thought of becoming a Christian some day, I kept feeling I was not ready to commit to the demands of a Christian lifestyle. But that morning I sensed the Lord saying to me, 'Dave, I'm giving you one last chance to decide in my favor.' Well, it's the best decision I ever made, and I want to affirm it with public baptism."

A Change of Nature
Light on the Pathway (John 1:11-13)

...Yet to all who received him, to those who believed in his name, he gave the right to become children of God—children born not of natural descent, nor of human decision or a husband's will, but born of God.

Upon repentance, regeneration follows. This describes God's activity wherein a new nature is implanted and the Lord takes up residence in the believer. Jesus taught that a born-again experience was necessitated by our inherent sinfulness. "For from within, out of men's hearts, come evil thoughts, sexual immorality, theft, murder, greed, malice, deceit, lewdness, envy, slander, arrogance and folly. All these evils come from inside and make a man 'unclean'" (Mark 7:21-23).

At times church leaders falsely assume that people can be educated into the Kingdom—that the key is simply knowledge. "Religious education," wrote E. Stanley Jones, the Methodist missionary, "can prepare us for this moment of surrender and faith; it can give us a thirst...but it cannot give the thing itself. That comes from a personal saving contact with a Savior, which in turn comes from decision, from repentance, from surrender, from faith, from appropriation. After one has accepted the gift, then religious education can cultivate the new-found life and nurture it, but it is no substitute for it."[25]

If children are reared in Christian homes, no dramatic life change may be noticeable. Some Christians say that they have believed as long as they can remember. It is true that some children have grown in their knowledge of God, and of Jesus Christ (living, dying and rising—for them) so gradually that they cannot define a time of commitment. After all, they never resisted the added truth.

Nevertheless, the inherent sinfulness of human nature is unarguable. My wife has devoted many years to a nursery ministry with babies and toddlers. She tells me, "No children need lessons on how to do evil. A selfish streak appears in the earliest stages of development. Inherently, kids know how to scream, hit, bite, or kick. And children, age three to five, very naturally lie and cheat to escape the awful embarrassment of losing face or losing a game."

Does everyone need conversion? Yes, because everyone has sinned. For many children the change will not be dramatic. Some will not know the exact time that they entered this "saving" relationship. However, by the time they reach their teens, they should be able to affirm (1) that they have decided to repent of all sin—in a world of good and evil—stepping over to God's side, (2) that they have accepted God's gift of salvation—believing in Jesus Christ as their own Lord and Savior, and (3) that they have embraced, as their own, the faith of their church and parents (providing the parents are believers).

A Change of Sphere
Light on the Pathway (Matthew 18:1-5) (John 5:24)

...[Jesus] said, "I tell you the truth, unless you change and become like little children, you will never enter the kingdom of heaven..." "I tell you the truth, whoever hears my word and believes him who sent me has eternal life and will not be condemned; he has crossed over from death to life."

Bent toward sin—selfish to the core—we're called to a major transition from death to life (John 5:24). Rather than aiding Satan's kingdom, disciples of Jesus, by means of repentance and childlike faith, deliberately cross over to the Kingdom of God. Basic orientations change. Life that once revolved around the big "I" now revolves around Christ (cf. 2 Corinthians 5:17). Christ becomes central.

In his excellent book, *The Upside-Down Kingdom*, Donald

Kraybill warns of the danger of cheapening and sugarcoating a costly gospel. "We slice off the call to discipleship and focus on spiritual fluff, froth and fizz....Just follow Jesus we are told, and we'll be successful....Be born-again and we'll win more beauty contests, hit more home runs, make more sales, and receive more rewards."[26] His underlying assertion is that conversion leads to a serious following of Jesus, a path that is likely to be difficult and counter-cultural, rather than easy and popular. Obedience to Jesus will likely encroach upon one's behavior.

When Dave accepted Christ, and joined his wife, Ann, in the fellowship of our church, he recognized the implications. His Sunday morning round of golf and his lawn mowing might be replaced by Sunday School and morning worship. He knew his leisure time might give way to Bible study and church activities. In fact, within one year he was a Sunday School teacher. In three years the church members affirmed his spiritual growth by electing him as chairman of the congregation.

A New Testament theology of salvation begins with the teachings of Jesus regarding the Kingdom of God in the Gospels, rather than with the Pauline teaching of justification by faith in the Epistles. The Gospels portray the Kingdom as a gift (Luke 12:32).[27] It is a sphere where the rules are different (Matthew 18:1-4); where priorities are shifted (Matthew 6:31-34); and where attitudes are reversed (Luke 22:24-27). We are all invited to that sphere where God reigns and his blessings overflow.

Conclusion

Now a moment of review: the lovingkindness of God is marvelous. Look at his rescue-operation—the mission of Jesus "to seek and to save the lost." In faith and repentance we run into the arms of a Loving Father. Our lives are transformed as we're born from above—by the power of the Gospel. The study of soteriology enlightens us, convicts us and ultimately enraptures us. It is God's "good news!"

We end with a teaching-testimony. Covenant-groups (8-12

persons) offer a nonthreatening way for teaching the assurance of salvation to adults. In a discipleship-nurture format, we included spiritual autobiographies. The leader shared his or her life-story in the first week. After that members took turns being the "Disciple of the Week"—to share theirs. The leader played a key role in discussing and affirming the story, and at times drawing the person out on certain deep-felt experiences. Everyone was participating. The leader treated each with equal regard, always ending with a prayer for the Disciple of the Week.

At times persons spoke rather nebulously in describing their religious stance, as though becoming a Christian was involuntary—like a flu to catch or an influence to rub off. After affirming key aspects, ever-so-gently, the leader asked some questions: When in life did God feel the nearest? When did your parent's faith become yours? Did you ever feel guilt over sin? Do you recall a time when you asked Christ into your heart? Have you had lingering doubts?

One night at ten o'clock Jose came to see me. "Pastor, tomorrow evening I share my life-story. I professed faith as a teenager and was baptized. Now I'm in my fifties and still suffer from gnawing doubts. I want to make sure tonight!" We pored over familiar scriptures and prayed together. The next evening he ended his story with: "Yesterday I went for spiritual counsel. Now I definitely know I am a Christian. I have no doubts anymore."

Questions for Discussion:

1. Discuss similarities/differences in the lost (sheep, coin, son) parables.
2. In your opinion, what brought about Dr. Ray Charles Jarman's conversion?
3. What aspect is most overlooked—Jesus' birth, life, death, resurrection?
4. Explain "saving faith." (John 3:16 offers eternal life to believers.)
5. How does your church help people who need assurance of salvation?

PRACTICING HIS PRESENCE: DEVOTIONAL PAUSE FOR BUSY DISCIPLES
Theme of the week — Born For Eternity

	Monday	Tuesday	Wednesday	Thursday	Friday
Light on the pathway	Luke 15:11-32	John 3:1-13	John 3:14-21	John 5:24-30	John 10:1-14, 25-30
Lesson for this day	Factor #11 Estranged	Factor #12 Supernatural	Factor #13 Incarnation	Factor #14 Believing	Factor #15 Conversion
Life in Jesus' way	Take time to pray	Take time to pray	Take time to pray	Take time to pray	Take time to pray

THIS WEEK — PRACTICE HIS PRESENCE AT CHURCH

Chapter

5

Fishing For People

16. Fishing
17. Acceptance
18. Commission
19. Sensitivity
20. Banquet

Introduction

The command of Jesus to be fishers of people is understood in a variety of ways. Some Christians visualize mass evangelism where persuasive speakers like Billy Graham expound the word and inquirers respond to an altar call. This idea was modeled at Pentecost. Peter preached; 3000 believed, were baptized, and joined the church (Acts 2:41).

In the mid-60's a Billy Graham Crusade came to the Los Angeles Coliseum. For our church and hundreds of others it was a high-point of "celebration." Serving as an advisor to the counselors I interviewed 51 persons who came forward to accept Christ. Many were sincere. Pastors in the follow-up task force noticed it was ideal when a convert was brought by a Christian friend. When they came alone and accepted Christ, it was nearly impossible to assimilate them into any church.

Other believers view their own pastor as the super "fisherman." Parishioners bring visitors, and the pastor preaches to win them. Many huge churches are built exactly that way. When the pastor urges people to evangelize, parishioners assume that they should bring their friends to church. In contrast to community-wide crusades, the advantage here is that the inquirers are already inside the walls of the church and are easily incorporated into the networks of that congregation.

However, I believe a full-orbed biblical evangelism requires that every Christian be a witness. Yes, the Great Commission is binding on all believers. Secondly, we also hold that some Christians have a spiritual gift of evangelism. As gifts are identified in churches, those with an evangelistic giftedness should be encouraged to reach new people, possibly winning them in their homes.

Others in the church, with gifts like leading, mercy, hospitality, and teaching, assume a pivotal role in establishing the new members. Ideally, the whole body of Christ becomes involved in nurture and convert-care. When Christ is Lord of the church, and the Holy Spirit fills each member, no part of the body is unengaged. In churches with good biblical input, a steady stream of people can be won, by way of Sunday School outreach, home Bible study, or personal witness.

This chapter on evangelism (1) opens on the theme of "fishing for people" and (2) proceeds to the attitude of "acceptance" in church outreach. Next (3), it looks at the Great Commission, and one denomination's 400-year experience with it. Finally (4), it details the need for "sensitivity" in evangelism, and (5) the need for urgency which the banquet-teachings suggest.

16. the FISHING factor

The recent writings of Reginald Bibby sent shock waves through the churches of Canada. Bibby claims that church attendance has dropped by half in just forty years. Christianity in Canada, he declares, is so infused by secular culture that its impact on the nation is negligible. More pointedly, he charges Conservative Protestants (evangelicals) for evangelizing only the already "initiated," for reaching only their own kind. Consequently, growing churches are not necessarily evangelizing. To put it bluntly, they are only "circulating the saints."[1]

The Birth of Vision 2000 in Canada

The severity of the spiritual crisis had long been felt by Outreach Canada. Together with several denominations they published a book in 1990: *Reclaiming a Nation: The Challenge of Re-Evangelizing Canada,* edited by Arnell Motz. In the process "Vision 2000" was born "as a strategy for mobilizing the whole Body of Christ in evangelism, with a focus on reaching [the] whole nation."[2] I attended a Vision 2000 meeting at Richmond, British Columbia in April of 1991, to hear the speakers and to conduct a discipleship seminar.

Each speaker had authored an evangelism book: Ray Bakke, Donald Posterski, Juan Carlos Ortiz and Keith Phillips. The final banquet was a kind of clincher—calling church groups to accountability. Some ten denominations, including my own, all outlined their 10-year goals for church planting and evangelism in hopes of reaching the cities of British Columbia for Christ.

As in Canada, so in the USA—church outreach lags. Evangelism is the heartbeat of any healthy church; yet one congregation after another requires jump-starting by some new impetus. It's a grave misconception to relegate witnessing to the most mature. In fact, new Christians grow and mature fastest if they are winning and discipling others. Even at that, Donald McGavran, in *How Churches Grow,* finds a prevailing bias in favor of comfortably settling down and perfecting the saints, rather than persistently reaching out to new people.

Light on the Pathway (Matthew 4:18-22)

As Jesus was walking beside the Sea of Galilee...."Come, follow me," Jesus said, "and I will make you fishers of men." At once they left their nets....

At first glance it may appear that this summons by Jesus to the four fishers, two pairs of brothers, was a call to strangers—a first contact. Far from it. As "the Relational Factor" of Chapter Two indicates, this is the second stage of discipleship development where occupations were abandoned.[3] The first stage came some six to eight months earlier as recorded in the opening chapters of John's gospel.[4] The initial stage called them to belief and led them into festive social interaction (e.g. the wedding at Cana).

While Jesus' call to "fish for people" did not come at Jesus' initial contact with these disciples, it did come in the middle of his first year with them. Very early in the discipleship training of the Twelve, Jesus began lessons on winning the lost—loving and caring, teaching and reaching. We make a major mistake if we wait until converts reach a certain level of maturity before we broach the subject of winning others. At the time of their conversion, believers have maximum contact with non-Christians, while also possessing a most exuberant contagious faith. Zeal cools off far too quickly when new believers take their cue from typical non-witnessing pew-warming Sunday-by-Sunday church attendees.

The Meaning of Fishing For People

A decade ago, Arthur McPhee's practical book, *Friendship Evangelism*, drew a comparison between present-day fishing and the fishing of Bible days—a comparison based in part on a 1973 article featured in the *Gospel Herald*. McPhee writes: "...We automatically think of angling (with a rod and a baited hook). But Jesus was speaking of net fishing. If we understood this properly, we would have a much-needed corrective to what often passes for evangelism these days...."[5] I draw four salient points from this comparison, and enlarge on them.

(1) Angling is a solo effort; net fishing is an enterprise of partners. When the weight of the catch is too heavy, fishermen call on their partners to help them (Luke 5:7). Evangelism, also, is basically a venture of partners. When each church member uses his or her spiritual gifts (e.g. hospitality, service, helps, evangelism, teaching and ministry) people are won and nurtured in a well-balanced manner. In the process, the love believers extend to each other, gives proof of true discipleship (John 13:35). The visible community is evidence that Christ breaks down the walls between Jew and Gentile, male and female, slave and free.

(2) Angling depends on trickery and violence. Fishing with concealed lines and baited hooks involves snagging fish by deception, and violently removing them from the water. By contrast net fishing involves lifting fish out of their natural surroundings. The implications for evangelism are important. Any outreach that uses entrapment comes under suspicion. The late George Peters said that at most, ten percent of a congregation can be trained in direct-confrontation evangelism while about thirty-five percent would be willing to practice friendship evangelism. Christians who are trained to share the gospel through clever Madison Avenue quick-sell schemes sooner or later get the uneasy feeling that their hard-sell approach is repulsive to unwilling souls.

(3) The angler fishes merely for sport; the net fisherman fishes for a living. The angler has trophies in mind. The net fisherman, on the other hand, needs the fish to maintain his family livelihood. In the same way the church does not fish for fun or trophies but for its survival. The church needs all the resources God provides—people, money, ability, spiritual gifts and wisdom.—for its very existence. God's gifted people must produce fruit, otherwise the church will wither and die.

(4) The angler is fascinated with his catch for today. The net fisherman, anxious about livelihood, is engrossed with his long-term needs. Good biblical evangelism is not a mere exercise in scalp-hunting, it has the long view in mind. It pays due respect to people as persons. It builds a bridge of friendship over which people can walk right into the church. It works for permanence— seeking to tie people into the church for the long haul through conversion, nurture, fellowship and service. New Testament evangelism shies away from "using" people; it bonds, it builds, it blesses.

So what am I saying? Our American concept of fishing conjures up ideas of trickery. Admittedly, even net fishing has an element of "outwitting" the fish. However, fundamentally, biblical evangelism is a task to pursue, not a trick to perform. Our caution here is not against boldness. God knows we need it. The caution is against devious methods that violate personhood.

Ponder this question: How does Jesus turn us into fishers for his kingdom today? The answer: (1) his teachings instruct, (2) his Holy Spirit prompts, and (3) his church discerns. As a whole, church-centered evangelism is the most lasting kind. Giving to missions, praying for others, and doing kind deeds all help.

The goal of fishing is to catch fish—to win new disciples for Jesus. Fishing by "presence" alone won't do it. Evangelism, at times, requires a verbal explanation and a closure—a prayer of commitment. Remember, all Christians are fishers. Those who feel incapable of drawing the net ashore can bring their "seeking" friends to a pastor or counselor or a mature sister in the church.

17. the **ACCEPTANCE** factor

Many smaller denominations face an overwhelming challenge—to move beyond the restricting limits of ethnicity while retaining the tenets of their biblical historic faith. When a church roots its identity in its common ethnic names, recipes and birthplaces rather than in the gospel of Jesus Christ, newcomers will feel like outsiders. (This could happen to Scottish Presbyterians, Swedish Baptists, Roman Catholics and German Mennonites.)

A Mennonite businessman from Los Angeles attended the annual Mennonite Central Committee relief sale at Fresno. He gave the high bid on a 1923 Chevy roadster: $5700. He overheard two local men: "Who bought the car?" "Oh, some Mr. Johnston from Los Angeles. Isn't it a shame some Mennonite didn't buy it!"

It is tragic when a man is valued, not for his life or character but for his name or ethnicity. "Johnston" does not sound like an insider to an Epp, a Friesen or a Swartzendruber. The man hoped "our kind" would keep this antique gem, forgetting the whole purpose of the sale. He could have remarked, "Praise God! Johnston gave five thousand dollars to help us feed the hungry."

This story hides a clue to a big obstacle in evangelism. Christians of a common ethnic group can develop a snob-complacency and smug-clannishness. A true Christian spirit is ethnically inclusive. A basic prerequisite to sound mission work worldwide is identification with others who differ from us. To be Christlike is to feel with all people, and to include them in our circles of friendship.

Now one of the Pharisees invited Jesus to have dinner with him, so he went to the Pharisee's house and reclined at the table. When a woman who had lived a sinful life in that town learned that Jesus was eating at the Pharisee's house, she brought an alabaster jar of perfume, and as she stood behind him at his feet weeping, she began to wet his feet with her tears. Then she wiped them with her hair, kissed them and poured perfume on them. When the Pharisee...saw this, he said to himself, "If this man were a prophet, he would know...she is a sinner."

This story, unique to Luke's gospel, reflects Luke's passionate aim: to show that Jesus accepted all humans, especially those that society ignored. He offered kindness to lepers, prostitutes, tax collectors, the poor and women in general. Jesus not only loved people; he sought them out to save them. This is Luke's plea (see Luke 19:10) that sinners who need a friend, need look no further!

Simon's Dinner Guests

A Pharisee named Simon invited Jesus for dinner. Who can guess his motive: curiosity, belief or entrapment? At any rate, all the guests were reclining on couches encircling the dinner table, with feet pointed outward, when a woman entered. It was common for poor people to enter banquets and sit on the fringes awaiting the leftovers. But this woman was a "notorious sinner," maybe a noted prostitute. Such people knew they were most unwelcome at a Pharisee's house.

As the meal proceeded, the woman wet the feet of Jesus with her tears, dried them with her hair, kissed them with her lips and bathed them with perfume. Simon observed in silence and shuddered. "Jesus must be unaware of her wickedness," he thought. Jesus read his mind and asked—if a moneylender cancels one man's debt of 500 denarii and another man's debt of 50 denarii—who will appreciate forgiveness the most? Simon guessed—the one forgiven most. Jesus said, "Correct."

Jesus went on to contrast Simon's meager show of hospitality (no kiss, no footwashing, and no head-anointing) with the woman's unusual outpouring of affection. Not that he was accusing Simon of rudeness, for hospitality rules have some flexibility; rather he was highlighting the incredible display of love, devotion, and faith shown by this woman. This he had not seen in his host, Simon.

This lady may have heard Jesus teach on other occasions, or even have sought his counsel. Jesus saw her tears as signs of belief, repentance and conversion. To Simon, Jesus announced that "...her many sins have been forgiven" (7:47). To the woman herself Jesus spoke assuringly: "Your faith has saved you; go in peace" (7:50). Her past sins were washed away as Jesus welcomed her into his eternal kingdom. While Jesus modeled warm acceptance, Simon could only muster rejection.

Acceptance and Church Growth

George Barna has a book for the church-shopper: *How To Find Your Church.* To form new relationships, sample the worship hour and Sunday School classes. Some Sunday services lack the personal touch and feel like funerals; others are upbeat and celebrative and joyous. Always note the interaction between members. Are you pleased? The clincher is—can you "...reasonably expect to be embraced as an equal and important part of that particular church family, given your circumstances?" In short—will you be accepted as a person?

This assessment is crucial, insists Barna, if your life situation is nontraditional—like being a divorced single parent, or being part of a racially-mixed marriage, or being a naturalized alien. "The sad truth is that some churches are not very tolerant and accepting of people who are different..."[6] Jesus, we know, lovingly mixed with the "fringe" people of society.

It is pathetic when churches cease being "Hospitals for Sinners" and become exclusive "Holy Clubs for Saints." Donald Posterski in *Reinventing Evangelism,* shares the heartbreak of one parishioner. "I know of a woman named Yvonne, who, after her husband had left her and their two children for another woman, was told by her pastor that 'her presence was unhealthy for the marriages of the people of the church.' Today, Yvonne is no longer a participant in any church and continues to wonder if God really is in this world."[7] As this God-given opportunity for ministry was mishandled three more persons became church dropouts.

In a forceful and engaging chapter, "Transcending Words," Posterski, a Canadian InterVarsity executive, urges churches to retool for evangelism: "...words that faithfully communicate the claims of the gospel will only ring true when those who "say" the truth, "do" the truth with the deeds of their lives."[8] His chapter radiates a fresh relevance for a timely witness.

A New Test on Acceptance

A Christian's acceptance-scale is being tested anew as immigrants of varied races stream into North America. Donald McGavran's monumental work, *Understanding Church Growth*, is helpful. His vision was to multiply churches and incorporate converts as reliable members. One of his claims drew worldwide attention, namely, that people prefer "...to become Christians without crossing racial, linguistic, or class barriers."[9] This idea sparked many heated debates.

A rebuttal is easy: the Gospel of Christ breaks down all barriers. Yet life is more complicated than that. In his book, *Church Growth Under Fire*, C. Wayne Zunkel, a Church of the Brethren pastor, offers a perceptive analysis of McGavran's view in a chapter titled, "That Offensive Homogeneous Principle." He speaks of two forms of blindness which are limiting to Christians. One is "people" blindness. This is a failure to see that people's culture—the food, the values, the language—gives them a separate sense of identity. The other is "kingdom" blindness. This is the failure to see that God wants to draw all people together as brothers and sisters within his kingdom.[10]

No church easily incorporates everybody. In my Kansas pastorate local people sponsored 15 Chinese-speaking Vietnamese refugees. We supplied housing and found jobs. Sunday worship had little meaning to them since English was not their language. So we engaged Ruth Epp, home from Hong Kong and fluent in Cantonese, to teach weekly Bible lessons at our house. The refugees loved it. On the final night all 15 accepted Christ! A few were baptized at our church; but most eventually moved to Vietnamese communities, apparently seeking a Vietnamese church.

18. the COMMISSION factor

In *Gentle Persuasion: Creative Ways to Introduce Your Friends to Christ*, Joseph Aldrich depicts the Great Commission as a standard for evaluating all methodology in evangelism. Christ mandates us to go "make disciples," not to win decisions. Thus our method is shaped by what actually produces disciples. The process includes whatever dynamics are necessary to bring people to Christ, to fold them into the church and to deploy them as redemptive people into the world.

According to Aldrich, among those who trust Christ and become faithful church members, 80 percent are led to the Lord by friends. Of those who trust Christ and drop out of church, 70 percent are led to Christ by strangers. Also, "almost 90 percent of those who 'drop out' are led to Christ by someone who perceived evangelism as a manipulative dialogue."[11] Those who remained faithful to the church had significant relationships with members before their conversions, and continued to build friendships in the church afterwards.

The Great Commission in History
Light on the Pathway (Matthew 28:16-20)

....*Then Jesus came to them and said, "All authority in heaven and on earth has been given to me. Therefore go and make disciples of all nations, baptizing them in the name of the Father and of the Son and of the Holy Spirit, and teaching them to obey everything I have commanded you. And surely I am with you always, to the very end of the age."*

This we call the "Great Commission." One imperative dominates: "make disciples." It is qualified by the participles: going, baptizing and teaching. Kittel writes "Mathetes [disciple] always implies the existence of a personal attachment which shapes the whole life of the one described as mathetes, and which in its particularity leaves no doubt as to who is deploying the formative power."[12]

Richard Gardner details the impact this text has had on history: "First...By anchoring baptism in a command of the risen Lord, it made this rite an indispensable ordinance of Jesus' community....Second, the great commission and related texts have propelled the church to understand itself as a community in mission. Jesuits, Anabaptists, and Pietists alike took their cues from the text, as did the great missionary movement of the nineteenth and the twentieth centuries."[13]

So it startles us to learn that great reformers like Luther and Melanchthon disavowed the Great Commission, relegating its discipling obligation exclusively to the original apostles.[14] They vigorously defended a medieval parish system with one official religion in each territory. Persons became members of the church and state, not by freedom of choice but by compulsory baby baptism. This makes American religious freedom (with its pluralism) more akin to the Left Wing of the Reformation—the Radical Reformers, than to the mainline reformers.

Reformation Perspective

What follows will be of particular interest to my Anabaptist readers. But because it relates to the church's implementation of the Great Commission, I believe it also speaks to the church at large. I am not planting divisive sectarianism; elsewhere I use numerous examples from traditions outside of my own. We as Christians stand together or fall together. We owe so much TO each other; we can also learn much FROM each other.

The Left Wing of the Reformation involved my own ancestors. Like a meteor sets the sky ablaze, so the fiery zeal of these spiritual pilgrims lit up the pages of history with a rare brilliance. They evangelized heroically under the banner of the Great Commission. They died in droves (by fire in Catholic areas, by drowning or sword in Protestant areas) for principles like the separation of church and state, which Catholics and Protestants alike today hold dear.

Dare I jolt my readers a bit? In Chapter 3, I told of a 50-year-old lady who joined my California parish and took up youth work. Had she joined an Anabaptist church group 470 years ago in parts of Europe, regardless of her origin (Catholic, Lutheran or Reformed) she would have been arrested, tried and executed! Why? Because she requested Believer's Baptism, when she had been baptized previously as a baby. Those ancient dynamics are very contemporary. In America today we all consider such freedoms as our God-given inalienable rights.

Reformation: Left Wing

The Anabaptist movement was spawned in 1525 in a home Bible study among the Swiss Brethren of Zurich, Switzerland. Their goal was to restore New Testament Christianity. In the first couple of years Hans Hut, the Billy Graham of the Brethren, baptized thousands, quoting the Great Commission at each baptism. "The Anabaptists were among the first to make the commission binding upon all church members," asserts Franklin H. Littell.[15]

On August 20, 1527, my radical forebears convened a strategy meeting at Augsburg—later named the Martyrs' Synod. Sixty leaders from South Germany, Switzerland and Austria assembled including Hans Hut. Their dream was to evangelize the whole of Europe.[16] However, only two or three of these 60 actually lived to see the fifth year of the Anabaptist movement. The Great Commission—the driving force to evangelize—cost them their lives. They paid dearly for freedoms most of us cherish today.

Among my Anabaptists forbears, ordinary church members spread the faith as well as missioners. Though women at the time were forbidden to preach or baptize, they were highly involved in evangelism. Take Liz Sedelmair of Bavaria. On a trip to Augsburg in 1528 she shared her faith with three inquirers. Elder Schleiffer of Vienna came to baptize them: Madlena Seitz, Anna Butz and son Hans.[17]

Years of Compromise

As decades passed, persecution shifted to religious tolerance. For two centuries, my people the Mennonites, heirs of Anabaptism lived as reputable farmers, the "Quiet in the Land." When Frederick the Great restricted economic and religious freedoms in West Prussia, many Mennonites opted for survival. They moved to the Ukraine around the year 1800. Rulers Catherine II and Paul I allowed free settlement and guaranteed "everlasting freedom."

The Ukraine was occupied by Orthodox, Lutheran and Catholic peoples. Settlement among them carried one binding stipulation: no evangelizing.[18] So our confrontationist stance was lost. In its place we spun a "germanic cultural cocoon" about ourselves, as Donald Jacobs called it, and carried our cocoon wherever we went. By the year 1900 it was rare to find a Mennonite, anywhere in the world, who didn't cling to the mother tongue of German or Dutch.[19]

Eerdmans' Handbook to the History of Christianity says: "Whether the mass of the Mennonites can rediscover the spiritual vitality, the evangelistic fervor, and the radical discipleship that made their forefathers such unique actors in the drama of the Reformation is a question that remains to be answered."[20]

Winds of Renewal Blow Again

Our migrations to North America, wave after wave, were distinctly providential. We were metamorphosed in the American milieu. Simply put: "We got revived." The combination of freedoms, resources, and a contagious American Revivalism affected a God-led turnabout. It was a 20th Century marvel.

Today Mennonites number 850,000 worldwide and worship

in 60 languages![21] One half of us live in Africa, Asia, and Central or South America.[22] On American soil we formed 33 mission boards that now support 1,133 missionaries overseas. We joined hands in a relief agency, the Mennonite Central Committee (MCC). Its staff numbers 1,000, of whom 527 work abroad.[23] (Another 1,000 Mennonites serve with "faith" missions or parachurch groups.[24]) It appears that our sisterhood of Anabaptist denominations makes an impact far out of proportion to its size.

Our evangelism is alive: (1) Gospel radio with Bill/Ruth Detweiler, (2) Mission retreats with Donald/Anna Ruth Jacobs, (3) Schools of Discipleship (Baltimore and Philadelphia) under the Eastern Board, (4) Vision-95 with 10-year goals of giving, praying, and evangelizing, (5) LIFE—Living In Faithful Evangelism, directed by G. Edwin Bontrager and Marilyn Miller. An Evangelism Academy trains people and Growth Workshops update them.[25] The Great Commission is operative.

My Little Country Church

A final testimony—my own grandparents were European farmers. They had no evangelistic vision. They emigrated to America and founded a congregation: the one that nurtured me. Last year that flock of 400 gave $500,000 to missions; in 118 years it has produced 100 Christians workers, many of them missionaries.[26]

In 1976 I addressed that church: "A century ago, Mennonite folk were planted on the Kansas prairies, destined by God to share food and faith with the hungry. In America's heartland, our Turkey Red wheat created a breadbasket for the world. In America's liberties, our faith blossomed into ministries of missions and relief, peace and service, mutual aid and disaster care. The blood of these early pioneers surges through our veins. Before they died, they handed to us the baton of faith. Let us renew our grip and run the race with dedication."[27]

19. the SENSITIVITY factor

Dr. Henry J. Schmidt, seminary president, convened a Church Growth Seminar in Canada to prepare for Century-21.

Later he wrote perceptively: "The greatest threat to evangelization is not external but internal. The greatest clue to effective church growth is internal (prayer, fasting, character, and obedience to God); not external (plans, strategies and techniques). The greatest struggle is not the motivation or mobilization of lay persons, but the nature of leadership."

Schmidt elaborates with some very pointed questions: "Will leaders model a direction that highlights relationships over position...empowering people over control-taking, mission over maintenance, risk over security, serving over lording, mutual trust over suspicion—in fulfilling our mission mandate?"[28]

The Evangelism Approach of Jesus

Look at the evangelism style of Jesus; he had no canned approach. Compare, for example, his nighttime chat with Nicodemus (John 3) and his high noon visit with the Samaritan lady (John 4). Here are two approaches but few similarities.

Nicodemus was a member of the powerful Sanhedrin. He had a prestigious reputation. He came to Jesus on his own initiative. Being courteous, he called Jesus "Rabbi," "a teacher from God" and "miracle worker." What a shock when Jesus abruptly told him that no one can see the Kingdom of God until he is born-again.

Jesus was noticeably blunt. Why? First, the "messianic consciousness" of Jesus is very evident in the gospels. He knew his purpose. He knew death was ahead. He knew the Jewish leaders were already plotting. Secondly, Jesus was getting down to basics. All the prestige in the world could never get Nicodemus into heaven. All people come into the kingdom humbly, on their knees, accepting God's grace and pardon. By the way, no on-the-spot acceptance of Jesus is claimed though Nicodemus later defended him (7:51) and assisted in his burial (19:39).

Jesus and the Samaritan Woman
Light on the Pathway (John 4:1-42)

....Jacob's well was there, and Jesus, tired as he was from the jour-

ney, sat down by the well. It was about the sixth hour. When a Samaritan woman came to draw water, Jesus said to her, "Will you give me to drink?" (His disciples had gone into town to buy food.) The Samaritan woman said to him, "You are a Jew and I am a Samaritan woman. How can you ask me for a drink?" (For Jews do not associate with Samaritans.) Jesus answered her, "If you knew the gift of God and who it is that asks you for a drink, you would have asked him and he would have given you living water...."

On this trip home Jesus took the three-day ridge route through Samaria. Most of his contemporaries, traveling from Judea to Galilee, chose the six-day road that crossed the Jordan and bypassed Samaria altogether. The hostility between the Jews and Samaritans was mutual and deeply rooted in history. When the Northern Kingdom fell in 722 B.C., the Assyrians deported many Jews and colonized central Palestine with citizens from Babylon. The resultant intermarriages created a mixed race (as the Jews viewed it) and a syncretized religion that meshed foreign deities with parts of the Jewish heritage.

Hungry, thirsty, and exhausted, Jesus sat on Jacob's well near the town of Sychar. As the disciples went for food, Jesus encountered a lone woman and asked for a drink. She was stunned— Jews seldom spoke to Samaritans, and never to a woman, much less ask for a drink from a common vessel! Jesus explained that if she knew his identity, the tables would be turned. She would be asking him for water—the living kind. She was listening with rapt attention.

Jesus' approach to the woman of Samaria was marked by rare empathy and tenderness. Normally, a Jewish rabbi carried a kind of hatred with racial overtones, and an open disdain for their "false" religion. Drinking out of a Samaritan cup would pollute his soul. What's more, the people of Sychar may have ostracized this woman for her five marital failures and her present live-in affair. (At any rate she chose to avoid the evening social hour at the well: the normal woman's high-point of the day.) The gracious attitude of Jesus enthralled her, and the conversation went deeper and deeper until she became a thorough believer in Jesus as the real and awaited Messiah.

In terms of a sound approach to evangelism, this account has four ideal features: (1) The conversation moves from the known to the unknown, from drinking water to spiritual water—a smooth natural transition. (2) The concern moves from past moral failures and the present immorality to stepping stones of forgiveness, hope and redemption; Jesus identifies himself as the Christ. (3) The fledgling believer immediately becomes an evangelist, gathering her friends to meet the Savior. What had been hearsay is now a firsthand experience. And finally, (4) Jesus models sound convert-care. He chose a 2-day stay to encourage them, to teach them, and to establish them.

An Exciting Venture In Evangelism

Rebecca Pippert's book: *Out of the Saltshaker & Into the World* (450,000 in print) has blessed myriads. In a delightful and contagious style she recounts her experiences as an InterVarsity staff person. Evangelism flows so naturally in her style that one supposes she has the Spirit's Gift of Evangelism. Here is a sample of her work at Stanford University.

When Becky started a dorm Bible study, a student named Lois promised to come but was certain that the Bible held no relevance for her! Lois lived off campus with her boyfriend, Phil, and brought him along to the first Bible study. Becky—not knowing who would come—had prepared to study John 4. To Becky's chagrin, the reading that fell to Lois was verse 17: "Jesus said to her, 'You are right in saying, "I have no husband"...for the man you're living with now is not your husband'" (RSV). Lois' eyes grew as large as saucers. She commented that the Bible was a bit more relevant than she had anticipated.

The next day Becky asked Lois whether there was any reason why she couldn't become a Christian? No—she said. "Well I can think of one," said Becky. "What will you do about Phil?" As they talked about becoming a Christian, Becky pointed out that

Christianity is a relationship and affects every aspect of life like values, lifestyle and sexuality. It became obvious that God had been pursuing Lois for a long time. Becky writes, "There were tears and struggles followed by an utterly sincere prayer asking Christ to come into her life as Lord."

Immediately Lois wrestled with her new dilemma: how to find another place to live. Miraculously, the next day a space opened up in the dorm, so she moved in. What a joy to find that her new roommate was a dynamic mature Christian. Lois' commitment to Christ had far-reaching effects. That night three girls on that dorm floor decided to get right with Christ. Phil, at first, was furious when Lois moved out; but three months later he too accepted Christ. He later credited Lois' obedience to Christ for affecting his own eternal destiny. This entire episode shows Becky's amazing sensitivity to the struggles of college kids.

Becky summarizes the event: "Lois' conversion was profound for her friends as well as for her. She recognized that becoming a Christian had tremendous implications. She came to see that if Jesus is Lord then the only right response to him is surrender and obedience. He is Savior and he is Lord. We cannot separate his demands from his love....Christ died so that we could be forgiven for managing our own lives. It would be impossible for Lois to thank Christ for dying for her and yet continue running her own life."[29]

20. the BANQUET factor
Light on the Pathway (Luke 14:15-24)

....Jesus replied, "A certain man was preparing a great banquet and invited many guests. At the time of the banquet he sent his servant to tell those who had been invited, 'Come, for everything is now ready.' But they all alike began to make excuses....Then the owner of the house became angry and ordered his servant, 'Go out quickly into the streets and alleys of the town and bring in the poor, the crippled, the blind and the lame'....'Sir,' the servant said..., 'there is still room.' Then the master told his servant, 'Go out to the roads and country lanes and make them come in, so that my house will be full....'"

Jesus gave a potent dynamic for evangelism when he compared a summons to the Kingdom of God with an invitation to a great dinner. Who would refuse a King's banquet? Yet, in Jesus' story people concocted excuses: going to look at land, trying out new oxen or getting adjusted to marriage. Three flimsy alibis!

Amazing—it sounds like our day! Why do people refuse Christianity? Materialism with its love for wealth bars many from a commitment. Crowded schedules take priority over the church. Family loyalties hold many persons back from an all-out involvement in God's Kingdom work. The story of Jesus is as relevant as the front page of USA TODAY.

For 20 years researchers studied the aims and values of incoming freshmen at the University of California at Los Angeles. The concern "being well off financially" showed the biggest upturn (from 40% to 70%) while during the same two decades, the aim of "developing a meaningful philosophy of life" showed the most dramatic decline (dropping from over 80% to 43%). So by 1990 the pursuit of money had replaced the pursuit for the broader meaning of life.[30]

The above correlates with the findings of Bibby and Posterski in Canada's Youth: Ready for Today, that a low value is placed on intelligence itself. "There is evidence to conclude that the inclination to think about life is being pushed aside by the desire to experience life. The gravitational pull is more toward titillating the senses than stimulating the mind."[31] All of these trends accent the difficulty North American Christians face in bringing people to Christ.

Jesus portrayed the Kingdom of God as a festive party, as a banquet hall to be filled . When respected people beg off, we must turn to others at the fringe of society. In the end, to fill the tables, we need to go to strangers and compel them to come. The door is open to all. Evangelism is urgent!

Banquet Invitation: Church Growth

Few leaders have so forcefully called the church to accountability in evangelism as have Donald McGavran and C. Peter Wagner. After studying the principles of church growth world-wide, they concentrated on American churches. Subsequently, they wrote: *Your Church Can Grow* and *Your Spiritual Gifts Can Help Your Church Grow.* They pinpointed procedures which growing churches tend to have in common. No more is church growth a hit-or-miss thing; it has become an exacting science.

More than once leaders in my denomination have said, "Maybe our particular mission is to stay small, but to exert an influence on other church fellowships—like salt flavors food." Isn't that a cop-out? Each denomination has influences to offer. And no one escapes the Lord's mission mandate. Church growth advocates have raised some tough issues we all must face. Are we evangelizing and assimilating converts? Are we planting church-es with a tested-strategy? However, church growth is more than implementing strategy. It "is a complex phenomenon surrounded by a measure of mystery and, if genuine, is directed and con-trolled by a sovereign God. We can discern the divine mind...only imperfectly."[32]

Banquet Invitation: World Evangelism

While both denominational and "faith" missions work hero-ically overseas, God is raising up facilitators at home. Roberta Winter's book, *I Will Do A New Thing,* tells how she and husband Ralph got the vision to buy (on faith) the 15 million dollar campus of Pasadena College to set up the US Center For World Mission. The purpose is to fuel a movement to reach the unreached. Agencies are invited to target certain people groups while church-es are urged to adopt a specific group.

Church planting that carries a "made in America" label faces opposition overseas. Moreover, it is expensive. Sending a North American family abroad for four years—to learn language, cul-ture, and people—costs a mission board $100,000 to $150,000. Therefore, John Haggai's approach of internationals training nationals looks like a good supplement to traditional methods.

Since 1969 The Haggai Institute For Advanced Leadership in Singapore has trained 5011 leaders from 116 countries, and these in turn have trained over 700,000 people. John Haggai's provocative book, *The Leading Edge,* states his goal: to train 10,000 nationals by the year 2000. Sponsors pay about $10,000 for the 4-week training of a Third World leader. World-renowned professors, like the late Dr. Chandu Ray, the Bishop from Pakistan, give superb training in an international setting. A training center is being developed in Hawaii as well.

Banquet Invitation: Urban Challenge

World evangelism can't ignore the cities—half of earth's 5 to 6 billions are city dwellers. Today 290 cities have over one million inhabitants.[33] Middle-class churches of all ethnic groups have fled to the suburbs, leaving poverty-stricken, gang-turfed, and rat-infested inner city areas unchurched.

The book: *The Urban Christian* is Ray and Corean Bakke's fascinating account of moving their family into Chicago's North Side in 1965 for a 20-year ministry. Ray's role model was Charles Simeon, a slum pastor in London 150 years ago. The Bakke boys (Woody 4, Brian 2) were a big "missionary" asset, building trust via a network of playmates, and later via students in high school. Chapter 8, "Bringing Up a Family in the City" is priceless. Some people chided the Bakkes for endangering their children (while others admired Elisabeth Elliot for raising her daughter in the jungle tribe that killed her husband). How inconsistent.[34]

One bright spot in ghetto-evangelism is World Impact of Los Angeles headed by Keith Phillips. Its 200 missionaries are healing the hurt of gangs, drugs and sex. The book *No Quick Fix* tells how Mary Thiessen won Patricia to Christ. Patricia was black, fatherless and poor. An uncle sexually molested her for years and threatened to kill her if she told. As ghetto girls chose between raising welfare babies and prostitution, Patricia modeled the option of Christian purity! She became a dynamic Club leader for World Impact—a radiant disciple.[35]

Banquet Invitation: Church Outreach

America has 350,000 Protestant and Catholic churches.[36] Normally when evangelistic zeal lags, we grab fresh cables for a jump-start. We elect a new committee, or set up a new crusade, or try a different "canned" approach. Alas, what churches really need is a stronger grasp on evangelism by friendship or lifestyle; not a grasp on some superficial fix-and-fail solution.

Joe and Ruthe Aldrich model lifestyle evangelism, always praying that their network of friends will trust Christ. Joe says, "I'd love to have a hundred bucks for every meal my wife has prepared for unsaved friends. I'd be delighted to have a dollar for every hour we've spent with non-Christians. I'd be glad to accept a gold bar for every tear we've shed...(with) these dear people..."[37]

Conclusion

My heart is warmed as I call to memory people Susan Joann and I have helped win to Christ. We shared our faith by weekly sermons, occasional altar calls, office counseling, discipleship groups at our house, neighborly kindnesses, persistent praying, gift subscriptions to *Guideposts*, and many other ways. Each contact symbolizes a beautiful story. It's a joy to sow and a joy to reap.

Sometimes evangelism begins WITHIN the church. During my third pastorate one member remarked, "Pastor, you preach evangelistically. We're not pagan; we're all on the church roll." My special burden was the young husbands who were irregular in worship, had little assurance, were nontithers, lacked enthusiasm for Jesus and were incapable of teaching their children spiritual truths.

Susan Joann and I opened our home to covenant-groups. This declared our home as being approachable, touchable—and fragile as others. Our 3-month course met two hours per week and climaxed in a banquet. Subsequently, each group became a monthly support group. Even seven nonmembers took the course, and four later joined our church. I kept a group for two years before delegating them to lay-leaders. Eventually, we discipled 128 men at our house. Speaking for Susan Joann and myself, we saw a little effort reap a good harvest of spiritual fruitfulness!

Let's wrap it up. Jesus promised to transform his disciples into fishers of people. Jesus is Lord and fishing on his team is adventurous. Christlike acceptance must replace sectarian snobbishness. At the core, the church is called to faithfulness—at home, in cities, and worldwide. The Great Commission is operable and obligatory. And all evangelism needs the "respect-for-personhood" that Jesus displayed at the well of Sychar. And lastly, all evangelism has an urgency. Our Heavenly Father wants the seats filled at the Banquet of Heaven. Winning people to Christ, therefore, is the greatest enterprise in this universe!

Questions for Discussion

1. If evangelism resembles fishing, is it net fishing, angling, or other?
2. What can we learn from Mr. Johnston's $5700 purchase at the relief sale?
3. What does the Anabaptist experience teach us on persecution & compromise?
4. Discuss sensitivity—Jesus at the well, or Becky Pippert in the dorm.
5. In Luke 14, God wants his banquet hall full. What can we do to help?

PRACTICING HIS PRESENCE: DEVOTIONAL PAUSE FOR BUSY DISCIPLES
Theme of the week— Fishing For People

	Monday	**Tuesday**	**Wednesday**	**Thursday**	**Friday**
Light on the pathway	Matthew 4:18-25	Luke 7:36-50	Matthew 28:16-20	John 4:1-42	Luke 14:1-24
Lesson for this day	Factor #16 Fishers	Factor #17 Acceptance	Factor #18 Commission	Factor #19 Sensitivity	Factor #20 Urgency
Life in Jesus' way	Take time to pray	Take time to pray	Take time to pray	Take time to pray	Take time to pray

PRACTICE HIS PRESENCE IN CHURCH THIS SUNDAY

Chapter

6

Showing Good Works

21. Salt
22. Light
23. Love
24. Child
25. Servant

Introduction

Recently we visited Disney World Epcot Center of Orlando, Florida. In the World Showcase, the China Pavilion fascinated us. While eating dinner at the Nine Dragon Restaurant we spoke with young adult workers from mainland China. All spoke English fluently.

We found the circle-vision tour of China a delightful experience—the Great Wall, the farmland countryside and the clean cities crowded with their millions. While waiting in the lobby a Chinese proverb caught my eye: "Hearing something one hundred times is not as good as seeing it once." That is performance with a capital "P". It's a good motto for any church.

The concept of "good works" being required of all Christians is rooted in Kingdom-theology. As the Sermon on the Mount opens, Jesus urges all disciples to "drive with their lights on bright," by displaying good works (Matthew 5:16). Before the sermon ends he says the Heavenly Father loves to do kindness in answer to prayer (7:7-11). Verse twelve begins with THEREFORE, linking the Golden Rule of kindness to others (7:12) with the gracious kindness of God to each of us. God showed kindness first— He set the example. So we live to imitate our Father!

Here I examine a Christian's witness "by performance" under five headings: being salt, being light, being a loving neighbor, being childlike and being a servant. I explore our influence, or even impact on others, and search the teachings of Jesus for recommended attitudes in this witness.

21. the SALT factor

Light on the Pathway (Matthew 5:13)

"You are the salt of the earth. But if the salt loses its saltiness, how can it be made salty again? It is no longer good for anything, except to be thrown out and trampled by men."

The functions of salt are well-known: (1) salt purifies, (2) salt preserves, and (3) salt flavors. Obviously, a Christian witness that is both faithful and healthy is also a corrective to society. It preserves the moral fiber. It offers a flavor of compassion. Often non-Christians and even agnostics choose a private Christian school to educate their children; they prefer residing in a community where the Christian principles that restrain evil prevail.

F. F. Bruce writes: "Since the disciples are spoken of as the salt of the earth..., as the light of the world and as a city set on a hill (Mt. 5:14), it is evidently their public life that is in view. They must be seen by others as living examples of the power and grace of God, examples which others are encouraged to follow."[1]

The early Christians had an impressive lifestyle. Jim Wallis of *Sojourners* elaborates: "To all who saw, Christian belief became identified with a certain kind of behavior. Unlike our modern experience, there was an unmistakable Christian lifestyle recognized by believers and unbelievers alike. That style of life followed the main lines of Jesus' Sermon on the Mount and his other teaching. To believe meant to follow Jesus. There was little doubt in anyone's mind: Christian discipleship revolved around the hub of the kingdom. The faith of these first Christians had clear social results. They became well known as a caring, sharing, and open community that was especially sensitive to the poor and the outcast. Their love for God, for one another, and for the oppressed was central to their reputation. Their refusal to kill, to recognize racial distinctions, or to bow down to the imperial deities was a matter of public knowledge."[2]

Reform: From Luther to Menno

In the sixteenth century radical discipleship emerged with the intent of restoring New Testament Christianity. True, the church had drifted far from its biblical pattern. Earlier many forerunners had recognized the need of reform. John Wyclif in the 1300s tried to make the Bible available to all persons in their own language; and Jan Hus [martyred-1415] accepted the authority of the Scriptures for the church—the church defined as the body of Christ.

Then came Martin Luther. A Catholic professor, he was dramatically converted while teaching the Epistle of Romans. It dawned on him that a person is justified by faith alone and not by works. He nailed 95 Theses to his church door at Wittenberg in 1517, challenging the See of Rome to dialogue. Luther lifted scripture above tradition.

In 1521 the Pope excommunicated Martin Luther, accusing him of advocating church innovations. In actuality, Luther was merely trying to remove heresies (e.g. atoning sins via indulgences and purgatory) clinging to the church from centuries of compromise and drifting. Luther became a champion of Justification-By-Faith, a most needed corrective in the church. His influence was immense.

A few dissenters claimed that Luther's reforms still fell short. These persons gave birth to the Anabaptist movement in Switzerland on January 21, 1525. Defying the order by the Zurich city council to disband, these radicals baptized each other at a prayer meeting, becoming the first Free Church of modern times. Franklin Littell alleges they made The Great Commission their mandate; and they fleshed out The Great Commandment via love, nonviolence, and mutual aid. Discipleship was their watchword—following Jesus in life.

In 1539 Menno Simons described behavior for persons who had passed from death to life (John 5:24): "For true evangelical faith...cannot lie dormant, but manifests itself in...works of love; it dies unto the flesh...it destroys all forbidden lusts...; it...serves and fears God; it clothes the naked; it feeds the hungry; it comforts the sorrowful; it shelters the destitute; it...consoles the sad; it returns good for evil...it prays for those that persecute it...."[3]

Christians as Salt in North America

As the church faces the 21st century, I am haunted by the comment of Jesus that salt can lose its saltiness. Is the church of North America a powerful force holding back the avalanche of evil, shaping foreign policy, and inciting compassion for the needy of the world? Has the church become insipid, leached out and tasteless? Or worse, is society salting it with corruption or fragmentation?

The salt of Christianity certainly flavored the history of North America. Its savor was long-lasting. In 1775 only 5% of Americans were church members; in 1850, 15%; in 1900, 35%; and in 1926, 50%. True, some standards of church membership were lowered. Notwithstanding, as mentioned previously, the Baptist evangelists and the Methodist circuit riding preachers had a strong civilizing effect in taming the wild western frontiers. Franklin Littell has observed that even the most crass form of evangelism was far preferable to the bloody political revolutions that hit European countries like France. Immigrants flocked from various faiths and nations to America, a milieu of freedom. The results were unprecedented church growth, financial giving, and mission-service activities.

Alan Kreider of London, England, calls the salt-and-light teachings of Jesus the charter for Christian involvement in society. He insists that biblical saltiness touches every area of life, even the sensitive areas of protection and provision. This raises provocative questions about the insurance we trust, the wealth we stockpile, the job-status we pursue, the food we eat, the clothes we buy, the toys we give; every deed impacts for God's Kingdom in some concrete way.

Kreider insists that Christians live under pressure as a minority group in society, and are susceptible to the twin temptations of withdrawal or compromise. "How will Jesus' followers know if they are being salty? Not by measuring their influence on the world, but by monitoring their similarity to their Master and their faithfulness to his teaching....Saltiness means putting into practice the will of the Father...."[4] Faithfulness is then a mark of biblical saltiness.

Insights From Chuck Colson

In 1988 NavPress published three small-group study booklets based on the writings of Chuck Colson. The need for these arose out of the discrepancy that existed between Jesus' admonition "to hear and to obey" (Luke 11:28), and the actual behavioral patterns of professing Christians. Late research indicated that, as regards divorce, child abuse, materialism and civic responsibility, Christians differed little from society in general. NavPress saw small-groups as the best avenue to offer the needed accountability to affect behavioral change.

In the booklet entitled, *Transforming Society*, Colson writes, "Christianity no longer enjoys a positive reputation in the main stream of culture; events of the past years have served to create a climate of suspicion and derision toward the church at large. Actions of the flamboyant few—television evangelists or pastors who abused their power and prestige—have created caricatures by which the rest of the church is now judged."[5]

Colson reminds us of God's command to help the poor, the homeless, the sick, and the suffering. The church by its presence must penetrate culture, and like salt, be rubbed in to save it. Colson calls the church back to its basics: to be the Body of Christ, to do the gospel, and to speak the good news with wise love.

22. the LIGHT *factor*

Light on the Pathway (Matthew 5:14-16)

"You are the light of the world. A city on a hill cannot be hidden.

Neither do people light a lamp and put it under a bowl. Instead they put it on its stand and it gives light to everyone in the house. In the same way, let your light shine before men, that they may see your good deeds and praise your Father in heaven."

When Matthew 5:1-16 is seen as a unit, one lesson is clear: the joy of the kingdom should radiate forth from Christians as distinctly as a city that is on a hill or a lighted lamp that is on a stand. Yet alas, the church too often resembles a car that has the transmission in neutral and lights off. It is obvious that Jesus expects activity and outreach. He wants disciples to "drive with their lights on bright." He takes pleasure in a visible witness.

Jesus clearly gives the "how" and the "why" of letting our lights shine. The method: a gracious friendly manner that illumines rather than obscures our good deeds done for the kingdom of God. The purpose: to glorify God with praise.

Shining Lights — Spontaneity

One day we had just arrived home when our doorbell rang. Two cars stood at the curb; and two men waited at the door. "Pastor Al," my parishioner said, "these people stopped by the church looking for the pastor." Turning to the stranger I asked what he wanted. He replied, "We're traveling through and need gas." I instructed him to go to the service station near Interstate 80. I promised to phone ahead to authorize ten dollars for gasoline. I sat down to my Sunday dinner, smugly satisfied that I had helped someone.

Only later did I hear the rest of the story. As my parishioner arrived at his house, his five children quizzed him: "Do those people have food to eat?" After some lively discussion Dad drove three miles to the Interstate to find the family filling up with gas. "Would you accept an invitation to dinner?" he asked. "Yes," they replied. So he led them back into town. The station wagon stopped in front of their house, and eleven people stepped out, including three full grown men. Our parishioners were cordial hosts—praying before the meal as usual and getting acquainted with the visitors while they ate.

My pastoral witness was like a pinch of salt. My parishioners, on the other hand, resembled a car driving with a high beam—all for the glory of God. First, here was the potential for impacting strangers with a Christian witness. Secondly, according to the research of Peter Benson, this was an ideal setting for Christian education; the incident would forcefully impact the five children of that Christian home. That one meal probably made a stronger imprint on them than one hundred admonitions—"Kids, do good, let your lights shine for Jesus!"

Shining Lights — Impartiality

Christians emit the very light that emanates from Jesus—the Light of The World. Their deeds, per se, are not the light; but loving deeds make the light more believable and understandable. As Christians flesh out the compassion of Jesus by their deeds; as they radiate the blessings of the Beatitudes, they give visible proof of Christ's rulership. The followers of Jesus embody His presence, and at the same time reflect the gracious benevolent character of God's kingdom.

A devastating tornado ripped through Grand Island, Nebraska on June 3, 1980. An unusual outpouring of Christian generosity was coordinated by Mennonite Disaster Service (MDS), and endorsed by the Grand Island Interfaith Task Force. During the 8-week cleanup period, 1,764 Good Samaritans converged on Grand Island with hammers, trucks, and chainsaws. They demolished, cleaned up, framed and shingled. It was Christianity in overalls. Some 674 volunteers came from out of state and slept in quarters provided by the Saint Francis Hospital.

The MDS cleanup shut down on August 2, having assisted 493 residents. Volunteers signing in donated about 24,380 hours of labor. "Money cannot buy what you gave us," wrote a 73-year-old couple, "that feeling of security that someone cares." Others wrote, "It's hard to find adequate words, but without your help we would still be digging out and probably be at the point of despair."[6]

I arrived at my new parish in Nebraska in 1981. As mentioned earlier, the church was large by our denominational standards: 1600 persons, including 500 children. The church typically gave $400,000 per year to benevolent causes (mission and relief projects). Hundreds of its members devoted time to the Grand Island tornado cleanup in the summer of 1980.

In April of 1981 the mayor of Grand Island requested that the leaders of our Nebraska Disaster Service appear to receive the Distinguished Service Volunteers of the Year Award! On May 8, August Franz of my parish joined MDS leaders from Grant, Milford and Schickley to accept plaques. To our surprise, the mayor presented a check for $10,000 on behalf of the Interfaith Task Force, to be used by MDS in their future projects. What a gracious affirmation!

For my congregation the Grand Island catastrophe was really a God-given opportunity to "shine for Jesus." This church was founded by 35 German-speaking families migrating from Molotschna, South Russia to Henderson in October of 1874. Due to its ethnicity, this church was at times viewed as a bit clannish. At Grand Island it had served anyone in need without regard for nationality, race or creed. Due to its custom of asking for alternative service to military duty, the church, at times, was viewed as unpatriotic. It was ridiculed, primarily by those who didn't understand our biblical deep-seated conviction that all war is futile. So this catastrophe became an occasion to express Christlike love and caring.

Shining Lights — Word and Deed

For Jesus—what one says and what one does is cut from one piece of cloth: "...let your light shine before men, that they may see your good deeds and praise your Father in heaven." When works of graciousness, kindness and love bolster our words of witness, the witness becomes much more attractive, effective, believable and powerful. Our light and deeds of love are inseparable.

Bishop C. N. Hostetter, Jr., of the Brethren in Christ denomination was a remarkable man. During his twenties he served as a church evangelist. From 1934 to 1960 he served as President of Messiah College of Grantham, Pennsylvania. No one worked harder at a synthesis between evangelism and social service than he. While in his 50s and 60s, his influence carried a two-fold thrust.

In The National Association of Evangelicals (NAE), Hostetter was nine years the President of the World Relief Commission (WRC). He vigorously challenged Evangelicals to follow the example of Jesus: to feed the hungry and aid the suffering. He insisted that many were making the same mistake that the Jerusalem church made when it concentrated on evangelism and neglected the Grecian widows (Acts 6). He urged Evangelicals to add overseas relief to their mission budgets.

Concurrently, Hostetter was chair of Mennonite Central Committee (MCC), a relief agency. He urged colleagues to make the gospel witness the basis for their social service: "We now expect our volunteers to give an unapologetic Christian witness in all the relief and service work they do."[7] This is a powerful combination, a radiant evangelistic witness, coupled with humanitarian acts of love!

Today, my brother John pastors the Emmanuel English Church of Hong Kong. He first went there in 1958 for a 3-year MCC stint, to distribute food to hungry children. His supervisors (Norman/Eunice Wingert) were skillful at blending evangelism and social service. At one school a grandfather heard the Bible story and accepted Christ. When he died, his family requested a Christian funeral. For the street procession, the band played, "What a Friend" and "In the Sweet By and By!"

23. the LOVE factor

Light on the Pathway (Luke 10:25-28)

On one occasion an expert in the law stood up to test Jesus. "Teacher," he asked, "what must I do to inherit eternal life?" "What is written in the law?" he replied. "How do you read it?" He answered: "Love the Lord your God with all your heart and with all your soul and with all your strength and with all your mind, and, Love your neighbor as yourself." "You have answered correctly," Jesus replied. "Do this and you will live."

This command to love one's God is an Old Testament statement (Deuteronomy 6:5), as is also the command to love one's neighbor (Leviticus 19:18). But notice the wording: loving with the totality of our being is reserved for God. We are not instructed to worship our neighbor with our whole heart. Love neighbor "as yourself" is the instruction. It is assumed that everyone will have a fair degree of self-worth, self-esteem and wholesome pride. The therapist Dr. Sullivan wrote in *The Reader's Digest* (January, 1974) that genuine love exists only if the well-being and satisfaction of others is as important to you as your own.

The Great Commandment, as we call it, is fresh, practical and relevant—it's really where "the rubber hits the road." Christianity, beyond accepting forgiveness, denotes living in newness of life. "If conversion to Christianity," writes C. S. Lewis, "makes no improvement in a man's outward actions—if he continues to be just as snobbish or spiteful or envious or ambitious as he was before—then I think that we must suspect that his conversion was largely imaginary; and after one's original conversion, every time one thinks one has made an advance, that is the test to apply. Fine feelings, new insights, greater interest in religion mean nothing unless they make our actual behavior better."[8]

My Grandpa and the Thieves

We can ardently talk about love, until we're blue in the face; but that love is fictitious and hypocritical if we don't, in concrete ways, actively seek the well-being of others. Take the example of my grandfather, John Epp Sr.

Grandpa migrated from Russia in 1883 to escape military conscription and took up farming in central Kansas in Butler County. The early years were tough and full of trials. One day he came home late at night and saw horses and a wagon rush away from his barn. Unknown to the thief, the hired man had sleeping quarters in the barn and witnessed the whole transaction. Grandpa left his shotgun untouched, and got a good night's sleep. The next morning he hitched up his horses, sacked some oats and drove to his neighbors. "Neighbor," said Grandpa, "I am bringing you some grain; I didn't know you needed it so badly. Next time feel free to come in daytime hours!"

A Serendipitous Lesson

Last summer on a trip to California we visited our children in San Jose. To our delight we were able to join them for their daily family worship. They used, *The ONE YEAR Book of Family Devotions,* from the Children's Bible Hour of Grand Rapids. At their church's bookstore we bought a copy for ourselves. Here's a sample: the April 16 page is captioned, "Love is Action." On the right side is the scripture (I Corinthians 13:4-13), and at the bottom, the memory verse (Galatians 5:22), "But the fruit of the Spirit is love..." On the left side is a contemporary story (ages 8-14), just right for our grandson, Josh.

Here's the story in capsule form: Helen's father was taking her to choir practice at church when they saw a bumper sticker: "Have you hugged your kid today?" "Hmmmph," Dad snorted, "That stupid bumper sticker makes me mad. I wonder how many kids have hugged their parents today!" Helen had been praying that her dad would become a Christian. Later that day she cleaned her room and washed the dishes. Dad said, "What's gotten into this kid?" Before going to bed she hugged both her parents. As she went to her room she overheard Dad say, "You know Helen is a nice girl. I think I'll go to church tomorrow to hear her choir sing." Helen hoped that love in action might some day win her dad to Christ![9]

Story of a Famous Helper
Light on the Pathway (Luke 10:29-37)

But he wanted to justify himself, so he asked Jesus, "And who is my neighbor?" In reply Jesus said: "A man was going down from Jerusalem to Jericho, and he fell into the hands of robbers. They stripped him of his clothes, beat him and went away, leaving him half dead....But a Samaritan, as he traveled, came where the man was; and when he saw him, he took pity on him. He went to him and bandaged his wounds, pouring on oil and wine. Then he put the man on his own donkey, took him to an inn and took care of him...."

Jesus had an uncanny way of making truth practical. Three philosophies of responsibility are at once mirrored: (1) thief—what's yours is mine, (2) priest and Levite—what's mine is mine, and (3) the Samaritan—what's mine is yours. The ending is a surprise: an outcast half-breed Samaritan is the hero. Jesus turns the tables on the Jewish lawyer and asks him to identify the true neighbor. The reply, "The one who had mercy on him." His lips refused to utter "the Samaritan!"

The lawyer and Jesus agreed on one point: loving God wholeheartedly and loving neighbor unselfishly was the standard of perfection. But alas no human can attain it; so redemption is essential. However, Jesus chose to zero in on the defective, selective, love of Jewry—helping only their own kind. When Jesus told the lawyer, "Go and do likewise," he was clearly requiring a love that cuts across and transcends lines of race, religion and nationality.

The instinctive benevolent response of the Samaritan illustrates four kinds of sacrifice: (1) Risk—he was in danger of being mugged, or being implicated in a crime, (2) Resources—he used his own oil and wine to treat the wounds, and pressed his donkey into ambulance service, (3) Precious Time—"he took pity" and helped, donating his care that day and all that night, (4) Money—he shelled out enough to prepay medical costs at the inn and guaranteed to cover added expenses later. Impressive! The bottom line—deeds of kindness validate words of witness.

Lessons From the Good Samaritan

In his *Teacher's Commentary*, Lawrence O. Richards tells a poignant story relative to this text. He visited a 21-year-old in the hospital who had shot himself with a rifle. As a child this young man asked a question at church: "When you're so proud of sending money overseas for missionaries, why won't you have anything to do with the poor people across the street?" He was told to leave.

Richards did not blame the church for his friend's drift to drugs at age 13, nor for his choice of bad company. But he wondered whether "our missionary budgets, our separation, our doings and duties, may at heart be expressions of an attempt to whittle God's standard of perfect love down to lists of things we can do, and in the attempt feel some pride?"[10] I would state it stronger. Churches habitually whittle down God's requirements and settle for vicarious things like sending money overseas, instead of donating time in sacrificial service at home.

In the section, "Link to Life: Children", Mr. Richards gives down-to-earth help for teachers: "Our neighbor is anyone in need. But how do children become sensitive to other's needs?...you can help them....Create a class 'get well' sign for a sick member. Visit and sing for an older house-ridden individual. Collect food for the hungry, and bring it to a mission or a soup kitchen, etc. Even young children are not too young to be exposed to needs..."[11] A creative teacher can help a child visualize how real caring is accomplished.

We cannot over emphasize the power of love in evangelism, church growth and general ministries of charity. Kind deeds authenticate our words. I repeat: merely accepting forgiveness falls short of God's ideal; Christians need to model a spiritual transformation with a love filled heart and a Spirit filled life.

24. the CHILD factor

Light on the Pathway (Mark 9:33-37)

...he asked them, "What were you arguing about on the road?" But they kept quiet because on the way they had argued about who was the greatest. Sitting down, Jesus called the Twelve and said, "If anyone wants to be first, he must be the very last, and servant of all." He took a little child and had him stand among them. Taking him in his arms he said to them, "Whoever welcomes one of these little children in my name welcomes me..."

The child becomes the symbol of the last and the least. Many of us remember those weekend picnics where we chose up sides to play ball. First chosen were the best pitchers and best batters. Next, it was the best catchers, best runners and best fielders. Finally, one kid was left. (Maybe it was you!) Suddenly, the embarrassed loner might volunteer to be the water-boy where everyone would need his services. According to Jesus, that child—the last of all—is the greatest in the Kingdom of Heaven.

Each of the Synoptics includes this child-lesson; but only Matthew adds the comment of Jesus, "...unless you change and become like little children, you will never enter the kingdom of heaven (18:3)." In Bible culture as well as ours, the child is the last to be consulted and the least to be reckoned with. While the disciples were dreaming of kingdom escapades and macho achievements in order to merit the gold, silver and bronze in the Olympian finals of Heaven, Jesus used shock therapy and advocated a conversion—where they become like little children!

A Prof Learns From Little Kids

Dr. Paul Welter teaches Educational Psychology. He and Kent Estes team-taught a class of forty-two students on "Learning From Children." At church he assisted with pre-kindergarten Sunday School and at home he specialized in his role as grandfather. The outcome is a delightful book, *Learning From Children*. He advocates that we view children as Master Teachers—our Spiritual Mentors.

Welter explains: "Young children model those traits which Jesus said are necessary to enter the kingdom of heaven. They are born free of those cultural restrictions and personal biases which are pressed upon us quite early in life. We are taught, for example, to compare ourselves with others, to be less than honest, and to be negative...When do children begin to lose their childlikeness? I think some begin to lose it in their second year of life. Others keep many of their childlike qualities on into older childhood and adolescence."[12] Some adults even seem to retain a childlikeness, insists Welter. At ninety they still show spontaneity and humor, courage and creativity.

Some twenty-two childlike traits are identified by Dr. Welter. In most cases each forms a chapter: humility, trust, honesty, optimism, courage, placing relationships over tasks, expressing love, caring, friendliness, sense of wonder, touch, laughter, sensitivity, forgiveness, mourning, ability to heal brokenness, moving, playing, singing, creativity, and the thirst for learning.[13] We look at four ways by which children model ministry for us.

Childlike — Healing Brokenness

A Mother writes: "I learned a deeper meaning of God's caring from my daughter who was three at the time. I had just lost my mother—a young mother in my opinion, fifty-six years of age. Although I had the assurance that she was in God's presence, I went through tremendous grief and had a terrible sense of loss.

On one occasion I had heard some music which touched me deeply. My daughter saw me crying. She came and put her arms around me and said, 'Mama, someone wants to talk to you on the phone [she handed me her play phone]. It's Jesus and he wants to tell you he's taking good care of Nana.' At that moment I believe some healing took place in my heart."[14]

That day when the disciples squabbled over greatness, Jesus took a child into his arms and reminded them that the willingness to be the least and the last opens great doors for creative ministries. Children in fresh imaginative ways bring healing and comfort to the broken, the sick and the hurting. Church members ready to use their spiritual gift of "showing mercy" are never unemployed!

Childlike — Empathetic Sensitivity

A child teaches the teacher. "It was Jeremy's first day in preschool....He found himself terrified and tongue-tied when the teacher asked him to talk during show-and-tell time. He stood, three and a half years old, silent, with twenty pairs of eyes on him....Another three-and-a-half-year-old got up, walked over, stood by Jeremy, and said, 'Mrs Walker, you should leave Jeremy alone because this is his first day in school and he needs more time just to be shy.' Mrs. Walker...went on to the next child. As a humble, open adult, she learned to be more sensitive. The child, as her teacher, was sensitive to Jeremy's needs (and also found the courage to be his advocate)."[15]

Children display amazing sensitivity. They have an eerie way of reading the feelings of people and responding appropriately. In the first group of men I discipled in 1982, one was affirmed by his peers to have the gift of encouragement. Later (1986), he lost both his farm and his wife. He was left with five children. With every trial and heartache, his gift of encouragement was only enhanced.

Childlike — Courageous Friendliness

John Haggai tells of a ten-year-old girl, Lori, and her mother, Linda. While living in Singapore Lori befriended a girl, Tracey, who used bad language. One evening in devotions Linda shared about Corrie ten Boom and the Jews. Tracey's family was Jewish; so Lori and Linda began praying for them. One day Tracey read Lori's Christian comic books from cover to cover. She told Lori that she wanted to become a Christian; Lori led her in a prayer of accepting Christ.

Next Lori got Tracey a Bible. Linda cautioned Tracey about telling her mother, but the girl wanted to. Soon the girls came running back to Linda, "It's all right to have a Bible; only Tracey can't go to church with Lori." The next day Tracey came to study the Bible. Later Lori reported to her mother, "Tracey has hardly said a bad thing all day, and she has started praying."[16]

Adults are fearful about witnessing to their own kind, much less to a Hindu, a Jew, or a Moslem. On the other hand, it never occurs to children that witnessing across cultural and religious lines will create any problem. Children are so open, honest and transparent. They visualize all people alike and this is exactly what Jesus wants his church to learn. Each human is a candidate for the kingdom!

Childlike — Need of Belongingness

John Drescher relates a story from the *New York Times*. A small boy was riding a downtown bus, huddled against a lady in a gray suit. His dirty shoes touched another lady, who promptly asked the first lady to have her boy get his feet off the seat. The lady in gray responded, "He's not my boy, I never saw him before." The lad squirmed, "I'm sorry...I didn't mean to." The ladies found out that the boy's mommy and daddy were both dead, and he lived with Aunt Clara, but was often shipped by bus to Aunt Mildred. The ladies, full of sympathy, told him he was very young to be shifted around. "Oh, I don't mind," he said, "I never get lost. But I get lonesome sometimes. So when I see someone that I think I would like to belong to, I sit real close and snuggle up and pretend I really do belong to them. I was pretending I belonged to this lady when I got your dress dirty. I forgot about my feet...."[17]

If the Barna Research Group is correct that one-fourth of Americans would accept an invitation to church if asked, there are thousands of people waiting for someone to touch them, to embrace them and to include them in their circle of concern! It is precisely these childlike traits of honesty and caring that Jesus wants his church to emulate—willing to be the last and least.

25. the SERVANT factor

Light on the Pathway (Matthew 20:20-21,25-27)

Then the mother of Zebedee's sons came to Jesus...."Grant that one of these two sons of mine may sit at your right and the other at your left in your kingdom." Jesus called them together and said, "You know that the rulers of the gentiles lord it over them,...Not so with you. Instead, whoever wants to become great among you must be your servant....just as the Son of man did not come to be served, but to serve and to give his life a ransom for many."

The Greatness of Servanthood

The disciples indeed believed that Jesus was bringing the Kingdom of God as he said. They speculated wildly on visions of spine-tingling power. First, as we stated earlier, the Master applied a little shock therapy by telling his pupils to become converted and childlike. If that wasn't enough, he now informs Mrs. Zebedee that for her sons to be the greatest—the best—they must pose as bond slaves. Can't you hear the self-talk of the other disciples: "See there, James and John; you deserved it!"

Liberalism tends to define evangelism as mere Presence or mere Performance—being there, or doing good. Fundamentalism often limits evangelism to mere Proclamation—speaking words and winning souls. The full-orbed biblical approach sees these wedded together. Social service is not an inferior form of witness if accompanied with a word of testimony, when appropriate. It's no either/or thing.

This issue was once vividly caricatured by a professor of mine: "Since the task of general charity is apparently unconnected with the work of saving souls, it rates low on the scale of fundamentalism. Handing out tracts is much more important than founding a hospital. As a result, unbelievers are often more sensitive to mercy, and bear a heavier load of justice, than those who come in the name of Christ. The fundamentalist is not disturbed by this, of course, for he is busy painting 'Jesus Saves' on the rocks in a public park."[18]

Being Servants to the World

Donald Posterski is General Director of InterVarsity of Canada. He writes a delightful chapter on "Transcending Words." He insists that words intertwined with deeds make our Christian message more believable. Christians demonstrating life in servant-style will create spiritual thirst. Words will be empowered. He pinpoints service-acts, especially hospitality, as key in helping internationals.

Posterski explains, "...the people of God begin by meeting

their new foreign friends at the airport and helping with the heavy suitcases. They help find apartments, give city tours, stand in registration lines, interpret what is meant by strange sayings and generally cultivate the art of helping people feel comfortable in a foreign land. Their acts of love and service are not a setup for Bible study, retreats and prayer meetings. They are acts of unconditional love for the sake of lifting the level of life in the name of Christ for people who have specific needs."[19] What a challenge as God brings the world to America!

The reticence of Evangelicals to engage in social services has clearly changed. World Vision, one of the evangelical social agencies, in 1990 helped 28 million victims of poverty, famine or political strife in 94 countries. Their child-sponsorships touched 1,000,000 children, community development helped 14 million, and their pastor's conferences blessed 95,000. Their *1990-Overview* says: "World Vision is, at the core, an evangelistic agency. Our fervent desire is to be our Lord's vehicle, touching the poorest of the poor with His mercy...."

MCC — Christian Resource for Human Need

The Anabaptists of the Reformation were zealous followers of Jesus. In an indirect way, their evangelistic zeal is today mirrored in the Southern Baptists, and related groups. In a more direct way, their concern for mutual aid, disaster care and compassion-ministries is reflected in the "MCC" of the Mennonites.

The Mennonite Central Committee, born in 1920 to aid Russian famine victims, is a "Christian resource for human need" with 1,000 service workers. Each has a two or three year term; and one-half serve overseas.[20] In 30 years (1956-1986) MCC distributed 364.5 million pounds of relief materials in 93 countries.[21] The day I phoned John Hostetler, MCC was loading supplies onto a chartered plane for Kurd refugees in Iran. Emergency relief is a perpetual concern.

Some Ideas That Work

The 36 annual American MCC relief sales are an interesting phenomenon. Whole families, even churches, get caught up in a festival of activities, making quilts, donating antique cars, selling crafts, baked goods, and many other items. The auction rings create excitement. The mood is generous. Through 1990, 542 regional auctions had netted MCC a whopping sum of $43,892,398 for world hunger. Celebrating with a smorgasbord of ethnic foods makes money-gathering fun.

The MCC SELF-HELP program is a novel job-creation system. Some 30,000 artisans in 40 developing countries earn part of their living by selling their products ($5.6 million in 1990) to MCC for sale in Canada and the USA. These items are sold in commercial stores, at relief auctions and in 150 MCC Thrift Shops supervised by 7,000 volunteers. Such work restores dignity to the artisan.

For the 50th birthday of MCC, Peter J. Dyck wrote about "A Theology of Service" (Matthew 20:28), "God has...transferred us to the Kingdom of his beloved son and serving others is part of our new nature. Such service does not distinguish between word and deed, between 'kerygma' and 'diakonia'...."[22]

One Foot Above the Rest

In chapel at Westmont College, Myron Augsburger, President of the Christian College Coalition, gave this example of humble service. In Madras, India, after preaching one Sunday morning at St. George Anglican Church, he and his wife walked with Pastor Azariah to Cathedral Road, a street lined with beggars and lepers. The pastor pointed to a man, "You must meet him! He is an umbrella repairman and shoe cobbler. His 8-year-old son is blind. His wife is dead. His two daughters board at a school. Some days he gets 20 rupees for his livelihood."

Once Pastor Azariah went to the cobbler with a proposal, "Our staff has raised 100 rupees for you. We want you to have a platform one foot above the street where you can sit and have a shelter from the hot sun." Gazing intently he retorted, "No thanks, just as soon as you lift me one foot above the sidewalk, my friends will no longer sit along side me and talk." Dr. Augsburger challenged the students to serve humbly—on the level of the people, and not arrogantly—one foot above the rest. Jesus taught that greatness stems from lowly service, not from regimenting, manipulating or ruling.

Conclusion

The cross of Calvary is our perfect portrait of self-sacrificing love. A generation ago, Dr. Jacob Enz, a son of my Kansas parish and until recently a professor at our seminary at Elkhart, Indiana wrote a book, *The Biblical Imperative For Discipleship*. He reenforced my aforesaid statement by writing: "The colossal error of modern Christianity is to welcome with open arms all the precious benefits of the blood of Christ so freely poured out for us, and then, sometimes ignorantly, often studiously, and sometimes even defiantly, reject the method by which redemption was wrought out— living, self-sacrificing love, to the bitter end and beyond."[23] It is true, the purpose of Christ's coming to planet earth was to live, to love, to serve and to give his life as a sacrifice for us all (John 3:16). This epitomizes Ultimate-Servanthood.

In 1987, on the campus of Union Biblical Seminary of Pune, India, Esther Augsburger of Washington D.C. made a nine-foot sculpture of Jesus washing a disciple's feet. A Muslim army officer quizzed her, "But you Christians claim that Jesus is God. God would never have stooped down and washed a person's feet!" She replied, "We believe that God came to us in Jesus, in self-giving love, forgiving us and accepting us as His own, and that He did express this love by washing the disciple's feet" (See John 13:1-17). The man stood in silence. Pondering this thought, he shook his head in amazement and walked away.[24]

To Jesus the last, the least and the lowest are the greatest in his kingdom. This is mind-boggling, a total reversal of human standards. As disciples of Jesus we are salt, we are light, we are love, we are childlike, and finally, we are servants! There it is—we flavor society, illuminating the way. We are neighbors to those in need, being spontaneously transparent. And finally, we do the most menial deeds. Like Jesus, we give our lives in service for God (Matthew 20:28)!

Questions for Discussion:

1. When do Christians become worthless salt (Matthew 5:13)?
2. Compare words and deeds as ways to drive with lights on bright.
3. Discuss the impact on children—the eleven unexpected dinner guests!
4. Evaluate the love-deeds of Grandpa Epp when facing his grain thieves.
5. Discuss the four child cases: healing, sensitive, friendly, belonging.
6. Consider the Augsburger story of the cobbler (one foot above the rest)!

PRACTICING HIS PRESENCE: DEVOTIONAL PAUSE FOR BUSY DISCIPLES
Theme of the week — Showing Good Works

	Monday	**Tuesday**	**Wednesday**	**Thursday**	**Friday**
Light on the pathway	Matthew 5:1-13	Matthew 5:14-16	Luke 10:25-37	Mark 9:33-37	Matthew 20:20-27
Lesson for this day	Factor #21 Be Salt	Factor #22 Be Light	Factor #23 Be Love	Factor #24 Be Least	Factor #25 Be Lowest
Life in Jesus' way	Take time to pray	Take time to pray	Take time to pray	Take time to pray	Take time to pray

PRACTICE HIS PRESENCE IN CHURCH ON SUNDAY

Chapter

7

Living By Prayer

26. Model
27. Intercessory
28. Power
29. Guidelines
30. Transmittance

Introduction

What aspect of North American church life has languished more in the last 75 years than the practice of prayer? The thought is disturbing. If the church's cosmic conflict requires supernatural power, then clearly, the Kingdom of God has lost ground. Frankly, a church operating in human strength alone fails Christ.

Dr. Henrietta Mears (1890-1963) was a prayer-warrior of our generation. A giant in Christian education, Richard Halverson dubbed her a "female Apostle Paul!" Lyle Schaller thought her to be "...one of the most influential figures in American Christianity in this century...!"[1] Regal Books honored her in 1990 by publishing: *Dream Big: The Henrietta Mears Story,* to mark the 100th anniversary of her birth.

While I was a seminarian in Pasadena in 1955, Susan Joann and I drove to First Presbyterian Church of Hollywood one Sunday to attend Miss Mear's college class. Amazing—a class of 300! As a master teacher she exuded love and fostered a godly self-esteem. Her biographer claims that she prayed 400 young people into Christian service based on Matthew 9:38.[2] One such person was Bill Bright of Campus Crusade. He said that she thought, prayed, planned and loved supernaturally. Others were the former actress Colleen Townsend, and her husband, Dr. Louis Evans Jr., Pastor of the National Presbyterian Church of

Washington, D.C. Colleen and Louis recall college prayer meetings with Miss Mears, "We learned there, from her example, to be bold before God, to ask great things on God's behalf and to do spiritual warfare from a bent-knee position."[3]

The accomplishments of Dr. Mears stand as monuments to the power of prayer. Forest Home was her "Miracle Mountain" where 2 million confronted her Saviour. Her Gospel Light Publications ministers to 20,000 churches, and her book, *What the Bible is All About,* has sold several million copies. Her literature is found in 100 languages.[4]

This chapter accents Jesus' teaching on prayer, followed by his own example. The power of prayer is shown through events in history. Prayer guidelines are listed. And finally, the chapter ends with ways to foster stronger prayer habits.

26. *the* MODEL *factor*

Cradled in the middle of the Sermon on the Mount is the Lord's Prayer (Matthew 6:9-13). In reality, this is "the disciple's prayer" as taught by the Lord. In context Jesus discredits the pagan-style of repetitious praying; so we conclude that he never expected his followers to repeat this prayer a thousand times over. Apparently, Jesus was giving the basic ingredients of a model prayer.

Light on the Pathway (Matthew 6:9-13)

"This is how you should pray: 'Our Father in heaven, hallowed be your name, your kingdom come, your will be done on earth as it is in heaven. Give us today our daily bread. Forgive us our debts, as we also have forgiven our debtors. And lead us not into temptation, but deliver us from the evil one.'"

Over the centuries this prayer has been analyzed and organized in a hundred ways. We simply accent six themes: (1) Adoration, (2) Submission, (3) Sustenance, (4) Forgiveness, (5) Temptation and (6) Deliverance.

*** **Adoration. "Our Father in heaven, hallowed be your name."** Some twenty times Matthew refers to God as "our Father in heaven." The Old Testament uses the "father" theme as an analogy, but not in direct address. Here Jesus breaks new ground. Here is adoration to God as the Holy-Sovereign One; and disciples can approach him as a caring, loving, and accessible Heavenly Father.

Praise and adoration are essential in praying—even in life's severe trials. Years ago I read a story of Harry Ironsides and his son playing "bear & boy." One day it was Dad's turn to be bear. He gave chase—under tables and over chairs. As the bear cornered him, the boy showed fear. Suddenly he relaxed, running into his dad's arms, "You're not a bear, you're my daddy!" Don't we often lose sight of God's love amongst our trials? Doesn't praise recapture "God's loving arms?"

*** **Submission. "Your kingdom come, your will be done on earth as it is in heaven."** In the early church, unbelievers were forbidden to say the Lord's Prayer or to partake at the Lord's Table. Submission was required. In kingdom-talk, this prayer asks God's saving rule to be extended as people bow in submission to him. They already taste the eschatological end-of-time blessings in salvation. They cry for the consummation of things.[5] They long to see the ruling reign of God in This Present Evil Age; they anticipate the Age To Come—a universal submission.

Some TV preachers sling the slogan: "Name it and Claim it!" For sure, people need reminders to come boldly to their Heavenly Father. Turning frustrations into prayer can prevent gnawing ulcers or higher blood pressure. However, when televangelists insist that the phrase, "if it is your will," be stricken from faith-building blessing-claiming prayer, the teachings of Jesus are being abused. Good praying is both bold and submissive. We do not always clearly discern God's will.

*** **Sustenance. "Give us today our daily bread."** After exalting God's name and coveting his will, the Lord's Prayer turns to four human needs. The first is food. First-century workers had a hand-to-mouth existence and were paid by the day. Life was precarious. By contrast, many affluent Americans are protected by guaranteed wages, unemployment benefits, and retirement plans. While our country has more than a million millionaires, one out of five households still lives on less than $10,000 per year.[6] Prayer for food is proper. It reflects a dependence on God. All of our health, livelihood, and heartbeats, are in God's hand.

While we have mountains of surplus food, some countries have abject poverty. My brother-in-law, with his wife, devoted 35 years to mission work in Colombia, Peru and Mexico. As a missionary, he tackled poverty via Self-Help projects: digging wells, raising poultry/vegetables, and getting land titles. Sad to say, in one country terrorists marked him for death. He had to leave! As in South America so in Africa, distributing food is complicated. Politicians starve enemies. So at times a prayer for food is tantamount to praying for a change in leadership.

*** Forgiveness. "Forgive us our debts, as we also have forgiven our debtors." The second need: forgiveness. Jesus weds divine forgiveness to human forgiveness. When people claim to have forgiveness from God—a gift of the kingdom, asserts George Ladd, yet refuse to forgive offenses against themselves, they deny their own profession of forgiveness and contradict the real character of the kingdom.[7]

The Lord's Prayer fits in with Israel's Jubilee Year. It has been argued that the phrase "...as we also have forgiven our debts" refers to monetary debt, and not to mere moral offenses. In Jesus' day a Jewish peasant risked losing his land due to a repressive debt system and high taxation. Lenders asked for land as security. Peasants, who lost their land became sharecroppers. Their unpaid debts kept mushrooming from high interest. Lenders could sell peasants and their children into slavery. Note—this Jesus who graciously forgave prostitutes, was adamantly unforgiving at one point—the grace of God is unavailable to lenders who refuse to forgive debts, to those who mercilessly enslave people.[8]

In church work, people have asked: "Pastor, how can you take that?" Persons have sometimes hurt intentionally. With each new church God gave me added grace, and hopefully, maturation. Whenever I was tempted to nurse a grudge, I thought of all God had forgiven me—that cured me every time! I left all vengeance to God.

The book *When Caring is Not Enough* probes deeply. It compares Fair Fighting (settling it) with Foul Fighting (gunnysacking grievances): "Of all the collectables, injuries are the most widely saved....The cost of carrying a set of open accounts...is (1) ongoing brooding, (2) unfinished business, (3) overloaded emotions, (4) past distances separating any present encounter, (5) fear...toward the future, (6) ...stress is converted into physical symptoms, (7) ...new difficulties...adding to old accounts...and...the energy required for all of the above."[9] Forgiveness is simply good therapy and Jesus, our Lord, mandates it.

*** **Temptation. "And lead us not into temptation."** Pardon for past sins is marvelous; but we also need protection against future sinning. That's the third need this prayer addresses. While God allows testing; his goal is never our failure (James 1:13). As bridge builders test work to prove strength, God tests us.

The human slant to this is: we pray as though it all depends on God; and we work as though it all depends on us. Jerry Bridges finds the American preacher, Jonathan Edwards a good model. Edwards made a resolution—not to do anything he would be afraid to do, were it the last hour of his life. "Are we willing to commit ourselves to the practice of holiness without exception?" inquires Bridges. "There is no point in praying for victory over temptation if we are not willing to make a commitment to say no to it."[10] Prayer—without honesty—is a farce.

*** **Deliverance. "Deliver us from the evil one."** The fourth need Jesus pinpoints is "deliverance." Matthew's first mention of the temptations (4:1-11) names the devil as the tempter. Later, the parable of weeds labels unbelievers "sons of the evil one" (13:38). Jesus teaches his disciples to seek deliverance.

He himself models victory through Scripture-use, Holy Spirit-enablement (Luke 4:1, 14), and willful resistance. In *The Screwtape Letters*, C. S. Lewis warned of two extremes—a total disbelief in demons or an unhealthy interest in them.

In the 1960s I heard talks by German Psychotherapist Kurt Koch. His hair-raising accounts sounded foreign to our ears. Of 20,000 counseling cases, 4,000 were linked to demonism, spiritism or the occult. In recent decades this has come to America with demon worship, weird occult acts and attacks on Christians.[11]

*** **Prayer Doxology. "For thine is the kingdom...the power...the glory..."** (Matthew 6:13 KJV). This beautiful ending may have been added by the church—it's missing in early manuscripts. The celebration of "the power and the glory" is always in order. As Oswald Smith once put it: "An hour's work in the Spirit will accomplish more than a year's work in the flesh. And the fruit will remain!"[12]

27. the INTERCESSORY factor

We have examined the model prayer Jesus taught his disciples in the early stages of their discipleship training. We turn next to the intercessory prayer of Jesus in John 17, just prior to his Passion. A messianic consciousness had been evident throughout his ministry. And now, his death for the salvation of the world was imminent, and he knew it. This was the prayer of a dying man—the very Son of God—who was about to place his whole kingdom-enterprise on the shoulders of his trained-but-untested fledgling disciples.

A. Jesus Prays For Himself (John 17:1-5)

Jesus begins with a personal concern, "Father, the time has come. Glorify your son that your son may glorify you" (17:1). Then he prays about accomplishing his threefold mission: to dispense eternal life to his followers, to complete his divinely appointed work, and to recapture the heavenly glory he had known in his preexistence. His prayer is intensely personal.

William Barclay gives this prayer theological perspective, under the caption "The Glory of the Cross." Jesus' obedience to the will of God was the "Gateway to Glory." The cross was the worst the world could do to him, and Jesus could have escaped it.

However, in his willingness to die, he demonstrated that the love of God had no limits, and that his atonement opened the gates of glory. The Resurrection was for Christ the capstone—his vindication.[13]

What do we learn about praying? Jesus did not shy away from praying fervently for himself (17:1-5). The typical church member in the USA and Canada, not generally known for praying, sounds so piously correct when he or she says, "I never pray for myself, I only pray for others." Wait a minute—STOP. Given the sinful nature of us all, proper prayer to a Holy Father (17:11) begins with confession and the seeking of cleansing. Only as our private needs are met, is our public ministry valid. It should spring like an overflow from forgiven lives.

In 1990, Search Institute took the prayer-pulse of 35 million church members by comparing the Southern Baptists to five mainline groups (Presbyterian-PCUSA, Lutheran-ELCA, Methodist-UMC, and Christian-UCC & Disciples). Pertaining to religious biography, one question asked, "As a teen, aged 13-18, did your home have family devotions?" Generally 65 percent said, "Never or rarely."[14] Also, 57 percent of mainline adults do not today engage in daily prayer and 66 percent never read the Bible when alone. By contrast, among Southern Baptist adults, 57 percent do pray daily and 74 percent do read the Bible when alone.[15]

Membership Profile II (1989) compared five Anabaptist denominations (with 232,275 members). While 90 percent usually pray at meals, and 78 percent claim to pray a time or two daily, 82 percent have no daily devotional pattern (private or family) where the Bible is read. Devotional customs, as well as worship attendance, showed a marked decline in the past seventeen years.[16]

Worthy habits and controlled lifestyles are often rejected by persons in the 1990's as too restricting. Here Olympic athletes serve as models: medals of gold and silver go to those who train. No disciple—NOT ONE—can excel in God's kingdom with a haphazard life of undisciplined slipshod devotional activities.

Jesus prayed fervently for himself; Christians need to pray continually for themselves.

B. Jesus Prays For His Disciples (John 17:6-19)

The second part of Jesus' prayer is clearly the longest (17:6-19), but very moving. Still looking heavenward (17:1), Jesus prayed aloud for the benefit of human ears. He affirmed his disciples warmly—as God-given, word-obeying, and assurance-possessing. Accepting the revelation of Jesus' divine origin, they had believed in the Heavenly Father who sent him. "Glory," says Jesus, "has come to me through them" (17:10). What positive affirmation these young followers felt. Never forget, Jesus led a high-risk venture. He moved with care, lest the disciples abort his mission. He prayed earnestly as though everything was at stake.

On the eve of the Crucifixion Jesus tenderly prayed for his disciples (17:9). What were his predominant concerns? We discover four: (1) Oneness—17:11. Unity among Christians is not something we "cook up" ourselves; it need merely be acknowledged, like the oneness between God-the Father and God-the Son. In Christ we are one! (2) Joy—17:13. Jesus wanted a full measure of his joy to indwell his followers. (3) Deliverance—17:15. Jesus prayed that his disciples would be protected from the evil one, and (4) Consecration—17:17-19. The sanctification of Jesus leads to ours as well. The Septuagint uses this verb to consecrate sacrifices or priests (Exodus 28). As Jesus set himself apart to do God's will (in dying); he sets us apart to do God's will (in living).[17]

As Christians, when we nurture converts, we must pray for them as Jesus prayed for his disciples. Increased activities can squeeze out prayer; but prayer is pivotal. Samuel Chadwick wrote: "The one concern of the devil is to keep the saints from praying. He fears nothing from prayerless studies, prayerless work, or prayerless religion. He laughs at our toil, mocks our wisdom, but trembles as we pray."[18] Jesus proved that to be true. When Satan wanted to "sift Peter as wheat" the prayer of Jesus shielded him from losing his faith (Luke 22:31).

In pastoral discipling, I found prayer to be absolutely essential. At one point we were three years into our discipling program. I was ready to recruit my fourth group in our large congregation. Susan Joann and I scheduled an introductory breakfast (6:30) for Thursday at our house. By Wednesday morning I had phoned 19 men; only nine had said "Yes." Four said, "Try me next year."

That noon my wife was in Lincoln shopping. I fed my invalid mother-in-law and decided, I—myself would "fast." Going downstairs, I devoted one hour to prayer, asking God for a complete group of 12. That evening I made three phone calls; each said, "YES!" The next morning at breakfast, all 12 enrolled. At our first gathering with its full-circle prayer, two of the last-minute recruits thanked God specifically for having been invited.

C. Jesus Prays For Future Believers (John 17:20-26)

Finally, Jesus prayed for the converts of the disciples—future believers. A thread of "glory" is woven into this prayer. There is glory in the church when disciples live in the unity of oneness. God is one with Jesus, Jesus is one with the disciples, disciples are one with each other and all are one with God. When believers witness to the world, their lives of oneness and love authenticate the gospel. Jesus' prayer for unity has an evangelistic motive. People will believe the gospel when they see it demonstrated in a loving church.

This prayer raises some intriguing questions. The first is: do people ever accept Christ and his gospel where prayer has not first preceded the witness? A knee-jerk response is—Yes, think of Saul of Tarsus—He was converted in a "lightning-stroke" kind of encounter with Christ. Note: Saul approved the stoning of Stephen; and Stephen in his last breath prayed for his enemies (Acts 7:54-60).

A second question casts the same issue into a broader framework. Do groups of people or geographical areas need concentrated prayers before evangelism can succeed? Thirty years ago, a pioneer mission worker, J. Arthur Mouw, from the jungles of Borneo, told my congregation his firsthand experience. One day he headed up a jungle river in his canoe to preach at another village. Suddenly, an unseen force began choking him. He turned back and postponed his trip for some months until prayer had overcome the power of Satanic opposition.

Ruth Veldcamp, Christian Reformed missionary in Nigeria, Africa, noticed that many Muslim leaders were linked to occult powers, often using witchcraft and sorcery. She enlisted one hundred American Christians to pray daily for the binding of Satan and for the building of churches in Muslim communities. There have been marvelous conversions among esteemed leaders. How did people come to belief in Christ? Often God miraculously communicated to them in visions and dreams.[19]

28. the POWER factor

Light on the Pathway (Mark 9:14-32)

....his disciples asked him privately, "Why could not we drive it out?" He replied, "This kind can come out only by prayer."

Effective ministries flow from times of persistent prayer. After a "glimpse of glory" on the mountain, Jesus and his circle of three came down to find their associates in major trouble. A man had brought his demonized deaf/dumb boy for deliverance; but they were powerless. The boy fell into another grand mal convulsion. The father pled for help and Jesus complied. The disciples learned a gigantic lesson. Right words are inadequate, when prayerlessness cuts them off from God's kingdom power-source.

1. Prayer & the History of Missions. Without fail, kingdom-advance stems from strong praying. The church goes forward on its knees. Prayer expels the forces of darkness, liberating people. Mission work and prayer are always inseparable.

One grand example is the Moravian revival. Coming suddenly on the German estate of Count Nicolaus von Zinzendorf (13 August 1727) this spiritual awakening melted and motivated a group with a twofold result: it spawned a 100-year around-the-clock prayer vigil. Think of it! For one-hundred years the Moravians divided the 24-hour day into segments, and prayed every minute. Also, a phenomenon was unleashed—a whole town of families (Herrnhut) had one single aim—to evangelize.

Fueled by the contagious leadership of Zinzendorf, this was the "most extensive of all missionary movements in which Pietism was a major factor," wrote historian Latourette. By the year of 1800 the Moravians had planted missions in Russia, India, Nicabor Islands, Ceylon, Gold Coast, Surinam, Central America, Greenland, Labrador, West Indies and the American Colonies—to the Indians.[20]

John Wesley was a trophy of Moravian evangelism. On April 26, 1738, according to Peter Boehler, Wesley came—weeping bitterly and requesting prayer as a "poor broken-hearted sinner." Later, on May 24, at a Moravian small-group meeting at Aldersgate, Wesley's heart was "strangely warmed." He writes: "I felt I did trust in Christ, Christ alone for salvation; and an assurance was given me that He had taken away my sins, even mine, and saved me from the law of sin and death." Wesley became a fiery evangelist. At his death in 1791, Europe had 72,000 Methodists, and America, 57,000.[21] These converts met in "bands" of six or more, confessing faults to each other, and praying for each other—based on James 5:16.

2. Prayer & the Great Awakenings. America has had many significant waves of revival, each linked to prayer. In 1727, Jonathan Edwards became co-pastor with Grandfather Stoddard at Northampton. He wrote: "...When God has something very great to accomplish for his church, it is his will that there should precede it the extraordinary prayers of his people."[22] This pattern appears normal.

The Great Awakening of 1858-1859 in Britain and America led to the formation of the China Inland Mission and The Salvation Army—two organizations of immense importance. In two years, two million converts were swept into churches. The movement paved the way for the Dwight L. Moody Revivals.

This awakening was precipitated by swarms of people praying. In New York on Fulton Street 10,000 businessmen met daily for prayer. Prayer groups sprang up everywhere. In Kalamazoo, Michigan an ecumenical prayer meeting was called, ranging from Baptists to Episcopalians. At the first meeting a request was read, "A praying wife requests the prayers of this meeting for her unconverted husband." Suddenly a man arose, "I am that man. I have a praying wife, and this request must be for me. I want you to pray for me." Seven men, in turn and in tears stood up: "I think that was my wife. I need your prayers!" The power of God fell mightily on the group. Before long nearly five hundred people were converted.[23]

3. Prayer & Political Oppression. For years Israel cried to God for deliverance. The most dramatic exodus of all times was Israel's migration from Egypt to Canaan, from slavery to freedom, across the dry bed of the Red Sea. In the annals of history, political oppression has often driven God's people to their knees. My people—the Mennonites—are no exception. They boast a dramatic faith-building migration of recent times: the Berlin Exodus.

Hitler's war-machinery plus the Potsdam Agreement (Aug-1945) signed by the Allied leaders created a refugee problem of colossal size—12 million in Germany alone.[24] The Mennonite Central Committee (MCC) set up a European feeding program, serving 100,000 daily at its peak.[25]

One day (1946) Peter and Elfrieda Dyck, MCC food-workers in Holland, got word from US Army Colonel Stinson in Berlin to come rescue Mennonites trapped in a bombed-out building. Peter found the group to be "Platt-Deutsch" German speaking Russian Mennonites with no legal status or food ration cards. They were fleeing the repatriation agreed upon at Yalta, fearing Siberian labor camps! As the Dycks supervised their feeding and housing, the group grew to 1000.

Colonel Stinson gave Peter a proposal: You find a ship and a country, I will promise an army-escorted train to the port at Bremerhaven. (Berlin was an island in the middle of the Soviet-held zone.) Through kindness, the Queen of Holland secured the ship "Volendam" for a fee of 375,000 dollars. After the USA, Canada, and Mexico all said, "No," Paraguay agreed to accept 3000 refugees—if Mennonite.

When all arrangements were final, Stinson called, "Peter, it's all off; Russia will not consent." Not to be denied, Peter went directly to General Lucius Clay, head of US forces in Europe. By sheer persistence he was allowed an hour with the General. "It is dangerous," said Clay, "even with my guards there will be shooting and your people will suffer."

On Monday of the target-week Peter gathered all the refugees and broke the sad news—the ship is coming to Bremerhaven, a train is enroute to haul us; but we can't cross "the Red Sea," the Russian zone! Peter started sobbing. One man comforted him, "Maybe it's not God's will, I will return to Siberia if I must. You have tried." One lady was introspective: "Possibly God is trying to speak to us." The Volendam loaded 339 refugees at Rotterdam and 1070 (from Munich) at Bremerhaven—then waited for the 928 from Berlin. Peter Dyck went there to the ship's farewell ceremony led by MCC's Mr. C. F. Klassen. (Hundreds of churches in North America were praying.) In Berlin the refugees met in prayer clusters, seeking a miracle. Expectancy was high. Sleep fled. Many started packing.

The farewell ended. The ship was about to depart. Suddenly Peter received an urgent call from General Clay, "Hold the ship— the train is cleared!" Peter asked for the ship's intercom, "Friends," he said with quivering voice, "God is doing a miracle; they are coming from Berlin!" A silence enveloped the ship, some fell on their knees, Peter stood speechless. All felt the awesome presence of God. Abruptly, Peter Dyck excused himself and rushed back to Berlin in his jeep.

One hour after Peter's announcement, the US chiefs of staff met to plan a midnight-exodus. At 6:00 p.m. Elfrieda Dyck was told to have people and baggage ready in three hours. That very day Soviet Marshal Sokolovsky had met with Clay and the

American ambassador, Robert Murphy, and had signed papers of permission, apparently as a gesture of goodwill. God alone knows how this all transpired!

Army trucks moved people to a 45-car freight train. Peter barely arrived before the train took off at 2:00 a.m. The orders were: "Low profile and silence." In the dead of night, in a "prayerful" hush, the 24-hour ride began. Once out of the Russian zone, a hymn erupted: "Now thank we all our God...who wondrous things hath done." As C. F. Klassen often said, "God can. It's not impossible!"[26]

29. the GUIDELINES factor

While prayer is powerful, it is also personal and intimate. We can refer to prayer as a relationship between a loving Heavenly Father and the subjects of his kingdom—the responsive disciples of Jesus, God's earthly children. This is not to say it has no guidelines. Clearly, Jesus gave us clues to effective praying.

Light on the Pathway (Matthew 7:7-11)

"Ask and it will be given to you; seek and you will find; knock and the door will be opened to you. For everyone who asks receives; he who seeks finds, and to him who knocks, the door will be opened. Which of you, if his son asks bread, will give him a stone? Or if he asks for a fish, will give him a snake? If you, then, though you are evil, know how to give good gifts to your children, how much more will your father in heaven give good gifts to those who ask him."

Near the end of the Sermon on the Mount, Jesus gave his disciples a triad of lessons on childlike simplicity—using the present imperative: keep asking, keep seeking, keep knocking. As a human father—so the Heavenly Father—uses these ways to educate his child in good manners, persistence and patience. If a child gets the response he or she seeks, it is because the child has learned something about what pleases the father.

Jesus said that fathers on earth, though innately evil, do not give their children stones or snakes when bread or fish are needed. The Father in heaven is pure, holy, and perfect. "What is fundamentally at stake is man's picture of God. God must not be thought of as a reluctant stranger who can be cajoled or bullied into bestowing his gifts..., as a malicious tyrant who takes vicious glee in the tricks he plays..., or even an indulgent grandfather who provides everything requested of him. He is the Heavenly Father, the God of the kingdom, who graciously...bestows the good gifts of the kingdom in answer to prayer."[27]

So from a Christian perspective, prayer boils down to the relationship that exists between the Heavenly Father and his children on earth, persons born-again by faith in Jesus Christ. With this mental portrait as backdrop, we sketch in five guidelines for praying as suggested by Jesus.

*** *Pray in Faith.* **"Have faith in God...if anyone says to this mountain, 'Go throw yourself into the sea,' and does not doubt...but believes...it will be done for him..."** (Mark 11:22-24, see also Matthew 17:20 & Luke 17:6).

The idea that faith "moves mountains" occurs several times, always in a different context. Teachers, of course, repeated themselves. Here was a common Jewish phrase for removing difficulties. It mirrors a faith that depends on God in the major problems of life. Jesus himself never moved a mountain into the sea; but he taught that a mustard seed of faith was powerful in removing obstacles.

*** *Pray in Jesus' Name.* **"And I will do whatever you ask in my name, so that the Son may bring glory to the Father..."** (John 14:13-14).

Banks honor checks with approved signatures. The bank of heaven honors the signature of the crucified, risen Christ. Here is a mind-boggling, spine-tingling kingdom offer, a blank check from our Lord. What a reminder of Psalm 23!

No doubt, Christians living close to God will more and more reflect the actual heart of God. Discernment on what will bring God glory comes from the Holy Spirit (John 14:26), and from our own inner conviction, as well as from the counsel of brothers and sisters in the community of faith. In my first church, Sam, an 80-

year-old man, came to the Deacons and Elders after morning worship to request prayer, "The doctors say I need surgery; but at my
age, I prefer to be anointed with oil, having you say the prayer of
faith based on James 5:13-16." We read the passage, shared together, and anointed him. God heard and God healed.

*** *Pray in Persistence. "...I* **tell you...because of the man's
boldness [or, persistence] he will get up and give him as much
as he needs"** (Luke 11:5-8).

In this parable, an unexpected traveler dropped in, and the
host woke up his neighbor at midnight to borrow some food.
"This parable teaches us to be persistent in prayer. It is not a story
about the nature of God. God is not in bed with his children,
asleep and reluctant to answer our prayers. Jesus is telling us to
approach God boldly as we would a neighbor and to ask repeatedly without giving up...."[28] Persistence in prayer proves our concern and real sincerity.

In the year of 1821 the youth at the Presbyterian Church of
Adams, New York prayed tirelessly for a 29-year-old lawyer,
Charles Finney. Their pastor, Rev. Gale, described Finney as
"hopeless;" but the youth persisted. One autumn day Finney left
his office. In the woods, on his knees, he claimed Christ's atonement for his sin-burdened soul. That evening joy flooded his heart
as the Holy Spirit infilled him—wave after wave.[29] Finney became
a renowned evangelist.

*** *Pray in Submission. "...if* **it is possible, may this cup be
taken from me. Yet not as I will, but as you will"** (Matthew
26:37-39).

We have accented three ideas that invite courageous praying.
This fourth guideline serves as a kind of caution. The place is the
Garden of Gethsemane where Jesus agonized over the will of
God. Such submissive praying, writes Psychologist Hart, "...is the
highest form of prayer because it recognizes that God knows better than you. It is the happiest form of prayer because it is the
prayer of complete surrender to a God you acknowledge as all-
loving....It is the healthiest form of prayer because it invites you to

subject yourself to God's will, whatever that may be—and His will is always good for you."[30] Excellent.

*** *Pray in Common-Agreement.* **"...if two of you on earth agree about anything you ask for, it will be done for you by my Father in heaven. For where two or three of you come together in my name, there am I..."** (Matthew 18:19-20).

If the "will of God" serves as one check to ward off reckless or selfish prayers, praying in twosomes gives another protection. Here is the marvelous **PROMISE** of answered prayer if "two agree" in their praying, and here is also the marvelous **PRESENCE** when "two or three gather" in Jesus' name. What a grand inducement to pray—in the oneness of a twosome—in the presence of Christ.

A transfusion of joy and freshness was injected into many prayer meetings thirty years ago by Rosalind Rinker's best-seller, *Prayer—Conversing With God.* Majoring on two themes: "Where two agree" and "Where two or three gather" she cured many ailments in group-praying. "Praying conversationally (that is praying back and forth on a single subject until a new one is introduced by the Spirit) makes prayer such a natural means of spiritual-togetherness that the healing love of God touches us all as we are in His presence."[31] In prolonged periods of prayer, Susan Joann and I, even today, use a modified version of this. In sum, Jesus' guidelines challenge us to powerful expectant praying, while cautioning us against prayers that either violate the will of God, or the advice of a friend.

30. the TRANSMITTANCE factor

How do we instill into people, prayer—as a habit? How do we transfer to our homes and churches a deeper prayer-commitment? How does a pastor transmit prayer patterns to his or her own leaders, and to the entire church?

This chapter began with a reference to the prayer life of Dr. Henrietta Mears. Her father's banking business in North Dakota kept him away from home much of the time. Each morning her mother withdrew to the bedroom to pray for an hour on her knees, with folded hands and lips moving. Henrietta observed her. Already as a toddler, she idolized her. While still a preschooler, she made it her goal as well. She took an alarm clock to her own bedroom. With closed eyes she prayed and prayed and prayed, for everything she could think of. Peeking at the clock, she found only one minute gone! How could mother think of things for a whole hour? To a little girl, mother's praying was awesome and contagious.[32]

Light on the Pathway (Luke 11:1)

One day Jesus was praying in a certain place. When he finished one of the disciples said to him, "Lord, teach us to pray, just as John taught...."

As disciples rubbed shoulders with Jesus, they saw how he often withdrew to pray (morning, evening or night). At other times he included them.[33] When they asked for teaching, Jesus gave them the Lord's prayer. (Luke's version is either a shortened form of Matthew 6:9-13, or was given at another time.) At any rate, Jesus added the parable of the midnight guests to demonstrate persistence in praying. Jesus' devotion to prayer made a lasting impression (Acts 6:3-4).

My Personal Pilgrimage with Prayer

During my years in Los Angeles, 200 pastors met annually in a 2-day mountain retreat—often at Mear's Forest Home. The Revival Prayer Fellowship under Armin Gesswein featured speakers like David Morken, J. Edwin Orr, Joe Blinco, Kurt Koch, and R. R. Brown. From many denominations these speakers all championed biblical church renewal. The prayer times were choice. I was blessed repeatedly and felt the afterglow for weeks.

Those retreats leavened the rest of my life. Robert Munger, a Presbyterian pastor from Berkeley once expounded Luke 4. Decades later, I remember it like yesterday: Jesus—in baptism, in temptation, in ministry—full of the Holy Spirit (4:1-15). Munger shared his own commitment to prayer: each Wednesday in a mountain above his church he prayed for each member by name.

I made a new covenant to pray. (Long ago, I learned that imitating others was risky, e.g. I thought of praying like John Wesley—at 4:00 a.m., until I learned that pre-electricity people went to bed at 7:00 p.m.) In this case I was hooked—I knew it was of God. I began praying for my 200 members each week. In my second pastorate, in the 70s, it was 900 members. And in my third parish, all through the 80s, it was 1150. This prayer habit took discipline but "putting my hand to the plow I never looked back." My preferred technique was to pray through the pictorial directory—family by family. In kingdom-language it was cross-bearing, serving Christ in the purpose for which he died. This was spiritually rewarding, psychologically therapeutic, and schedule-wise exacting.

The life of Jesus jars and jostles us. Just think—in the hills he prayed all night and in the morning chose his Twelve. Once, in my first church, I invited the Deacon/Elder Board to join me for a night of prayer. I still chuckle. They concocted a clever plan, "Pastor, one of us will come at ten, the second at 11:00, etc." I prayed with them, one by one. For six hours the leaders and I prayed, touching a host of crucial concerns. But as the last one left (4:00 a.m.), I felt so drowsy, I went home as well. In evaluation, two things came to me: (1) harness daytime hours first, and (2) try all-night vigils when the burden of prayer chases sleep away. The bottom-line issue really is—all of church work requires supernatural wisdom, power and blessing. The church operates on prayer.

In the last 35 years, in three separate parishes, I led an old fashioned midweek prayer service. The attendance generally ranged from 40 to 85. In each case we had vigorous praying. Our sessions had three equal parts: Bible study, sharing and prayer. The writing of all requests on a blackboard, and the sharing of PTL's taught accountability. Always, we prayed for all the sick, all of our missionaries, and all urgent concerns. At times we divided into cells of four, so each one could pray. To model prayer as a priority, I as pastor led the service.

Prayer and a Small-Group Format

A small-group format is ideal for teaching people to pray. I have already stated how Susan Joann and I opened our home to covenant-groups: (1) how we recruited 128 men, (2) how we used life-stories to help clarify salvation-assurance. Now (3), I add our prayer-experience. Each session gave 20 minutes to prayer. On the "Common Prayer Page," requests were listed, dated, and all answers were recorded. We went full-circle adding and updating requests each week.

Group-experts frequently advise praying in cells of two or three. I have no objection; but most of our men preferred full-circle prayer. Here is why it worked well, even though each group had 8 to 12 people: (1) Brevity: we suggested at most 5 or 6 sentences, (2) Specificity: we suggested picking 2 or 3 items from the list, so no one was caught in fear trying to think up a prayer, and (3) Group Dynamics: hearing each one pray had a bonding effect, fostering a healthy togetherness. (Note: in the recruitment call, we forewarned people that we had full-circle prayer and they were welcome to use a pre-written prayer, at first.)

I'll never forget one group's first meeting. We began collecting requests for the Prayer Page. The first 5 requests were trivial and totally safe. Some said, "I pass." Number six shared deeply. Then number one interrupted, "Now I see what we're doing, let me add another request: I am not satisfied with my job situation and plan to apply elsewhere." Remarkable! In our small community that is sensitive info—needing absolute confidentiality. As the twelve united in prayer, week by week, you can imagine the jubilation when he announced, "I have a new job; you can mark down a PTL!"

At one "graduation banquet," a 31-year-old father shared: "I joined a Discipleship Group and was so nervous....I had never prayed in front of twelve people before. When I saw the Common Prayer Page with a place to record PTL's, I thought, 'Would it not be embarrassing if we got only a few?' I was surprised as the weeks went by at the PTL's we got—in a few instances it was miraculous. This really made me a believer in the power of group-praying."

Every Christian needs to give priority to prayer by scheduling it into his or her daily calendar. During their high school days, two of our sons were influenced by their Youth Pastor, to make lifetime commitments to a five-minute daily Quiet Time (QT). That is a good start. While writing this book, my wife and I devoted one hour to prayer each evening (after exercise, dinner & news). Praying aloud, we alternated in 5-minute segments, using prayer lists. We both loved it!

Some Elementary Suggestions

1. Pray each day at the same time. Consistency counts! Jesus is waiting.
2. Prepare your heart with devotional reading. Some Bible reading is best.
3. Pick a place as your special praying place. This will be meaningful.
4. Pick a favorite posture—sitting, standing, walking or kneeling. The best posture is the one that keeps you alert and concentrating.
5. Pray aloud. Silent praying was not a normal practice in Bible days and is not helpful for most of us. Audible praying helps keep us on track.
6. Pray to God in a conversational style. Talk to God like you talk to any special friend. This eliminates any special lessons. Talking is natural.
7. Pray whether you feel like it or not. You need this communion with God and God longs for your fellowship. Just take these facts by faith.
8. Pray about the big things, and all the little things. Your Father cares.

Conclusion

Our generation has witnessed an unbelievable miracle—the opening of Eastern Europe to the Gospel. Somebody's prayers have prevailed. This earthshaking change—sad to say—can hardly be linked to Canada or the USA, where people, always on the run, snatch a prayer here and catch a prayer there. Possibly the prayers of Christians elsewhere (e.g. Koreans pray for hours, days, weeks.) have prevailed.

A few days before Desert Storm broke loose, Canadian mission professor, Levi Keidel, wrote: "Can prayer change the course of history? The Persian Gulf crisis is a call to persevering prayer. If we believe that our primary conflict is with the rulers of the darkness of this world (Eph.6:12), a war in the Middle East could be a diabolical scheme to shunt a horde of souls into eternal darkness, and to render impotent all subsequent efforts originating from the West to evangelize the world's 900 million Moslems."[34] Churches world-wide—beseeching the Lord of the Harvest—have a gigantic task!

Myron Augsburger, likewise, urges the church to confront the mind-boggling issues of our day with united prayer: "This solidarity with one another as disciples, when expressed... between denominations, or across national lines in the global community, can change the world. Such prayer can remove the gulf between the races, between the haves and have-nots...and can...correct the apartheid, terrorism, and wars which plague the world."[35] The prayer life and prayer teachings of Jesus encourage us never to give up.

The church, in every generation since Pentecost, has felt that an avalanche was about to engulf it. Today's threats run from A to Z: affluence, abuse, AIDS, abortion, broken families, chemical dependency, demonism, ease-seeking, etc. If a Henrietta Mears can make a difference, so can you and I. If each pastor would model praying, if each church would multiply its prayer groups, if each Christian family would place Bible reading and praying at the center, if each individual disciple of Jesus would double his or her prayer time—God would bless!

Questions for Discussion:

1. How do you think Jesus intended the "Lord's Prayer" to be used?
2. What key lessons do we learn from Jesus' prayer in John 17?
3. Do you believe all conversions, awakenings and renewals stem from prayer?
4. We listed five prayer guidelines of Jesus. Which challenges you the most?
5. How do we best transmit good prayer habits and patterns?
6. What has been your most dramatic answer to prayer?

PRACTICING HIS PRESENCE: DEVOTIONAL PAUSE FOR BUSY DISCIPLES
Theme of the week — Living by Prayer

	Monday	Tuesday	Wednesday	Thursday	Friday
Light on the pathway	Matthew 6:1-15	John 17:1-26	Mark 9:14-32	Matthew 7:7-11	Luke 11:1-13
Lesson for this day	Factor #26 Our Model	Factor #27 Intercession	Factor #28 The Power	Factor #29 Guidelines	Factor #30 Transmission
Life in Jesus' Way	Take time to pray	Take time to pray	Take time to pray	Take time to pray	Take time to pray

PRACTICE HIS PRESENCE IN CHURCH ON SUNDAY

Chapter

8

Forgiving Without Limits

31. Love One
    Another
32. Turned Cheek/
    Second Mile
33. Forgive 70 x 7
34. Love Your Enemy
35. Forgiving
    Process

Introduction

In his delightful book, *Learning From Children,* Paul Welter tells how naturally children forgive. He recalls the time his two girls (age two and four) taught him an adult lesson: "When big sister was disciplined for hurting little sister, big sister cried for her blanket (the special one that comforts her). I did not let her have it for a few minutes, so little sister, who had just been hurt by big sister, went and brought her the blanket."[1] What a beautiful quality this child displayed—instant spontaneous forgiveness!

But adults—how different! Forgiveness comes so painfully, so agonizingly. I recall my encounter with an elder in my first parish. We tangled in a phone conversation. It was heated and abrasive. "I think I'll come over to clear this up," I fumed in desperation." "I think you better!" he retorted. On the freeway I called on heaven for wisdom. I knew this man was godly, but I suspected his real motives. Basic issues separated us. I took our youth to our church camp 200 miles away; he liked a nearby camp. I wanted our youth to have interaction with our inner city churches of Los Angeles (where some youth were black or Hispanic); he felt that was too "dangerous." I suspicioned prejudice, and felt the situation demanded more than a BAND-AID quick-fix.

He met me courteously and we talked. I raised basic issues. "Huh, I can see there will be no reconciliation here today!" he rebutted. After more excruciating words—issues I didn't want swept under the rug—I made two unconditional promises: "Brother, any time your name comes up in a conversation, I'll put in a good word for you. Secondly, whenever you enter my thoughts, I'll pray God's blessings on you." He arose and embraced me. Every year since—twenty years straight—until his recent death, he sent us a lovely Christmas greeting! (My one-way unconditional promise was made at a point of desperation, and is not meant here as the perfect model. For further insight, see page 175.)

I begin this chapter by examining forgiveness as a bequest of Jesus to his disciples. The heart of the chapter centers on what is perhaps Jesus' toughest requirement: unconditional forgiveness. The chapter ends with a sixfold elucidation of the forgiveness process, always easier to discuss than to implement. Notwithstanding, forgiveness is the genius of Christianity. God did it first!

31. the LOVE-ONE-ANOTHER factor

The cattle on the western prairies are branded with the insignia of their ranch. Last year on a speaking-mission to Oklahoma, I had a meal at the ranch of Jack Sawatzky. His special brand was a "lazy-J" with an "S" attached. When he registered his brand, he got approval since none of the other 18,000 permits in the state of Oklahoma had that precise shape. According to Jesus, the decisive trademark of his followers is LOVE (John 13:34-35). No other religion in the world has this insignia—love shaped like the cross—attached to the empty tomb.

In the supermarket housewives buy many items according to the brand name. Food on the grocery shelf is identified by its label: Folgers coffee, Kellogg's corn flakes, Sunkist oranges, Campbell's mushroom soup, Gerber baby food, and so on. All shoppers are attracted to their favorite brands. What is the label that attracts the outside unbeliever to a healthy church? At the top of the list is that quality of love that cares, helps, and forgives.

Redemptive Christlike forgiveness springs from wholesome therapeutic love.

Light on the Pathway (John 13:34-35)

"A new command I give you: Love one another. As I have loved you, so you must love one another. All men will know that you are disciples if you love one another."

We lived in the Los Angeles area when our sons were ages eight, five, and three. One day they had a noisy scuffling brawl in the backyard. I ordered them into the house. "Boys," I said, "We are Christians. What will the neighbors think? Jesus said, 'By this shall all men know that ye are my disciples if ye have love one for another!'" (John 13:35 KJV). "Boys," I continued with stern emphasis, "Not one of you will leave this room until you have memorized this verse." Repentant, they complied. One by one they left the room—having learned one of the greatest utterances ever given to the church of Jesus Christ.

Christ's Parting Concern

Chapters thirteen to seventeen of John's Gospel are often called the Upper Room Discourse. Most likely, the occasion was the Passover meal and the Last Supper as recorded in the Synoptic gospels. In this specific context Jesus spoke of his own glorification—a reference no doubt to his dying, rising and ascending (13:31). And secondly, in this context he called himself a pattern to follow: "As I have loved you, so you must love one another" (13:34).

Why did Jesus seemingly link a love-and-forgiveness theme to his approaching ascension? The answer is simple. He would soon place the entire work of his kingdom onto the shoulders of his disciples. But they were a frail crew. Jesus knew that Peter would falter in the impending arrest and trial. He knew that James and John were vying for top seats in his kingdom; he recalled their prophet-like idea to call down fire from heaven to scorch pagans in Samaria. Jesus knew that the disciples, human as they were, required solid tutoring on love and forgiveness.

God's dramatic redemptive acts come alive on the pages of Holy Scripture. While being righteous, God is also compassionate. Love and forgiveness irradiate from the church's key memory verse: John 3:16. God loves; his children must love.

The True Marks of Love

The nature of love baffles people. *The Reader's Digest* (January, 1974) carried an article "Do People Really Marry For Love?" Psychiatrist Sullivan gave many reasons why people marry: (1) fear of being unloved, (2) fear of loneliness, (3) search for financial security, (4) the desire for sexual fulfillment, and (5) the hunger for approval. Each reason is self-serving, if not self-gratifying.

What then is real love? According to Dr. Sullivan, real love exists when the satisfaction and security of another is as important to one as one's own satisfaction and security. That's biblical. Here then is the acid test for the church. Do I love my neighbor as myself? Is our out-going love, concern, and acceptance of others, just as obvious, just as tangible, just as unmistakable, as the personal pampering we bestow on ourselves? Do the visitors who show up at our church instinctively sense a genuine heart-felt love?—or does it feel skin-deep?

Forgiveness in Church: Rooted in Love

Jesus underscored that the distinguishing trademark of his disciples would be LOVE. A teacher today might put it this way: "As surely as a steam engine runs on water, and a car runs on gasoline, and a vacuum cleaner runs on electricity, the Church of Jesus Christ runs on love!"

How do outsiders actually perceive the church? What is the prevailing view? George Barna's nationwide research suggests that on any Sunday 15-20 million of unchurched people, one out of four, would be willing to attend church if some friend would simply invite them. That's the good news. There is solid potential. If churches could swap their smug indifference for a Christlike caringness, many people would walk into the church. A simple act of inviting is all it takes.

Alas, the bad news is that the bulk of unchurched people perceive the church as an uncaring, unloving, unforgiving institution. "Millions of Americans have turned their back on Christian churches because they believe it is hypocritical for churches to preach love, but exhibit rancor and division regarding denominational lines, theological distinctives, or ethnic differences. Skeptics that we are, Americans are not about to patronize an institution which appears incapable of living what it preaches."[2]

Church Squabbles and Forgiveness

Several decades ago, a plane ride from Los Angeles to Portland, Oregon landed me in the middle of a heated church squabble. As a district rep I was joined by a denominational leader from the east. Together we conducted a preaching mission in the evenings. Daytime hours were filled with prayer, interviews, and reconciliation-talk. Since slander and gossip were cheap, we held people accountable. We discounted hearsay, and required people to speak for themselves. We verified each accusation, and discovered a hopelessly-entangled skein.

The pastor of this 325-member church had walked out with 50 parishioners in a protest move. As we went from charge to counter-charge, the members were laying on each other special conditions for forgiveness and reconciliation. It became so involved we knew we could never unravel things this side of eternity. There I learned one basic superb lesson: unconditional love, with no strings attached, is an absolute prerequisite for healing, harmony and happiness. Making the score even, tit for tat, never satisfies an unloving-unforgiving soul.

All weasel wording in churches needs to be scrutinized, especially the kind that says: "Sure, I love everyone, but I certainly don't like them all. In fact, I can't stand the sight of some, and heaven forbid if I'm ever placed on a committee with them!" Wait-a-minute. Feeling closer to some than to others is normal;

but true love sees each person's potential "in Christ" and so to love someone is to like that one.

In church work, I have long felt that forgiveness grows out of a healthy, mature biblical love. Theologian Ladd confirms this: "Another evidence of the life of the Kingdom is a fellowship undisturbed by ill will and animosity. This is why Jesus had so much to say about forgiveness, for perfect forgiveness is an evidence of love. Jesus even taught that human forgiveness and divine forgiveness are inseparable (Mt. 6:12)."[3] We reiterate: forgiveness is first and foremost rooted in mature love and becomes a full-blown expression of that love.

32. the TURNED-CHEEK/SECOND-MILE factor

Our basic Christian stance of mutual love and unlimited forgiveness forms a launching pad for a God-honoring response to hostility. Turning a cheek or going the second mile is a positive action, utilizing creative Christlike approaches.

Light on the Pathway (Matthew 5:38-42)

"...If someone strikes you on the right cheek turn to him the other also. And if someone wants to sue you and take your tunic, let him have your cloak as well. If someone forces you to go one mile, go with him two miles. Give to the one who asks you and do not turn away from the one who wants to borrow from you."

Jesus picks a few examples from a catalog of grievances and at once elevates personhood above possessions—helping above hoarding, giving above guarding, blessing above balking, smiling above smiting. They are vexations common to anyone's daily schedule: a personal altercation, a lawsuit, forced labor, and a pesky borrower. Yet the solution is consistently the same. Live so unselfishly that the presence of Jesus will radiate from your life. Openhanded generosity will be multiplied 100-fold when we cross the threshold of death; but hoarded gold and goods will be devoured by vultures of greed.

Christlike Love Turns the Cheek

If struck on the cheek, a disciple absorbs the insult and pain. Turning the other cheek will startle the enemy. It is not an act of cowardice; it is a symbol of courage and love. It is a clever strategy to break the cycle of revenge—a true protection for the forgiver.

In 1941, due to ill health, the father of Myron Augsburger moved his family for the winter to Newport News, Virginia. He worked as a foreman on a house construction job. Bearing a German name and being a conscientious objector to war, he became the object of some criticism. One day, Bob, one of his severest critics, was laid off by another foreman. Some days later when Mr. Augsburger needed two more workers, he intentionally chose Bob, knowing he needed food for his family. Fifteen years later, Myron was invited to conduct an evangelistic crusade at Newport News. On the first Sunday evening, at the invitation to surrender to Jesus Christ, an older man came down the aisle. He said to Myron, "Do you know Clarence Augsburger?" "Why, yes," said Myron, "he's my dad!" Tearfully the inquirer continued, "That man is why I'm here!"[4] Turning the other cheek—more often than we dream—wins people to Jesus Christ.

Christlike Love and Lawsuits

Jesus urges us to exceed expectations, letting generosity outdo what is required by law. Cultivating friendships is far more important than accumulating funds. Losing a few bucks can be a good investment.

A parishioner of mine in California (we'll call him Joe) once joined two other lenders to give a man capital to start a new cement-concrete firm. Eventually, the enterprise collapsed. "Joe," said the lenders, "let's sue this rascal to recover our money!" Joe replied, "I refuse to sue another Christian brother." The two lenders took the beleaguered man to court. As he took legal action to protect himself, the prosecution lost the case. Many years passed. One day Joe received a letter. "Dear Joe," it read, "I have never forgotten your kindness when I started my cement business. Recently I retired; we have sold our house. My wife joins me in sending you the money you loaned us so many years ago. We hope you are in good health. Thanks again!"

Christlike Love Goes the Second Mile

Roman soldiers habitually commandeered Jewish civilians to carry their goods one Roman "mile." The Greek word "impressment" means to "press into service." Simon of Cyrene was forced to carry the cross for Jesus precisely that way (Matthew 27:32). Jesus urged his disciples to exceed expectations and go two miles.

Going the second mile is now a famous phrase for going beyond the call of duty. It holds marvelous potential for therapy, evangelism, and conciliation.

When Susan Joann and I took our first pastorate in the Los Angeles area in the mid-50s, we tried to go the second mile with some tough cases. One member on the church roster (we'll call him Willie) hadn't attended for years. On a visit to his home in Paramount, I found his wife studying with Jehovah Witnesses. She gladly accepted my offer for some home Bible studies. One day I had the joy of leading her to faith in Christ. However, her health declined. I visited her at the Long Beach hospital the day she died.

Willie turned bitter—to God, the church and the pastor. He asked a stranger to conduct the funeral. At times I chatted with Willie at his service station at the corner of Lakewood and Artesia—all to no avail. After years of boycotting the church the elders asked: "Is you membership meaningful to you, or shall we drop it?" He retorted, "Who are you to play God? Hassle me and I'll transfer membership back to Newton, Kansas, where I was baptized as a teen, shortly before my army tour." Eventually his name was dropped.

In 1971 we accepted a pastoral call from a 900-member parish at Newton, Kansas. Imagine our surprise—Susan Joann and I were invited to Ramada Inn one Sunday evening to have coffee with Willie and his new wife, a childhood sweetheart. The moment we sat down, Willie began: "Pastor, I apologize for the way I treated you in L.A. I long admired you two for attending my wife's funeral after I intentionally snubbed you! According to Steps Five and Nine of Alcoholics Anonymous I'm making amends wherever possible." "Willie, I never held a grudge," I said, "but thanks for your apology; we warmly forgive!"

How did Willie get to Kansas? California authorities had sent him to a cousin's farm at Whitewater to dry out. Leaders of AA at Newton had picked him up twice a week for their meetings. Eventually, Willie bought a house three blocks from the church of his childhood, and opened a home for alcoholics. We as a church bought 800 dollars worth of wood and built a fence around his house so his alcoholic friends would have some privacy.

A Prodigal Returns Home

Once I preached on the Prodigal. Barely home, the phone rang. It was Willie: "Pastor, I heard you on radio. I'd like a cassette. That's my story. The first year in AA, I was so bitter I refused to say 'God' in the 12 steps of AA!"

One day Willie gingerly asked, "Can I take communion at your church?" My response was: "If you believe in Jesus Christ—his death and resurrection for you, and desire to live for him, you are welcome! This is the Lord's table." But on Communion day, Willie was hospitalized, and could not attend.

When released, he and Sue invited me and a deacon to the house to observe Communion. There we sat in a circle—Willie and Sue on the bed and Deacon Herman and I on chairs facing them. After Bible reading we shared. "This means most to me," mused Willie, "since I have been forgiven the most. I have not taken communion since my baptism 38 years ago!" Then his wife chimed in: "I have come through a long drug rehab, but I remember clearly the day my daughter died. I could not overcome my bitterness until it dawned on me that children are only loaned to us. Then I could thank God." Yes—a most memorable communion!

One day Willie cautiously asked: "Pastor, you know my

background—army, divorce, and alcohol. I ask no special favors; but do you think Sue and I could join your church?" With joy I responded, "Willie, we are a hospital for sinners, not a holy club for saints. As you join us in serving Christ, we'll join hands with you in helping alcoholics!" Thus (4-7-74) Willie and Sue joined our church, some 17 years after I started praying for Willie in California. Going the second mile had paid off—beyond our wildest dreams.

33. *the* FORGIVE-70-TIMES-7 *factor*

Jesus, the master storyteller, unveils another pungent parable. As he poignantly taught the lawyer about neighborliness through a story of a roadside beating, he now graphically teaches Peter forgiveness via a story of an unpaid debt and the threat of jail. Once again Jesus locks in a theological gem—our gracious Heavenly Father holds us accountable to forgive others as he has forgiven us!

Light on the Pathway (Matthew 18:21-35)

Then Peter...asked, "Lord, how many times shall I forgive my brother when he sins against me? Up to seven times?" Jesus answered, "...the kingdom of heaven is like a king who wanted to settle accounts....Then the master called the servant in. 'You wicked servant,' he said, 'I canceled all that debt of yours because you begged me to. Shouldn't you have had mercy on your fellow servant just as I had on you?' In anger his master turned him over to the jailers to be tortured, until he should pay back all he owed. This is how my heavenly Father will treat each of you unless you forgive your brother from the heart."

Forgiveness: a Biblical Basis

Reflect on this parable carefully. A king decided to settle accounts. He called in a man who owed an enormous debt—10,000 talents, in our currency millions and millions of dollars. When the man could not pay, the king proposed to sell him into slavery, together with his wife, his children and all his possessions. The man fell on his knees and pleaded for his life. The king was moved with pity and let him go scot-free.

The forgiven man found a servant who owed him a mere one hundred denarii (one hundred day's salary for a common laborer). He demanded payment. The man pled for patience. The forgiven man refused to listen and had him cast into prison. The other servants were deeply upset and reported this travesty to the king. In anger the king denounced the man for not showing mercy, sent him to jail, and ordered him tortured until he repaid his enormous debt.

Kenneth Taylor (Living Bible) lists the big debt as ten million dollars compared to the smaller one of two thousand. The ratio is 500,000 to one. Several lessons are obvious: (1) if the king represents God and the debt we owe him is huge, then his forgiveness demonstrates his enormous grace—all undeserved, (2) if we have been forgiven by God, any human offense against us, no matter how serious, by comparison is trivial; it requires our merciful forgiveness. Finally (3), all forgiveness is costly. A college professor once asked our Ethics Class, "If a debt is forgiven, then nobody pays—true?" Wrong! The forgiver pays. The king actually paid the cost, that is, he absorbed the loss. So too, our forgiveness has cost God dearly; as His son, Jesus Christ, absorbed our sin, suffered the dregs of hell in our place, paid the price, and set us free.

This reference of Jesus to a "70 times 7" kind of forgiveness is an affirmation that forgiveness is endless, never affected by recurring failures and never harboring a residual grudge. Of course, this supernatural Jesus-Way ethic presupposes supernatural enablement. And contrariwise, decreeing severe punishment (18:35) does not violate God's character. "Jesus sees no incongruity in the actions of a heavenly Father who forgives so bountifully and punishes so ruthlessly, and neither should we...he is a God of such compassion...he cannot possibly accept as his those devoid of compassion...."[5] The lesson is explicit. Forgiven people are to duplicate that generosity. Forgiveness is nonnegotiable.

Forgiveness: a Theological Basis

One scholar links forgiveness with kingdom-theology: "The point of this parable is that when a man claims to have received the unconditioned and unmerited forgiveness of God, which is one of the gifts of the kingdom, and then is unwilling to forgive relatively trivial offenses against himself, he denies the reality of his very profession of divine forgiveness and by his conduct contradicts the life and character of the kingdom....It is therefore the church's duty to display in an age of self-seeking, pride and animosity the life and fellowship of the Kingdom of God and the Age to Come."[6] Thus the church mirrors God's intent.

The New Testament insists that imitating Jesus ultimately narrows down to one's attitude regarding forgiveness and servanthood. Paul never lifted up Jesus as a role model for his celibacy or his tent-making livelihood. The New Testament idea of imitation is consistent "...at the point of the concrete social meaning of the cross in its relation to enmity and power. Servanthood replaces dominion, forgiveness absorbs hostility...only thus are we bound by New Testament thought to 'be like Jesus.'"[7]

Forgiveness: a Sociological Basis

On the American scene, salvation-concepts tend to be individualistic and lack the biblical dimension of community. In church history, the Left Wing of the Reformation saw forgiveness as a reconciling relational process rather than a private individualistic spiritual act. "Anabaptism sees forgiveness in communal context as defined in Mt. 18:25ff. and the goal is not the personal release of guilt...but regaining the brother and sister. In stressing relationship, Anabaptism moves forgiveness...toward solidarity with the forgiven...[and] demands that sustaining the body of Christ and nurturing community are the essence of a discipleship that works for shalom."[8] This kind of Christian community, of course, implies a whole gamut of blessings, e.g. discerning God's will together, holding each other accountable, and practicing mutual aid.

While parachurch groups of North America have provided some necessary emphases, few have done justice to the communal dimension of the gospel. When God's forgiveness is seen merely as a private personal transaction, a key element is overlooked. The isolation from others of like faith deprives one of an environment for growth, nurture and accountability which the church ideally provides. Salvation-forgiveness binds one to the Body of Christ.

In his provocative textbook, *Pastoral Counseling Across Cultures,* David Augsburger, examines forgiveness more deeply. One chapter is titled: "Inner Controls, Outer Controls, Balance Controls—The Theology of Grace."[9] He argues that three control patterns (1. Anxiety, 2. Shame, 3. Guilt) are present in all cultures; but that each culture tends to emphasize one over the other two. He cites the opinion of Margaret Mead (1946) that Western culture is guilt-oriented and the Japanese culture is shame-oriented. Later, scholars termed this an oversimplification, since each culture has all three qualities to some degree. However, all three find resolution in authentic forgiveness.

A person's theology of grace may stress any one of these three controlling motifs: (1) anxiety-punishment-release, (2) shame-alienation-reconciliation, or (3) guilt-condemnation-forgiveness. As God's grace—his steadfast love—moves all creatures toward wholeness, trust replaces anxiety, acceptance restores shame, and forgiveness resolves guilt. God's all-inclusive love affirms us holistically.

Augsburger has observed that Western writings have avoided both "guilt" and "shame" in the past half century. Writings generally label such emotions as very repressive—influences to be ousted—in the interests of liberation. They fail to see the constructive and instructive aspects that the emotions of guilt or shame can bring. In either case, the ultimate solution is God's forgiving grace.

To summarize, in theology forgiveness is essential; in secular psychology it is largely omitted. When Peter quizzed Jesus about repetitious forgiving—up to seven times—Jesus startled him with the "70 X 7" idea, and clinched the lesson with the story of a king who forgave a huge debt (until the man refused to reciprocate). The Bible accents forgiveness; yet according to Psychologist Archibald Hart, a dozen current psychology textbooks don't mention it.[10] That is surprising! Certainly, anxiety and guilt drive thousands to the therapist.

34. the LOVE-YOUR-ENEMY factor

In three years of teaching Jesus obviously covered important themes numerous times. These passages from Matthew and Luke are virtually identical. An excellent overview is offered by D. A. Carson in the *Expositor's Bible Commentary*.

Light on the Pathway (Luke 6:27-36, Matthew 5:43-48)

"...Love your enemies, do good to those who hate you, bless those who curse you, pray for those who mistreat you....Then your reward will be great, and you will be sons of the Most High, because he is kind to the ungrateful and the wicked. Be merciful, just as your Father is merciful."

"...But I tell you: love your enemies and pray for those who persecute you, that you may be sons of your Father in heaven. He causes his sun to rise on the evil and the good, and sends rain on the righteous and on the unrighteous. If you love those who love you, what reward will you get?..."

We select two key ideas. First, when God sends sun and rain on all, we must not conclude that his love will send salvation to all. Jesus was explicit about that (Matthew 25:31-46). Since Calvin's day, favor without distinction (such as sun and rain) has been called "common grace" (5:44-45). God could justly condemn everyone; but chooses to show favor in this Present Evil Age. This we emulate.

Then secondly, to be persecuted for righteousness sake aligns one with the prophets (5:12); but to bless and pray aligns one with God (5:45). Dr. Plummer once said it succinctly, "To return evil for good is devilish, to return good for good is human, to return good for evil is divine."[11] The following four stories are concrete examples of how people loved their enemies.

Case No. One — David Jacobsen

David Jacobsen, head of West Beirut's largest hospital, was accosted by three hooded men with machine guns and hustled to a hide-out. The hostages, led by Catholic Father Jenko and Rev. Benjamin Weir, founded the "Church of the Locked Door," their one true freedom while being held in captivity. Late in 1986, after severe beatings, Jacobsen was kept in isolation for 45 days. Sensing God's presence and reciting Psalm 27 and 102, he suddenly had the hunch that he would be released on November 2, 1986. And so it happened.

Instead of seething with anger and fantasizing about revenge, Jacobsen and his friends, according to *Guideposts'* account, reflected some of that blessing and praying that Jesus spoke of: "I found that no one's faith was weakened by the hell we found ourselves in....Grasping hands, we'd quote Scripture and pray. Oddly, our guards seemed to respect our ritual. Our togetherness in prayer showed me that when the Holy Comforter is called, he answers....It [prayer] is the greatest weapon known to man."[12] Hate consumes a lot of energy; instead, these hostages chose to pray.

Case No. Two — Lazaro Udubre

Marian Hostetler's book, *They Loved Their Enemies,* recounts the courageous witness of an aged African Christian, Lazaro Udubre.[13] In the late 1960s, near the Blue Mountains in the Congo Republic (Zaire), Simba insurrectionists fought against the new government and looted villages. One day near Lake Albert the rebels announced that they planned to kill someone to show their authority. They chose a young leader, one of Lazaro's sons. Everyone was horrified; women wept.

Lazaro stepped forward and begged that his son be spared— he had a family. "If someone must die, let it be me! I'm old. I've lived my life. I'm a Christian. I know that I will go to heaven where it is more beautiful than anywhere on earth. So kill me." In disbelief, the rebel chief had him tied and put into the truck. His sons rushed to kiss him good-bye. "Don't try to change my mind," he insisted, "I know what I'm doing. We'll see each other again in heaven..."

Lazaro was taken to a clearing in the forest. He saw bodies strewn everywhere. Soldiers were loading guns to shoot more men and boys. The rebel chief called to the firing squad to wait while he asked this Christian—willing to die for his sons—to preach to this group. Lazaro stepped forward urging the whole group to believe in Jesus, like the thief on the cross who in the last minute accepted salvation. While some of them were still sobbing out prayers the firing squad silenced them. Later that day the rebel leader told Lazaro to preach to two more groups before their executions. Still they spared Lazaro.

Day after day this horrible butchery continued. Lazaro despised it. Each time he was asked to preach to another group. One day a rumor spread through the rebel camp that government forces were closing in. The whole camp fled into the forest, and Lazaro escaped! After peace was restored, the local Christians demonstrated the Good News of Jesus Christ with the story of Lazaro Udubre—the man who was willing to die for his sons. Christ's death became understandable.

Case No. Three — James Graham

Years ago, Dr. James Graham, Presbyterian missionary from Taiwan preached in my pulpit. David Swartz shares a touching story about Mr. Graham. In the Boxer Rebellion 100 missionaries and families were killed in the Shansi Province of China. One day Graham returned to the area to see if it was now "safe." Late at night the executioner of these Christians came to him: "How can I atone for my sin?" He was deeply shaken; many Christians died singing praises to Jesus!

Graham knew that this man had killed his close friends. Suppressing his rage, Graham explained the gospel: "Your sins are great—Very Great. But God's mercy is even greater. Jesus is his son who came to earth to die for sinners like you. I too am a sinner....And because he died for you, for Jesus His Son's sake, God can forgive you."[14] That night a missionary brought a murderer to Christ, who like Saul (Acts 8:1), had the blood of Christians on his hands.

Case No. Four — Bishop Festo Kivengere

In 1977 the ruthless dictator of Uganda, Idi Amin, began attacking the church. His troops searched the house of Archbishop Janani Luwum at gunpoint. They arrested all religious leaders and herded them into an open area. Hundreds of irate soldiers encircled them. There, in the tropical sun, the mob tiraded them, accused them of smuggling weapons from China, threatened to kill them—for six hours, without food or water. Soon all were released except Archbishop Luwum.

The Archbishop was taken to President Amin and asked to sign a confession; but he refused. Instead, he started praying for his captors. Amin ordered him shot. When the soldiers refused, Amin shot the Archbishop himself, plus two of his own cabinet members. The TV news reported the deaths as car accident victims.

The late Bishop Festo Kivengere, one of the foremost evangelical leaders of Africa, fled to another country. One day he was interviewed by the Western press. "What would you do if you were alone in a room with President Amin and you only had a gun?" According to Don Jacobs of Mennonite Christian Leadership Foundation, a close friend of Festo, his reply was straightforward, "I would say, 'Here, you take the gun. My weapon is love.'" Festo even wrote a book, *I Love Idi Amin* (Revell-1977). Here are his words, "I love Idi Amin. I have never been his enemy. Anyone who loves humanity must seek the constructive reconciling way. God did it. Who am I to stray from his way? So that's why I love Idi Amin. As long as he is alive, he is redeemable. Love can heal. Pray for him."[15] Festo modeled for us how to love our enemies!

Normally enemies anticipate hatred, retaliation, cursings, and violence. Instead, Jesus advised his followers to handle an enemy with love, with goodness, with blessing and with prayer. The theological underpinning again comes from our role model—our Heavenly Father—who is kind to the wicked and the ungrateful.

35. *the* FORGIVING-PROCESS *factor*

It appears we all need help in learning the techniques of forgiveness. Almost unawares, we are strict with others, but lenient on ourselves. According to Jesus we overlook huge flaws in ourselves while being overly-critical of small faults in others. We forget that all judging will be reciprocated.

Light on the Pathway (Matthew 7:1-5)

"Do not judge, or you too will be judged. For in the same way you judge others, you will be judged, and with the measure you use, it will be measured to you. Why do you look at the speck of sawdust in your brother's eye and pay no attention to the plank in your own eye? You hypocrite, first take the plank out of your own eye, and then you will see clearly to remove the speck from your brother's eye."

(1) Don't Treat Others Unfairly

In his bestseller, *The Friendship Factor*, Alan Loy McGinnis writes about the need of fairness: "If we are to forgive freely, we need a tolerance of others as generous as that tolerance we display toward our own errors. It is remarkable how understanding we can be of our own flops in interpersonal dealings—we didn't intend the error, or it happened in a moment of stress, or we weren't feeling right that day...."[16] We excuse ourselves most liberally.

It seems human to judge others strictly, accurately and precisely—by their ACTIONS, and all the while judge ourselves loosely, tolerantly, considerately—by our INTENTIONS! So the starting point to any meaningful forgiveness is to admit that we must all function by the same rules (see Golden Rule, page 204).

(2) Don't Short-Circuit Forgiveness

At a minister's "Mental Health" seminar at Fuller's School of Psychology, I heard lectures by Dr. Archibald Hart on themes like depression, self-esteem, stress and anger. To him forgiveness is, "I surrender my right to hurt you back."

The tendency for people to ignore, or minimize their hurts, or even to deny them, gives rise to Hart's major concern that persons not short-circuit forgiveness. We do have the right to feel hurts deeply and the right to retaliate. So before we surrender that right as Christians, he suggests this fivefold exercise of don'ts—to assure that forgiveness genuinely resolves the issue.[17]

As a starter, don't channel the anger elsewhere, venting hostility to others is a tragic misplacement. Next, don't ignore hurt feelings; to identify them and feel them is wholesome. Thirdly, don't try to initiate some act of reconciliation at this point; your attempt to "talk things out" will likely end in deeper hurt, including the temptation to apply a bit of revenge. Next, don't try to forget the hurt by absorbing it. Fifthly, experience the hurt genuinely, so you can identify clearly what needs to be forgiven. Only after these five steps are taken should you surrender back to God the right to retaliate, just as Jesus did on the cross.

(3) Don't Leap Too Far—All At Once

Forgiveness is a Christian's objective; but it needs to be broken down into manageable chunks. That is the assertion of David Augsburger, prolific writer on forgiveness themes: "In spite of the pain, hurt, loss and wrongdoing that stand between us, we are encouraged to forgive in a single act of resolving all by giving unconditional inclusion. Such a step becomes too large for any human to take in a single bound. Forgiveness is a journey of many steps, each of which can be extremely difficult...."[18] Many a task is easier when reduced to small bits.

We summarize Augsburger's six steps for making forgiveness more manageable: (1) Despite the wrongdoing, see the other person as having VALUE, (2) Despite the pain caused, in LOVE, see the other person as being precious, (3) Accept reality and CAN-CEL DEMANDS, (4) Actually forgive via reciprocal TRUSTING and mutual repentance, (5) Forsake ironclad guarantees for the future, OPENING THE DOOR to choice, risk and spontaneity, and (6) CELEBRATE LOVE through the bonding of a renewed relationship.[19] As always, words come easy; reconciliation comes hard.

(4) Don't Sacrifice Assertiveness

Unresolved festering relationships may appear harmless, but they taint other relationships, and tend to make us dysfunctional. Each of us must free ourselves from hate, vindictiveness and all desire to hurt back. This, however, does not mean we become doormats. Healthy self-esteem requires that we display a healthy degree of assertiveness. The teachings of Jesus on not-judging, cheek-turning, and going-second-miles do not rule out "tough love" or "bold love" or plain "Christian Love." In homes, firm standards hold children within bounds and keep them from "being spoiled." When a teenager shoots dope, a good loving parent says, "Go to rehabilitation and counsel, or find another home. We refuse to finance your habit of drug dependency." In essence—true Christlikeness oozes with loving creativity, and is devoid of rancor, revenge, or ruthlessness.

(5) Don't Overlook a Forgiveness-Strategy

In three decades of pastoral work I occasionally faced opposition, even direct animosity. When tempted to withhold forgiveness, as stated earlier, I thought of God's warm gracious forgiveness of all my sins; that was all I needed.

What was my coping strategy? First, I set a goal—never to retaliate (see Genesis 50:20 and Ephesians 4:32). Next, I reserved the pulpit for positive blessing, not selfish advantage. Thirdly, in crisis or illness calls I treated everyone with equal regard. Fourthly, I urged the pastoral staff and the Elder-Deacon board to work together to model the love of God. And fifthly, my trump card for coping was prayer. For thirty years I prayed each week for members—by name—mentally "imaging" their potential in Christ. In response God gave a lovely ministry with fruit that lasts (John 15:16). Genuine prayer dissolves hatred.

(6) Don't Offer Blind-Naive Forgiveness

My chapter title, "Forgiving Without Limits" may lead some to think that I advocate unconditional forgiveness with no guidelines. In the Introduction I told of my efforts to restore harmony with an alienated church elder. Fortunately, in that case, my one-way unconditional promise resulted in a mutual resolution. However, truth has many sides. There are times when no good is served if people forgive naively, fail to confront, or when reconciliation is not pursued.

Here again, the book, *Caring Enough to Forgive,* is helpful. It lists five conditions where forgiveness should not be given blindly. "Forgiveness as it is frequently practiced is a process of denial, distortion, isolation, or undoing which leads to behaviors of avoidance, distancing, and spiritual alienation. Any stance of superiority, super-spirituality, or unilateral self-sacrifice reduces the possibility of real repentance and reconciliation."[20] It is precisely this kind of faulty forgiveness that deserves a warning.

The five cautions are reflected in the chapter headings— Don't Forgive When Forgiveness—(1) "Puts You One-Up," (2) "Is One-Way," (3) "Distorts Feelings," (4) "Denies Anger," and (5) "Ends Open Relationships."[21] Of special interest here are the titles of chapters (1) and (2). They reveal a crucial insight!

The healthy approach to forgiveness is to treat others with equal regard. If we forgive condescendingly, we make the other person forever indebted to us for our having offered the favor of forgiveness. That makes the other person the lifetime cheater, lifetime adulterer, lifetime liar, or lifetime thief, or whatever—whom we graciously forgave. Real caring does not thrive on this kind of "earned one-way" forgiveness, where persons are accepted on an inferior basis. Wholesome forgiveness says: "I too am a sinner. I forgive you as God forgave me!"

Conclusion

Forgiveness is the genius of Christianity. It promotes peace and justice. It releases us from hurts and gives protection. Forgiveness is healthy, wholesome, and conducive to happiness. Yet alas, 80 percent of our population is unhappy, and unforgiveness seems to be a major contributing factor![22]

Pope John Paul once awed the world, as he extended forgiveness to the man who tried to kill him. *Time* Magazine (1-9-84) asked "Why Forgive?" The article read, "...If one does not forgive, then one is controlled by the other's initiatives and is locked into a sequence of act and response, of outrage and revenge, tit for tat, escalating always. The present is endlessly overwhelmed and devoured by the past. Forgiveness frees the forgiver!"[23] Beyond question, our age needs role models on forgiveness and Pope John Paul clearly is one.

In my third parish a lady named Sylvia utilized discipleship groups to give how-to-do-it help on forgiveness. After she had taken our new discipleship course, she discipled another 25 ladies (in three groups) and included some hands-on training for handling unresolved conflicts.

God had prepared her heart at an earlier Karen Mains-Seminar. She learned the art of surrendering all blaming, accusing and bitterness—a basic clearing of the slate. During a week of sewing, Sylvia remembers jotting down item after item of life's hurts, and presenting the list to the Lord, asking for release from the pain. Her motto was "Hold on and grow bitter, or release and get peace!"

In her teaching sessions, Sylvia also used a technique gleaned from a book by H. Norman Wright, *Making Peace With Your Past*. She advocated placing Jesus in a chair opposite you, and pouring out to him the list of grievances against persons, one by one. Affirming that Christ is a loving-accepting-forgiving Lord brings comfort. With his strength all anger is released. Finally, the list is burned in the fireplace. As a bell still goes ding-dong a few times after you quit ringing it, says Sylvia, so memories of bitterness will act up, at times, until you have said, "I forgive" often enough—until you have gotten the victory.

Questions for Discussion:

1. Jesus made the trademark of his church: love. (John 13:35). Why?
2. What irritates you the most—a lawsuit, a pesky borrower, or forced jobs?
3. Why is God insistent—if you want forgiveness, you must forgive others?
4. Discuss the three control patterns of culture: anxiety, shame and guilt.
5. James Graham offered heaven to a man who killed 100 of his friends. Why?
6. How do we keep today's anger from overloading tomorrow's circuits?

PRACTICING HIS PRESENCE: DEVOTIONAL PAUSE FOR BUSY DISCIPLES
Theme of the week — Forgiving Without Limits

	Monday	**Tuesday**	**Wednesday**	**Thursday**	**Friday**
Light on	John	Matthew	Matthew	Luke	Luke
the pathway	13:31-38	5:38-48	18:21-35	9:46-56	17:1-10
Lesson for	Factor #31	Factor #32	Factor #33	Factor #34	Factor #35
this day	Love Others	Turn Cheek	Forgive 70X7	Love Enemies	The Process
Life in	Take time	Take time	Take time	Take time	Take time
Jesus' way	to pray	to pray	to pray	to pray	to pray

PRACTICE HIS PRESENCE IN CHURCH ON SUNDAY

Chapter

9

Giving With Generosity

36. Management
37. Firstfruits
38. Emulation
39. Motivation
40. Reciprocal

Introduction

C enturies ago God warned his people about forgetting him in days of prosperity. Deuteronomy 6:10-12 is a classic! It served as the text for my Centennial Sermon to my home congregation. I reminded my people that Grandfather Harder, one of 55 families, had swapped beautiful farmland in Prussia for the buffalo-grazed prairies of Kansas. He sought religious freedom and their first church services met in his barn. In my sermon titled, "Lest We Forget," I told my relatives that adversity is tolerable but prosperity can be lethal.[1]

Affluence in the American church could be without its equal. On the plus side the church has unprecedented resources; on the minus side Christians could be addicted to materialism, even numbed or anesthetized by it. Two televangelists, with a Jaguar in the garage, a yacht in the harbor, and a mansion in the mountains, were only disciplined by their church for sexual misconduct, and not "...for their open and scandalous perennial prostitution of possessions, ostentatious lifestyle and illicit money making."[2] How typical!

Jesus devoted one quarter of his teachings to the subject of possessions. In fact, he spoke more on wealth than he did about heaven and hell or even about peace and forgiveness. Therefore the wise use of money for today and estate planning for tomorrow are ideas to be preached from every pulpit, discussed in every class and prayed over in every small-group. Countless people need help in corralling the runaway horses of consumer spending. Their purchasing habits race out of control.

Daniel Kauffman and John Rudy studied eleven churches regarding money and economic issues. The top five areas where churches asked for help, listed in the order of the frequency of mention, were: (1) basic biblical teaching on Christian stewardship, (2) personal/family money management, (3) principles for estate planning, (4) conflict resolution over money matters, and (5) responsible Christian lifestyles.[3] This is a most practical list indeed.

This chapter will answer five questions in turn: Who are God's managers? Is firstfruits tithing relevant for us today? How should believers model Christlike generosity? What are proper motives in giving? And finally, in what way are faithful stewardship practices actually reciprocal?

36. the MANAGEMENT factor

As a Kansas farm boy in his early teens, I was helping Dad husk corn when a car stopped nearby. A man crawled over the fence and came toward us. It was Milo Kauffman, president of Hesston College. "Albert, finish both rows and come for lunch," Dad instructed as he left. Once home I asked Mother, "How much did Dad give?" "Five hundred dollars," she responded (half the price of a new Chevrolet)!

Later I attended Hesston College for two years. As time passed President Kauffman increasingly spoke and wrote on stewardship. So when I began discipling people by twelves in my third pastorate, I made Mr. Kauffman's book, *Stewards of God*, required reading. Though a bit repetitious, the first one hundred pages said pointedly that all of life is a stewardship—owned by God and loaned to us. The rest of the book was replete with vivid accounts of Christians using their money for God's vital causes.

Jesus' parable of the Shrewd Manager might be his best and strongest statement on the proper use of money. A certain manager, so the parable goes, was about to lose his job. Being too weak to work and too proud to beg he devised a fast scheme. He summoned his master's debtors and reduced one debt by fifty percent, the other by twenty percent. The master was impressed by the manager's cleverness. Obviously, the debtors would help this unemployed rascal later.

Light on the Pathway (Luke 16:8-15)

"The master commended the dishonest manager because he had acted shrewdly. For the people of this world are more shrewd in dealing with their own kind than are the people of the light. I tell you, use worldly wealth to gain friends for yourselves, so that when it is gone, you will be welcomed into eternal dwellings...No servant can serve two masters...both God and Money."

One central lesson emerges—"people of the world" manipulate money matters to achieve their goals. If Christians, "the people of light," utilized spiritual wisdom as non-Christians utilize worldly wisdom, they would harness every financial opportunity for the cause of Christ. But alas, the children of grace are not always as motivated as the children of greed.

Two exegetical points, says E. Earl Ellis, help explain the story, but in no way alter its lesson: (1) the debt-reduction may be the steward's profit (usury) which he foregoes to ingratiate himself with the debtors, and (2) the term "dishonest steward" is misleading. The Greek only says "unrighteous." He was merely a human who lived like others in this Present Evil Age.[4]

The Money-Management Crisis

In *Master Your Money*, Ron Blue gives superb help for personal/family money-management. The typical American family, he states, is in a serious dilemma. Here is proof: "...only 2% of Americans reaching age 65 are financially independent; 30% are dependent on charity; 23% must continue to work; 45% are dependent on relatives. Additionally, 85 out of 100 Americans have less than $250 when they reach 65. According to Devney's Economic Tables, fewer men are worth $100 at age 68 than they were at age 18—after 50 years of hard work."[5]

These figures reveal a crisis in money-management. In one of the richest countries, 98% of the people at age 65 exist hand-to-mouth, with little security, no savings, and no financial independence. So in an ocean of wealth the life jacket of ambition buoys us up, but in the final analysis we're pulled under by the high cost of our easy-credit and the heavy weight of our debt load.

Our problem of mismanagement is compounded by the problem of misdirection. As Christians in America we fight to gain control of our budgets, while spending an inordinate amount on ourselves. This consumerism shows up in a hundred subtle ways: (1) we urge college youth to take courses that lead to the highest paying jobs, (2) we urge youth to build a financial base rather than give two years to voluntary service, and (3) we urge our sons and daughters to stay home and take over the family business rather than to consider God's call into career mission service overseas. We have blessings; but we hoard them.

The Case of the Rich Fool
Light on the Pathway (Luke 12:13-21)

....Jesus replied...."Watch out! Be on your guard against all kinds of greed; a man's life does not consist in the abundance of his possessions."

And he told them this parable: "The ground of a certain rich man produced a good crop. He thought to himself, '...I will tear down my barns and build bigger ones....And I'll say to myself "You have plenty of goods laid up for many years. Take life easy...."'

The "Rich Fool" was a symbol of success, the envy of the countryside. His office wall, no doubt, displayed a "Farmer of the Year" award. He was a whiz at farming, an expert at wheeling and dealing—and he turned a profit. But he ignored God. According to Jesus—he died just as he had lived—a fool!

Why? He stockpiled his wealth for personal security, high-style living, and a luxurious retirement. He flunked God's management test: (1) of allotting resources for God's kingdom, (2) of releasing funds for the needs of people, and (3) of planning for dying. In short, he failed in estate planning.

In context, this parable of Jesus was a caution against greed. The joy and meaning of life, he said, are not wrapped up in accumulating wealth. Of course, a selfish greedy poor man is no better (or worse) than a selfish greedy rich lady. While Jesus nowhere said that money, per se, was evil, he did hint that it was hazardous to handle. Its allure can seduce us.

The Christian education task seems awesome. How do we teach a biblical perspective on money? Tony Campolo, in *Wake Up America* tells of the Russian Deputy Minister of Education who came to Philadelphia—requesting to see social services enacted by religious groups. Tony showed him many projects and last of all a Christian school for disadvantaged children. At the debriefing, the Russian expressed surprise that children spoke so much about "making money." He remarked, "...Since they are Christians, I expected that they would be concerned about spiritual things. Instead, they are more materialistic than the Marxist youth in my country!..."[6]

Children Will Have It Tougher

The American Dream sees every couple owning a three bedroom house. According to Century-21, Phoenix, AZ and Orlando, FL offer such houses for $83,000. In other states costs can be much more. (A 30-year loan of $100,000 at 10% interest will cost a whopping $315,720 over the time of the loan.)[7]

Few Christian writers have grappled as realistically with alternate lifestyles and the maximizing of money for God's kingdom as has Tom Sine. His book *Wild Hope* is a virtual religious *Future Shock*. I call it required reading for every church leader. He asserts: "We have programmed the Christian young to expect to have everything economically that their parents had and a little more. But while their parents could typically buy the split-level and everything that goes with it on a single income, such lifestyle today requires at least two incomes."[8] Christians need to cope in new and creative ways.

Walking with Jesus as Lord is more than claiming forgiveness; it mandates walking in newness. It behooves every Christian family to set monetary priorities, to take control. The parable of the shrewd manager reminds us that we should make our money serve the noble goals of God's kingdom. We must pray boldly and plan astutely. In addition, the rich-fool parable suggests that making preparations for dying will affect profoundly how we live. In fact, my up-to-date will is my ultimate witness to the values I hold.

37. the FIRSTFRUITS factor

From Genesis to Malachi, the Old Testament teaches that all blessings of life fall from heaven and that Jehovah God desires the first and the best portion of our earnings. In the New Testament, Jesus our Lord never rescinded such spontaneous giving; it is our response to God's grace. However, Jesus taught financial stewardship from a Kingdom perspective, as we have already seen in the two parables above. Authentic discipleship means that Jesus is Lord of all.

Cain and Abel brought their offerings in worship to God (Genesis 4:2-5). Cain brought "fruit of the soil" and Abel brought "fat portions from some of the firstborn of his flock." In their commentary on Genesis, the Hebrew scholars, Keil and Delitzsch, assert that Abel brought his best, the firstfruits. A Greek expert, Thayer, translates Hebrews 11:4 as saying that Abel brought a sacrifice "greater in quantity." So it is possible that this is an allusion to firstfruits giving or tithing, rather than to a sin offering as many had assumed.

The Hebrew patriarchs Abraham and Jacob were tithers. Moses gave elaborate laws on firstfruits giving, tithing and Jubilee practices. In spiritual awakenings under Hezekiah and Nehemiah tithing practices were restored. The Old Testament ends with a challenge by the Prophet Malachi to restore the customs of tithes and offerings (3:6-12). Graphic rewards were promised—like the protection against crop failure—and the open floodgates of blessings from heaven.

The Divine Purpose in the Tithe

The practice of tithing from crops and the giving of firstborns from flocks (Deuteronomy 14:22-23), taught people how to put God first (Living Bible) or "so that you may learn to revere the Lord your God always" (NIV). The actual giving of the firstfruits was either in raw form as cereal and grapes, or in a prepared form as oil, flour and dough. Restating the purpose: firstfruits giving was a way to avow "...that the land and all its products were the gift of Yahweh to Israel, and [were offered] in thankfulness for his bounty...."[9]

An excellent biblical overview of firstfruits giving and Jubilee living can be found in Daniel Kauffman's book, *Managers With God: Continuing the Work Christ Began*. This book is somewhat autobiographical—the product of a lifetime of fundraising and stewardship teaching. It is a practical resource for any church.

Kauffman reduces Old Testament firstfruits teaching to five summary statements: (1) God is owner through creation and redemption, (2) Men and women are stewards, (3) We are to return a portion of our wealth to God, (4) We are responsible to God and society for the management of this trust, and (5) Faithfulness in this stewardship will bring blessing and prosperity; unfaithfulness will bring curse and tragedy.[10]

What about Jesus? He spoke much about money matters, but said little about tithing or firstfruits giving. Yes, one time when the Pharisees tried to trap him he said, "Give to Caesar what is Caesar's, and to God what is God's." Some listeners may have taken that to mean: pay tax to Caesar and tithe to God. However, only once did Jesus specifically use the word tithe—in a command.

Light on the Pathway (Matthew 23:23)

"Woe to you, teachers of the law and Pharisees, you hypocrites! You tithe a tenth of your spices—mint, dill and cummin. But you have neglected the more important matters of the law—justice, mercy and

faithfulness. You should have practiced the latter without neglecting the former" (cf. Luke 11:42).

While Jesus did not invalidate the concept of tithing, he placed it in perspective. Pharisees, fanatical in their legalism, even tithed garden items. It seems that tithing was so overdone that Jesus didn't need to urge it. In fact, the only other time we hear Jesus use the word tithe is when he quotes the self-righteous Pharisee in Luke 18, "God I thank you that I am not like...this tax collector. I fast twice a week and give a tenth of all I get."

For New Testament believers the only argument against the tithe is to go beyond the tithe, that was once the view of Milo Kauffman. Jesus did not abrogate firstfruits giving; rather, he likely expected his redeemed followers to measure up to and even outgive the Old Testament saints. Under Mosaic law several tithes were given; one went to the poor. Since American tax is used for welfare, some believers today consider ten percent giving as a valid minimum starting point.

Serious Givers — Approach No. 1

Among Christians who take discipleship seriously—who seek to develop a Christlike generosity, several approaches to giving prevail. One approach uses the firstfruits tithe as a starting point, a symbol of putting God first. Over time, when possible, this is gradually increased—say to twenty percent. Added to this, occasionally, extra thank-offerings are given—to urgent mission projects or to human disaster needs. This kind of scheme somewhat parallels the pilgrimage of Susan Joann and myself. Some of our friends follow a similar pattern.

Serious Givers — Approach No. 2

A second approach, often building on the biblical theme of Jubilee, starts with the launching of Jesus' deliverance ministry (Luke 4:14-21). This ties in with Leviticus 25. In the 50th year—the Year of Jubilee—debts were cancelled and land was returned to its original owner. In essence, no land could be held in perpetuity, since God was the owner. Applying this to stewardship concepts the reasoning runs like this—If God owns all, the legitimate question is: How much will I keep (not how much will I give). What are my own real needs?

I recall a marvelous speech given some years ago at a father-son banquet. The speaker was a businessman, a recent convert to Christianity. In his spiritual commitment he vowed to live on a set amount and give the balance of his company's earnings to Christian causes. His business was in a good profit cycle. That year [when we adjust the figures to the economy of the 1990's] he and his family took for their own use $40,000. At years-end they had $360,000 left over to give away!

Serious Givers — Approach No. 3

A third approach—the graduated tithe—is really a blend of the above two. (A notable advocate is Ronald J. Sider.) It sets a minimum tithing base as well as a maximum consumption limit. For example, if a family chooses a baseline figure of $30,000, it tithes 10 percent on that amount. On each additional one thousand, the tithe is raised by five percent, until it reaches a plateau at $48,000. After that every dollar is given away to the cause of Christ.

What is the real significance here? "At $48,000, a family following this scheme would have given $13,350 and retained $34,650 for personal use and savings. Under the traditional tithe, they would have given $4,800 with $43,200 left over. A graduated tithe embodies the Jubilee spirit and nudges us in the direction of generous stewardship."[11]

The Summary

In summary, firstfruits, firstborn and Jubilee legislation were all signposts, vivid reminders to Israel that Jehovah God deserved preferential recognition. After all, God had lovingly and providentially led them, and redeemed them, as his precious possession. His lovingkindness warranted a grateful submission.

This meshes clearly with New Testament discipleship theology. Incarnated, Jesus became one of us. Crucified, he died for us. Rising, he became the firstfruits of eternal blessings—I Corinthians 15:23. We as Christians declare Jesus as Lord. So each specific commitment as part of a disciplined accountable lifestyle becomes a reminder of whose we are, and whose kingdom we serve.

38. the EMULATION factor

Light on the Pathway (Luke 19:1-10)

Zacchaeus...said..."Look, Lord! Here and now I give half of my possessions to the poor...if I have cheated anybody...I will pay back four times the amount.' Jesus said..."Today salvation has come to this house...."

The conversion of Zacchaeus instantly affected his financial holdings. He publicly declared his plan to give to charity. Jesus in no way imposed the left hand/right hand formula of secrecy, nor suggested that Zacchaeus' open disclosure forfeited his future rewards. And imagine, Luke wrote this for the whole world to read! It becomes apparent that in the right situation a stewardship testimony may be just as valid as a salvation testimony or a service testimony.

Our Family Stewardship Pilgrimage

In our personal family history, my paternal grandfather, John Epp Sr., serves as a role model on firstfruits giving. He started a flow of God's blessing that has trickled down to the third and fourth generation. The source, however, is one's commitment to Jesus Christ—the giving flows out of that.

The First Generation (John Epp Sr., 1862-1943)

* He migrated from South Russia to Whitewater, Kansas at age 21 (1883).
* A devoted Christian, he came for religious freedom—to avoid conscription.
* His first wife and children died. Next, he married Anna (6 March 1890), the oldest daughter of Preacher Cornelius Regier of Elbing.

Story: Things were tough. Grandpa's dad-in-law, Preacher Regier suggested, "John, you had better give up farming. It appears like you are not going to make it!" John was not about to quit. He wanted one more chance. This time he made a vow with God—to begin tithing on all he got. He wrestled in prayer, asking for help, committing his whole farming operation into God's hand. Things began to change. Soon he was able to reduce his loan from the Bernhard Harder family by $1,000 per year. The final payment was made in 1904.

The Second Generation (John Epp Jr., 1901-)
* The 7th of nine children, he married the daughter of Bernhard Harder.
* His wife, Marie, was youngest of 4 girls; John took over the Harder farm.
* Annually, John farmed about 400-560 acres and fattened 100 or more steers.
* Active Mennonite church members—enthused over evangelism/missionary work.
* Of their 8 children, five became pastors, missionaries or pastor's wives.

Story: John got married at age 26 and Marie already had her inheritance, so they started farming with fair momentum. They worked hard to get ahead—to buy more land, and still be faithful in giving to the church. John later testified that the 1941 tornado, which demolished their farm, was a turning point. In rebuilding, they started farming for Christ and no longer for wealth. At age 75, while still farming, John uncharacteristically showed his latest IRS-1040 to his oldest son. The adjusted gross income was $27,000; contributions were $9,300.

The Third Generation (Albert H. Epp, 1931-)
* Third child of 8. At age 21 he married Susan Joann Walter of Yale, SD.
* Susan—daughter of Joe/Susie Walter from the Krimmer Mennonite Brethren.
* Pastor: 200 members-California; 900 members-Kansas; 1150 members-Nebraska.

Story: Susan Joann and Albert were married with four years of college/seminary to go. From the start they agreed to practice firstfruits tithing. They got a bit behind during the first year but caught up again in seminary days. The real crunch came in 1964, eight years into the first pastorate, when the boys were 7, 4 and 2. Family giving had been reviewed annually. When the church added a missionary budget, Al suggested an added faith promise. So, at this point, the giving took about a 20 percent bite out of a modest pastor's pay.

One day Susan Joann complained, "We need furniture but can't afford it. I'm tired of sewing the rips in the couch." Al retorted, "What we really need is some investment to plan for our boy's education." Two days later, Albert was home alone. He agonized in prayer: "God, am I a fool for giving? Should the needs of my family come first? Our tithes could buy a lot of furniture!" He paced back and forth, oblivious to time. A favorite verse came to mind, Malachi 3:10: "Bring all the tithes...prove me...says the Lord..if I will not open you the windows of heaven..." KJV. It was a sacred moment of commitment. Albert decided to continue giving—to continue leaning ever more heavily on "the Lord of Hosts."

As Susan Joann and Albert look back to that crisis some 30 years ago, they stand in awe. Some things seem too sacred to disclose. God saw them through. He provided a new Maytag clothes dryer, free of charge. He provided a rental property as a cushion for the future. And as to furniture, Susan Joann bought it with money from a two-year child-care job which God brought into her own home.

The Fourth Generation (Steven W. Epp, 1957-)
* Firstborn. College degree (math); and master's degree (computer science).
* Math teacher turned Computer Programer for Xerox. Lives in San Jose, CA.
* Wife, Kimberly Molinar, discipled by Oak Park Foursquare of Arroyo Grande.
* Steve/Kim have two sons; they help with children's work at their church.

Story: As Steve took his first teaching job at Atascadera, California, he consistently gave a tenth of his paycheck. After marriage, Steve and Kim moved to San Jose and anchored into a church. They continued this giving pattern. Not long ago they gave $600 above the tithe to help a family in their church. Some days later Steve arrived home from work with a check in his pocket for $660—an unexpected bonus from his employer. Was this coincidental?

Kim also exudes joy when she talks about her personal first-fruits giving—off the paycheck from her job at school. The tenth came to $60 per month and was committed to a mission project.

Then she made a pivotal decision—stay home with her two boys—becoming a one-income family once more. In faith, she decided to continue her mission pledge, trusting God to help her raise the $60 each month via miscellaneous odd jobs that come her way.

The Fourth Generation (J. Gregory Epp, 1960-)
* 2nd born. College B.A. (Business Ad); Work—Certified Public Accountant.
* As a CPA, he is Controller for Poland Oil Inc. of Grand Island, Nebraska.
* Wife, Caroline Huenefeld, grew up at Pleasantview Bible Church of Aurora.
* They have 4 children. Greg, at times, teaches Sunday School at his church.

Story: Greg and Caroline began marriage with a covenant on firstfruits tithing. After three years they came to a tight spot. They were $45 behind in their tithe. Here was the squeeze: (1) they had a baby to feed, (2) some bills were coming due the next week, (3) Greg had taken his CPA exam but didn't know his score, (4) he had no prospect of work, but was knocking on doors full-time taking his resume to prospective employers, and (5) they had a mere $65 in the bank. At that moment they decided to give the $45 and trust God based on Malachi 3:10. Two days later the bank notified them that an anonymous donor had placed $500 into their checking account. While still praising God, a couple weeks later, they received a letter from Grandpa Epp in Kansas—he was giving special gifts to his grandchildren and hoped they could use the gift he was enclosing.

In summary, as a family we have bared our souls a bit, allowing the reader to look into a very private aspect of our lives. As I spoke with my dad, my spouse, and two of my sons, I was awestruck by the sincerity, conviction and above all, enthusiasm with which all spoke about their financial pilgrimage. Our love for Christ, we hope, has shone through. Apart from his grace we are nothing.

39. the MOTIVATION factor

The subject of "motivation in giving" is about as tricky to handle as is the greased pig at a county fair. We cannot espouse the health and wealth gospel (that all good Christians are rich and well), but contrariwise we affirm positively that God has promised special blessings for faithfulness in financial steward-ship. A proper balance calls for much Bible study and dialogue.

MOTIVE NO. 1 Giving out of Gratefulness

The Reformed tradition perpetuates a grand insight: The chief aim of humankind is to glorify God and to enjoy him forev-er. How motivating! What higher goal than to transform all of our living and giving into one big praise-expression!

As a lad Daniel Kauffman dreamt of being an executive at Ford or John Deere. Instead the Lord led him to a 40-year stint in money-management for the Kingdom—mostly in Anabaptist cir-cles, though not exclusively. He chose II Corinthians 8 and 9 as best epitomizing New Testament stewardship ideas.[12] The starting point is a total self-dedication to God and his people (8:5). This negates giving sparingly or reluctantly. It does, however, embrace giving voluntarily and cheerfully, calculatingly and proportion-ately, lovingly and generously. It's not as specific as Old Testament tithing, but surely it's not giving at a lower level.

Light on the Pathway (Luke 8:1-3)

After this, Jesus traveled...the Twelve were with him, and also some women...cured of evil spirits and diseases: Mary (Magdalene)..., Joanna...; Susanna....These women were helping to support them out of their own means.

Luke highlights the compassion of Jesus toward the neglect-ed—the poor, the lepers and the women. Mary, Joanna and Susanna were three among many, who apparently contributed to the common purse of Jesus and the disciples. The motive was clear. These ladies had experienced deliverance from demonism and disease. As always, when deep spiritual needs are met, purs-es are opened to spread the news.

A family began attending my West Coast parish. The lady urged me to visit her 50-year-old mother dying of cancer. On my visit, I learned she was a member of a mainline church in town.

Apologizing, I offered to call her pastors. She objected, "My church sends weekly offering envelopes, that's all; no pastor has come for six weeks." I provided pastoral therapy for her final nine months.

When church budgets lag, boards tend to beef up their collection technique, without upgrading their level of care to members. Pastors may badger members with guilt-producing sermons rather than equipping the laity. A Lutheran leader, Waldo J. Werning astutely asks: When does a church panic—when half don't come to worship, when less than 20% are in Bible studies, when less than 10% witness, or when the budget isn't met? There is the real tip-off whether the church is in a survival maintenance mode or in a genuine mission mode![13]

MOTIVE NO. 2 Giving out of Compassion

The disparity between the haves and have-nots is growing rapidly. The average income (USA) before taxes is about $28,000 while one out of every five households lives on a yearly income of less than $10,000. "The richest 20 percent of the land are getting 44 percent of the nation's income, while the poorest 20 percent get less than 5 percent of the aggregate income."[14]

Tom Sine calls Christians to a "whole-life stewardship," a concept he seldom hears advocated in either evangelical or ecumenical churches. It is a reordering of priorities in order to place the values of God's kingdom first. A medical doctor in Denver who sold half of his practice serves as an example. "He supports his family very comfortably on a twenty-hour a week income. He spends his other twenty hours running an inner-city health clinic for the growing number who can no longer afford access to even basic levels of health care."[15] Sine insists that prayer retreats are useful in redirecting life away from its usual rat race!

Light on the Pathway (Matthew 6:1-4)

"Be careful not to do your 'acts of righteousness' before men, to be seen by them. If you do, you will have no reward from your Father in heaven. So when you give to the needy, do not announce it with trumpets, as the hypocrites do....They have received their reward in full. But

when you give to the needy, do not let your left hand know what your right hand is doing...."

In the Sermon on the Mount, Jesus spoke of leaders who were generous almsgivers and yet had little compassion for people in need. Jesus did not necessarily forbid the publicity that naturally happens in the course of giving. He rebuked ostentatious publicity meant to merit applause from peers, or to enhance one's public image. Both the trumpet and left hand idea seem figurative. Jews were not known to blow trumpets, and disciples surely weren't forbidden to keep records (cf. Matthew 5:16). It is self-aggrandizement that is the issue.

In our Kansas pastorate a member asked our mission board for a list of projects of crucial need overseas. He chose one and funded it with a one time gift of $10,000. At my invitation, he shared a giving testimony with our Sunday morning worship audience. It was discreetly done. Later one brother quipped, "Well, he's had his reward!" Wait-a-minute. Was the motive a heavenly reward? The donor gave to alleviate desperate need—to further Christ's kingdom. It became apparent that devoted church members got a bit uneasy when giving was modeled that openly. Our intention was pure—to inspire others to love and to do good (Hebrews 10:24).

MOTIVE NO. 3 Giving out of Duty

Good giving flows out of joy and appreciation, not out of guilt, compulsion or duty, we are told. But does not biblical motivation include duty? We seem so gun-shy of legalism that we slight obligation. Yes, any spiritual discipline is oppressive when the heart is not in it. But the solution is not in dropping "duty" from our vocabulary. We dare not amputate the legs of accountability in our theology of stewardship.

Light on the Pathway (Luke 17:1-10)

"Would he thank the servant because he did what he was told to do? So you also, when you have done everything you were told to do, should say, 'We are unworthy servants; we have only done our duty.'"

According to the Internal Revenue Service, in the United States 1.7 percent of income is given as contributions. Among church attenders 2.2% of income is given. In two larger groups in Anabaptist circles, giving hovers around 5 to 6%. Since a small group in any typical church gives half of the total, it follows—the rest give miserly!

How do we instill vision—our Christian responsibility toward a needy world that lacks food, medical help, education and especially the Gospel of Christ? When our three sons were teenagers, Susan Joann and I once called a family forum. (We had just turned an investment; before reducing debt and reinvesting, we wanted to acknowledge our God.) I said something like this, "Sons, God has been very good to us. Mom and I have decided to send $6,000 to an urgent mission need overseas. This is above our regular commitments to our church. For Mom and me it is both a joy and a duty to honor God in this way. We want you boys to know it."

The responsibility of Christians is staggering. In just the USA, there are one million millionaires. Households earning in excess of $75,000 have doubled in the past decade. Barna writes about people over 50: "Although this age group constitutes 25 percent of the population, they possess 70 percent of the nation's worth; [and] 77 percent of all financial assets...."[16] What a source to tap!

Where does Christian duty begin and end? First, if we don't do faith-giving at the start, when it's tough, we won't part with the greenbacks when we're rich. Secondly, at each stage in life we must renegotiate our future. All persons over 50 should reexamine the needs of self, family and church—and readjust goals.

40. the RECIPROCAL factor

Next we look at the blessings which accrue to the faithful steward. In our discussion of motives for giving—gratitude, compassion, duty—we never included the acquisition of riches nor the achieving of salvation. Regarding the latter, the Bible is amply clear that Christ's atonement, not our attainment washes away our sin. Salvation is unmerited. It is a gift accepted by faith.

Neither do we give to get, nor tithe to gain material wealth. In fact, most persons with a greed-motive are too greedy to part with a tithe in the first place. At any rate, the idea of giving some—to gain more—does not fit into the New Testament framework of stewardship. Giving is an act of appreciation by accountable stewards of the gospel, by ambassadors of reconciliation. We give to further Christ's work and to advance the cause of his kingdom.

Let me repeat—we don't give to get. Yet the teachings of Jesus are filled with the reward motif. Hospitality to Christians gets a reward. The cup of cold water gets a reward (Matthew 10:41-42). Suffering for Jesus gets a reward. Loving enemies gets a reward. Lending to enemies gets a reward (Luke 6:23,35). Sometimes the scriptures add "Great is your reward in heaven."

We must say, in all honesty, the Old Testament did promise material rewards to tithers (Proverbs 3:9, Malachi 3:10). Jesus also promised overflowing blessings for giving (Luke 6:38), but these go beyond the material. The New Testament framework appears to be this: put God's kingdom first and you're entitled, even encouraged, to expect God to supply your needs in daily life (Matthew 6:25-34). In essence, it is giving to God in faith and leaving the outcome to him.

Light on the Pathway (Luke 6:37-38)

"Do not judge, and you will not be judged. Do not condemn, and you will not be condemned. Forgive, and you will be forgiven. Give, and it will be given to you. A good measure, pressed down, shaken together and running over, will be poured into your lap. For with the measure you use, it will be measured to you."

Fourfold Reciprocity

Jesus states reciprocity in two forms. Negatively, if you avoid the behavior of judging and condemning, you'll be spared of the same. Positively, if you practice forgiveness and generosity, you are guaranteed the same.

Then Jesus says, "give," and follows it with a fourfold promise of return. This proverbial expression came in part from Hebrew sayings. When buying grain or flour in the marketplace, the container for measuring was filled level full, pressed down and shaken—and then, if the seller was really generous, filled to over-flowing. This was poured into a person's lap—a pocket formed by pulling up the outer robe and hanging it over the girdle.

As a grade school kid in the tiny village of Brainerd, Kansas, I remember the country store, a stopping-off place owned by Oscar. I have long since forgotten his face or his faith or even his family. But after 50 years I still recall his generosity. When buying peanut clusters, he tossed in an extra scoop. While weighing out four and a quarter pounds of grapes he only charged for four. And with each bushel of apples, he piled on some extra. And always candy for kids.

We say it again: "For the measure you use, it will be mea-sured to you." The same sized shovel we use to scoop blessings into the lives of others, will be used by God to shovel blessings our way in return. Yes, giving is reciprocal.

Case No. 1 The Willards — The $20 Bill

Finally, we draw lessons from three cases of reciprocity. The first comes from Dallas Willard's book, *The Spirit of the Disciplines*—a book which I read with a yellow marker in my hand. As a California professor at USC, he draws a comparison between frugality and sacrifice. Frugality is abstaining from the use of money merely to satisfy our cravings for status, glamour and luxury. Sacrifice by contrast, is actually abstaining from some-thing necessary to life, like the widow of Luke 21:2-4 who gave all she had and cast herself on God's care.

"Once while in graduate school...in Wisconsin," says Willard, "my wife and I decided to give away what we had left after pay-ing the bills at the first of the month. It was not much to give away, but we did it. And we told no one. How odd then that a twenty-dollar bill was found pinned to the steering wheel of our car a week or so later! With hamburger at thirty-nine cents a pound, we lived like royalty until the next month,...enjoying the provisions of the King."[17]

When we exercise the discipline of sacrifice, God often rewards in unexpected ways. Faith becomes immeasurably stronger because of the experience.

Case No. 2 The Munsons — The Hailed-Out Crop

Another story comes from *Guideposts*. Cliff and Betty Munson are dry-land farmers who started "crop-tithing" in their most disastrous year. Their pastor preached a sermon series on giving back to God. Until then, God got the leftovers; the expenses ate the income. Puzzled, yet intrigued, the Munsons called the pastor over and asked a lot of questions on tithing.

Some Montana farmers plant wheat in strips, leaving half the land fallow to conserve soil moisture. On a pledge card the Munsons made a faith-promise, not to give a tenth after harvest but designating two specified strips as the Lord's. Soon a farmer's worst nightmare occurred. Hail shredded the whole crop—except the two tithe-strips on the east side. They stood unscathed! How heartrending—harvesting the two strips and giving every cent away as covenanted! The next year was the toughest ever—with bank-borrowing, credit-buying, and praying for shoes. Cliff did custom cutting in the fall and machine repair in the winter. When the holiday looked very bleak, a friend gave a turkey for Christmas as a bonus for work![18]

Four lessons stem from the Munson episode: (1) Our giving commitments are occasionally tested. (2) The greatest blessings are spiritual and not material—the Munsons testify to a deeper level of trust in God's care. (3) We need to stand on scripture; the Munsons hung onto Malachi 3:10. And (4), Giving is reciprocal. The Munsons kept on tithing—believing God returns a blessing!

Case No. 3 Homer Rodeheaver — The Golf Caddy

The final case of reciprocity I owe to a Sunday sermon. One Sunday my wife and I attended the Rosemont Alliance Church of Lincoln, Nebraska. The pastor's sermon centered on the use of money. His biblical exposition skillfully navigated the sermonship through the straits—denying that all good Christians get health and wealth, but still affirming the blessings that grow out of giving. He told a story.

Homer Rodeheaver invited a teenager to hear a noted evangelist on a certain Sunday. The boy said that he was a caddy at the golf course and had to work. "How much do you make in a day?" Homer asked. The boy told him. Homer persisted: "If I gave you that amount would you be able to come?" "Yes, I suppose so," was the reply. So he paid the lad the money. Years passed. One day at a meeting, a man approached Rodeheaver, "Do you remember me?" "No, I don't think so," he responded. "Well, I'm the caddy you paid to miss work. I have not only given my heart to Jesus Christ but I've given my life for service—I am presently attending seminary in preparation for the ministry!"

For a generation short on patience—three insights catch the eye: (1) many kingdom investments are long-term, (2) many rewards are nonmaterial, and (3) many rewards [by inference] will be revealed in the life hereafter.

Conclusion

A story told by Bruce Larson illustrates the dynamics of generosity. A friend built a house in the mountains of Vermont. He hired an old-timer to divine for water with a stick. The man found the spot and said, "Dig fourteen feet straight down....When you hit water pump it out every day." The homeowner found water and pumped it daily. The water level rose to eight feet and leveled off. He left the water alone for several months while finishing the rest of the house.

The day came to turn the water on. The first day there was plenty, the next day none! Efforts to revive the water-flow failed. In despair an artesian well was dug at the cost of three thousand dollars. Later he told his disappointment to the old-timer. "You fool," the man retorted, "I told you to pump it each day. Underground rivers have thousands of capillaries. They open and enlarge with use. Once you allow things to stand for a while, the water backs up, the capillaries close and the river runs elsewhere!"[19]

That's the life of a Christian disciple. In a holistic sense we manage our money, our time, our loving relationships, and our spiritual gifts for God. Generosity enlarges with use. When stinginess, selfishness and miserliness set in, the capillaries of compassion close up and the river runs elsewhere. This is basic discipleship stuff: sound stewardship stems from a commitment to Christ as Lord. From this unbroken relationship flow streams of living water (John 7:38)!

Questions for Discussion:

1. The typical American works 50 years and is poorer at 68 than at 18. Why?
2. God initiated tithing (Deut. 14:22-23) as an aid to remembrance. Discuss.
3. Jesus said that giving reaps overflowing blessings (Luke 6:37-38). How?
4. Is a giving testimony as proper as a service or witness testimony?
5. How can we teach our children to put God first—giving right off the top?

PRACTICING HIS PRESENCE: DEVOTIONAL PAUSE FOR BUSY DISCIPLES
Theme of the week — Giving With Generosity

	Monday	Tuesday	Wednesday	Thursday	Friday
Light on the pathway	Luke 12:13-21	Matthew 23:13-24	Luke 19:1-10	Matthew 6:1-4	Luke 6:37-42
Lesson for this day	Factor #36 Managers	Factor #37 Firstfruits	Factor #38 Emulation	Factor #39 Motivation	Factor #40 Reciprocity
Life in Jesus' way	Take time to pray	Take time to pray	Take time to pray	Take time to pray	Take time to pray

PRACTICE HIS PRESENCE IN CHURCH ON SUNDAY

Chapter

10

Building Reconciling Relationships

41. Golden Rule
42. Christlike Spirit
43. Hostility Control
44. Classical
    Reconciliation
45. Relation
    Transformed

Introduction

When human relationships become irritating, strained or even broken, who is responsible to mend them? Who should initiate healing? The answer of Jesus may surprise you. First off, if you have wronged someone, it is your duty to right it—to seek forgiveness and to make amends. Secondly, if someone else wrongs you, it is again your duty to take the initiative to bring about reconciliation, to demonstrate a spirit of forgiveness, and to harmonize your differences. **Under all circumstances, the followers of Jesus are required to claim ownership to their own rapport with others.**

Guideposts tells of an occasion when Dr. Norman Vincent Peale was driving a rented car. He was lost and running late; he risked missing his plane. While speeding down a freshly oiled road he sprayed another car with tar. The offended driver roared past him, moved to the center of the road, slowing to a crawl. As Peale felt the awful urge to blast his horn, a verse flashed into memory: "A soft answer turns away wrath, but grievous words stir up anger" (Proverbs 15:1 KJV). So he prayed for patience and turned the controls over to God.

The car ahead stopped, blocking the road. The irate driver shouted, "Where do you think you are going?" Peale responded with utmost kindness: "I am sorry I sprayed your car. I am lost. I am about to miss my plane. I can't find the airport entrance." Slowly the man relaxed, "I was about to wring your neck but if you're lost, I will lead you to the airport." With that he sped on ahead. In all relationships, the blessing of love goes miles further than the blasting of hate.

This chapter highlights four principles from the teachings of Jesus about shaping solid God-honoring relationships: (1) disciples live by the Golden Rule, (2) disciples embody a Christlike spirit, (3) disciples control hostility, both in what they overtly express and what they personally absorb, and (4) disciples learn from the noted Reconciliation Procedure as taught by our Lord. Finally, the chapter ends with down-to-earth examples of building rapport redemptively.

41. the GOLDEN RULE factor

Light on the Pathway (Matthew 7:12; cf. Luke 6:31)

"So in everything, do to others what you would have them do to you, for this sums up the Law and the Prophets."

As alluded to in the opening of Chapter Six, our Heavenly Father, like our earthly fathers, loves to give good gifts to children upon request—doing kindness in answer to prayer (Matthew 7:7-11). In the Greek text, the opening words of verse twelve are "all things therefore" or "so in everything" (NIV) and proves that the Golden Rule of kindness to others hinges on the gracious kindness of God to us. God sets the example and we are to pursue his pattern of behavior. As God loves to answer prayer; we love to do kind deeds in response to requests.

Rules and Regulations

It is typical for people to be lenient with themselves—judging flexibly by intentions. At the same time, they judge others strictly by precise actions. In a nutshell: they pamper themselves but handle others critically. This is not fair. Jesus requires everybody to operate by the very same rules.

Churches have standards to uphold. Christians are to advise, admonish and correct each other in redemptive-mutuality. According to Jesus all "church discipline" must be handled with fairness. In the fourth book of the "Caring Enough" series, David Augsburger makes a basic observation, "A relationship is as healthy as its understandings are just, fair, and trustworthy; to yield these without effort in the name of unselfishness is to work for injustice. To surrender in the name of love without resisting evil is to destroy the integrity of human connectedness which keeps love alive."[1] Clearly, the starting point for solid biblical standards in the church is that all must live by the equality-idea inherent in the Golden Rule. This is a fundamental fact.

About the year 1960, a pastor-friend of mine took a small church in the Northwest. A distressed couple came to him. They had been dating and she was pregnant. They wanted forgiveness from both God and the church. The pastor helped them pursue God's forgiveness and counseled them about the implications of their actions. The pastor hoped that a few church leaders, appointed to assist him, would bring this couple through their crisis and restore them to the church—fully forgiven and accepted.

To his surprise, the church board insisted that a historic custom be upheld: the couple would appear one Sunday morning before the whole church to confess their wrong and ask forgiveness. Out of deep remorse and guilt the couple readily agreed. The appointed day came. At the close of the morning sermon, the pastor called the couple forward and gave them the floor.

Very sincerely and discreetly they told the church of their dilemma and asked its forgiveness. To the pastor's dismay, the congregation did not swarm forward to embrace, to forgive and to reassure. The parishioners—like scared rabbits—headed for the exits. The pastor told me, "Never again will I use this method of restoration. Why single out a few people? Why single out a few sins? It's simply unfair."

Traditionally, many churches required strict accountability for certain sexual sins, but no accountability for other sins like:

shoplifting, character-assassinations, income tax fraud, the use of alcohol, drunk-driving, giving liquor to minors, the nonpayment of personal debts, outright lying about government crops and quotas, sex-parties in colleges, doing drugs, abortions—the list is endless!

Careful Restoration

The Golden Rule of Jesus is simple: "...do to others what you would have them do to you...." Don't get me wrong, the Bible upholds high standards. But to be fair, all parishioners need to operate by the same rules. Confession, forgiveness and restoration need to be handled in a discreet redemptive manner.

The ideal way to handle moral-behavior issues is in the context of pastoral counseling. When a church appoints deacons, elders or especially gifted couples to assist the pastors in working through individual cases, you have an ideal combination. Forgiveness and restoration are best handled in conjunction with counsel in an atmosphere of acceptance, empathy, and forgiving love. Often support groups are a great help in reassuring persons through Bible study, prayer, and affirmation from one's own peers.

God wants open, honest, transparent relationships. People often assume that if they admit any weaknesses and request prayer, others will look down on them. The opposite is true. People identify most with persons who freely admit their needs (with discretion, of course). In any covenant-group, the disciples who are most honestly transparent, are the most respected. They immeasurably deepen the trust level for the whole group.

Fighting in Fair Ways

Living by the Golden Rule not only suggests that we live by the same rules and guidelines; it also suggests that we confront each other actively. Such confrontation will prove most helpful if we understand and pursue a common procedure. The book, *When Caring is Not Enough,* is a delightful manual with a thirty day experiment contrasting clean-fair fighting versus dirty-foul fighting. The imagery is cast into a New Testament mode of the "Old Self" with all of its devious slick tricks versus the "New Self" with a redeemed honesty and transparency. On 30 subjects, one per day, the author illustrates in a graphic way the route that healthy relationships need to take. I commend this most practical educational tool on how to build healthy relationships.

The chapter, "Day Ten: Gunnysacking" is alone worth the price of the book. As Augsburger puts it—the Old Self collects hurts, accumulates slights, remembers injustices, broods on injuries, and keeps grievances on file to justify any actions in the future. But not so the New Self. It says—I will finalize my anger on the past. I won't allow the anger to seep over into my future. Here and now I will work through this anger. I willingly accept all risks up ahead.[2]

The two fighting codes differ widely from each other! The "Dirty Fighting Code" says "I saw that, I felt that, I'll save that. I'll use it when I'm good and ready. Meanwhile, I'll let it grow inside me until the right time for it comes along!" The "Fair Fighting Code" looks like this: "I will let go of what was, let be what is, let come what will. Each day's anger is sufficient for that day. I will carry over as little as possible from day to day."[3]

Effective confrontation between persons requires that all relationships be kept current. As all banks balance their books daily, recording the debits and credits, and clearing all checks by nightfall, so our human relationships need daily clearing. Such up-to-date balance sheets finish anger carefully, swiftly, and properly. Today's anger should not shape or distort tomorrow's choices. Unfinished anger always spills over to the next day and taints relationships.

No Passive Doormats

Christian love does not require that we be passive doormats, repressing our own feelings; but it does mean that we all operate by the same Golden Rule and that we follow fair procedures of confrontation. Jesus was both firm and fair. Nowhere are his attributes more clearly defined than in the biblical quotation that follows.

42. the CHRISTLIKE SPIRIT factor

Light on the Pathway (Matthew 12:17-21)

This was to fulfill what was spoken through the prophet Isaiah: "Here is my servant whom I have chosen, the one I love, in whom I delight; I will put my Spirit on him, and he will proclaim justice to the nations. He will not quarrel or cry out; no one will hear his voice in the streets. A bruised reed he will not break, and a smoldering wick he will not snuff out, till he leads justice to victory. In his name the nations will put their hope."

Jesus is highly honored in this quotation (42:1-4), the longest from Isaiah found in Matthew. He fulfills God's lofty ideals. Israel, God's servant-nation, had fallen far short of these standards. The "voice" at the baptism declared that Jesus was elected and loved, the delight of his Father. As the Son of God, he came as the "Suffering Servant" rather than the reigning Davidic king. God's highest purpose was fulfilled in Jesus' role as an obedient servant.

We highlight three items. First, God put his Spirit on him. In context Matthew says that Jesus drove out demons by the Spirit of God (12:28). Jesus said this action proved that he was inaugurating God's kingdom. The blasphemy of the Holy Spirit becomes an unpardonable sin. An accent on the Holy Spirit is again needed today. A supernatural ethic requires that the church be supernaturally empowered. The Holy Spirit can do in an hour what we struggle to do in a lifetime!

Secondly, God's chosen servant will proclaim justice to the nations (12:18). Ideally justice is the basis of society. For a Christian perspective on justice, I recommend Myron Augsburger's chapter, "Conscience and Justice" in *The Christ-Shaped Conscience.* He decries poverty and injustices that cause it. He urges the affluent to simplify lifestyle—to give more to relief and evangelism.[4]

Thirdly, with no arrogance or fanfare, and no boisterous

shouting in the streets, the Lord's Servant comes triumphantly with utmost gentleness, humility and compassion: bruised reeds he will not break; smoldering wicks he will not snuff out. Implied in the rhetoric is the opposite—a tender care that props up a weak soul, a vision that mends broken lives, and an endless love that breathes life into a feeble flickering flame. It is to nurture hope where despair abounds.

A Story From Real Life

Early in my ministry, three brothers started riding our church bus to Sunday School. After Hilda, our Church Visitor, contacted the home the mother began coming also. To our joy, she made a profession of faith in Christ and affiliated through baptism. As for her husband, Jimmy—that was another story. He was in prison. Apparently, he had a record of alcoholism and forgery.

When Jimmy was released, men from our church befriended him. They took him to Christian businessmen's (CBMC) meetings, and eventually won him to Christ. He found local Alcoholics Anonymous (AA) meetings helpful. More than once I joined him for encouragement. On a day in August he followed the Lord in baptism and joined our church. It was thrilling to see this whole family grow in Christ.

One day Jimmy came to me with a heavy heart: "Pastor, I'm in trouble. I found a personalized checkbook and forged four checks at lumberyards where I get my construction materials for my odd jobs. I know they're after me. I should not have done it. But now it is too late." We bowed in prayer asking God to forgive. We asked God for help. In a matter of days, he was arrested and charged. He was released on his own recognizance awaiting the date of trial.

Fanning a Flickering Flame

As a young pastor I asked God for wisdom—to be realistic and redemptive at the same time. First, Jimmy and I had a long talk. Next, I approached our church leaders with a proposal:

"Jimmy is willing to go with me to each lumberyard to apologize and I would like to pay the bill in each case with a church check!" The size of the debt was the big concern. The answer: $2,000 (figure adjusted for inflation). Our leaders "lost their false teeth." "Pastor, do you trust an alcoholic?" Another observed: "Once a paperhanger, always a paperhanger!"

I explained our once-in-a-lifetime opportunity to encourage this fledgling Christian. Here was a golden occasion to be redemptive and Christlike. We could teach him accountability, we could show the court that churches can make restitution; and finally, we could show this family that we were willing to sacrifice in hopes of keeping their breadwinner out of jail. Was his failure a reason for our abandoning him? With a measure of caution and reserve the board reached full consensus.

Jimmy and I went to four lumberyards—four times he apologized and four times I paid the debt. The church board explained to Jimmy that their help was a symbol of their love, but that church membership also entails accountability. To remain a member in full standing, he would need to reimburse the church as he was able. This he began doing immediately, bit by bit, from his odd jobs.

The lawyer, whom Jimmy hired, postponed the trial several times—until the lawyer's fee was fully paid! On the day of the trial, several church leaders and I drove to the huge impersonal Los Angeles County Court. As the case of Jimmy was summoned and pushed through, we were deeply disappointed that the lawyer said nothing of Jimmy's restitution; his new church involvement; nor his church's wish for him to stay in town so that they could be a therapeutic community aiding in his rehabilitation! The judge quickly sentenced him to six months in the prison work camp at Saugus (sixty miles away). Jimmy did indeed look like the typical run-of-the-mill repeat offender.

Protecting Bruised Plants

While incarcerated Jimmy volunteered to assist the chaplain

and experienced good spiritual growth. The act of ministering to others not only afforded a good pastime; it was good spiritual therapy. Soon Jimmy was back, working in our community and worshiping in our congregation.

In the meantime, his three sons accepted Christ and followed the Lord in baptism. It was unfortunate, though I suppose to be expected, that these sons found it difficult to forgive Dad, to accept him, or even to relate to him. Simply put—through the eyes of a teenager, Jimmy was an outright failure.

The church, however, displayed a healthy acceptance of Jimmy and continued to nurture him toward spiritual maturity. Gradually, he repaid every cent of his monetary debt. In terms of his overall performance, praise to God, Jimmy remained alcohol-free and forgery-free, the rest of his life! All the risks we took were richly compensated, though right or wrong is not measured by success. Only one thing matters—were we truly faithful to Jesus Christ?

It was said of Jesus that he would not extinguish flickering lights, nor would he break bruised plants. How is it with you my Christian friend? Are you allowing the Holy Spirit to build into your life a concern for gentleness, for caring, or for healing? Are you a bridge-builder? Are you a fence-mender? Are you becoming like Jesus?

We are all prone to react to any situation with a spring-loaded response. However, what the church of today needs is a fresh filling, anointing or baptism of the Holy Spirit. As Jesus manifested the fruits of his Spirit-baptism, we too need that divine touch, to practice true justice in a spirit of true compassion. Old familiar responses are not adequate. The complex issues of our day call for a new godly creativity, a new effectiveness to blaze a trail of caring.

43. the HOSTILITY-CONTROL factor

We began with two basics in healthy relationships: (1) treat all with equal regard (Golden Rule), and (2) adopt a Christ-likeness that mends broken lives. Now a third principle: (3) keep hostility under control, both the anger-feelings that mushroom in our hearts, as well as the anger vented towards us (be it via deeds or lawsuits). In all cases, we must claim ownership of our rapport with others.

Light on the Pathway (Matthew 5:21-22)

"You have heard that it was said to the people long ago, 'Do not murder, and anyone who murders will be subject to judgment.' But I tell you that anyone who is angry with his brother will be subject to judgment. Again, anyone who says to his brother, 'Raca,' is answerable to the Sanhedrin. But anyone who says, 'You fool!' will be in danger of the fire of hell."

From angry hostile feelings, to abusive language, to blatant condemnatory cursing, so moves the progression of feeling. Mere anger accompanied by some destructive behavior may place one before the local court, which in Bible times consisted of some 23 members. Going a step further, calling someone "Raca" (Aramaic for simpleton, stupid or block-head) may land one before the supreme court (the 71 member Sanhedrin which eventually condemned Jesus to death). This kind of derogatory speech withholds the respect all humans deserve. Angry thoughts can be checked, but words of insult can never be retrieved. Such insult can cut as deep as calling someone an "imbecile;" it can trigger bitter resentment, even precipitate violence.[5]

Worst of all, to call a person "Fool" is so serious that no earthly court is qualified to pass judgment. F. F. Bruce suggests that this non-Greek word has a religious meaning like "Rebel against God" or "Apostate" and resembles our phrase: "You godless, worthless fool!" This is a despicable depreciation of a person's worth and character. Says Jesus—this can merit "the fires of hell."

Our word "hell" comes from the Greek word, "gehenna" and refers to the valley south of Jerusalem where King Ahaz and King Manasseh sacrificed babies to the god, Molech. After Josiah's day it became a perpetually burning incinerator used as the city rubbish dump. It became a symbol of the final destiny for the wicked who had rejected the revelation of the Old Testament patriarchs and prophets. Supremely, hell is the eternal abode prepared for the devil and his angels, and of all people who reject Christ's rule in God's kingdom. Jesus says in effect that those who incite murderous violence via demeaning, devilish and derogatory speech will ultimately be held accountable before the eternal tribunal judgment-bar of God. In the end, the defiant rebels get a "Christless" eternity.

Light on the Pathway (Matthew 5:23-24)

"Therefore, if you are offering your gift at the altar and there remember that your brother has something against you, leave your gift there in front of the altar. First go and be reconciled to your brother; then come and offer your gift."

Fifty years ago many denominations had a healthy sense of accountability. Seeking to be biblical, they suggested that brothers or sisters in the church, who refused to talk to each other, due to grievances, should not partake of communion. Many churches— near the year 2000—have lost this accountability. Alas, some churches have grown large and impersonal, some cold and indifferent, and some permissive and lenient. We need a return to biblical accountability.

Once again the Sermon on the Mount provides shock therapy. Of all things, Jesus tackles the church offering. God doesn't want one dime or one dollar if our brothers or sisters have something against us and we have not taken steps toward reconciliation. The teaching is clear: God first of all prefers loving relationships, and secondly a generous offering. How radical! Since God so mercifully extends forgiving grace to us, he expects us to graciously reciprocate the same.

Light on the Pathway (Matthew 5:25-26)

"Settle matters quickly with your adversary who is taking you to court. Do it while you are still with him on the way, or he may hand you over to the judge, and the judge may hand you over to the officer, and you may be thrown into prison. I tell you the truth, you will not get out

until you have paid the last penny."

Jesus urges a prompt and expeditious handling of all reconciliation matters. Procrastination can be costly! "In the ancient world debtors were jailed till the debts were paid. Thus v.26 is part of the narrative fabric and gives no justification for purgatory, universal restoration, or urgent reconciliation to God. It simply insists on immediate action: malicious anger is so evil—and God's judgment so certain (v.22)—that we must do all in our power to end it."[6]

Churches need to provide fence-mending, bridge-building and injury-bandaging opportunities to restore damaged relationships. Unsolved problems can fester for years; but as a physician lances a boil to guarantee healing, so a Christian therapist, or even a concerned brother or sister in the church, can facilitate the repairing of broken relationships and everybody benefits.

Revival Meetings in Minnesota

Some years ago two neighboring churches in Minnesota invited me to come as evangelist and Bible teacher for some old-fashioned renewal meetings. I have never forgotten one Monday night. My topic centered on "facilitating caring in the church," enabling people to liberate each other through confession and forgiveness, seeking to keep the lines of communications open.

I wanted a kind of altar call that could benefit the whole church as well as any individual—where the Holy Spirit had freedom to move. I felt led of the Lord to say, "As we end this service, we give opportunity for any people to stand and share a prayer request. Either Pastor John or Pastor Joe will pray for you, or they will assign someone else to pray." The response was beautiful.

A sixth-grade lad, sitting between Mom and Dad, stood and requested prayer for more victory in his life. Pastor Joe prayed for him. A lady in her thirties arose. She spoke of her singing ministry, and the criticism she received from her own church when she sang at other churches. So I called for a volunteer—some lady who had been critical. A woman arose and led in prayer. Then a second lady arose and confessed that she too had harbored a critical attitude and requested forgiveness. A third person, an elder, confessed his own lack of caring.

The response—etched deepest in my memory—came from a man about sixty years of age. He stood to his feet in that packed church and spoke with trembling but sincere voice: "Please pray for our family. Since my parents died, my family has been caught up in a terrible inheritance squabble! It is nothing short of an awful disgrace to God. If anyone needs prayer, we desperately do." (The pastor told me later, "That had to be an enormous burden. That man is very shy. He never speaks up in public.") We asked Pastor John to "field" that prayer request.

Helping as Church Leaders

Pastors, elders and deacons have a special duty, admittedly difficult, to alleviate the friction areas of the church. Of course, it's embarrassing to have church leaders invade our private lives and request information regarding unsolved grievances. However, what is public knowledge is no more a private matter. The New Testament concept of the church—being one body—is helpful. An injury in any one part of the body sends shock waves of pain to the rest of the body.

Estrangement, bickering or even avoidance between members can damage the witness of any church to the outside world. The unchurched are never attracted to a feuding church. Never forget: as a car runs on gasoline, the Church of Jesus Christ runs on love! It was Jesus who gave his insignia as LOVE. It was Jesus who urged followers to settle disputes quickly—avoiding festering relationships.

44. the CLASSICAL RECONCILIATION factor

Light on the Pathway (Matthew 18:15-17)

"If your brother sins against you, go and show him his fault, just between the two of you. If he listens to you, you have won your brother over. But if he will not listen, take one or two others along, so that 'every

matter may be established by the testimony of two or three witnesses.' If he refuses to listen to them, tell it to the church; and if he refuses to listen even to the church, treat him as you would a pagan or a tax collector."

Jesus outlines three simple steps; they constitute the classical Anabaptist approach to reconciliation. Step one is a confidential ego-saving maneuver to privately resolve a conflict—just between the two of you. Step two is an accountability-measure. Having a third party present, he or she can help interpret what happens and can mediate where the two may be emotionally talking past each other. Significantly, the third party becomes an eyewitness if all attempts fail.

Step three is an integrity-measure to preserve the unity and witness of the church. As a final resort the matter is brought before the whole congregation. If no repentance and cooperation is evidenced, the recommendation of Jesus is nothing short of excommunication. (The instruction to treat the offender as a pagan or tax collector is evidence that Matthew was writing to Christians with a Jewish background.) Even here the goal is to salvage a life—to be redemptive, rather than retaliatory—always praying and hoping for repentance and return.

Christ's Procedure For Our Good

In Chapter Eight, I told a story growing out of my first pastorate. An elder and I got entangled in a phone conversation—in a heated verbal debate. Because of the distance between us, we decided to meet personally to reconcile. For both of us, a knowledge of Matthew 18:15-17, was the precise reason we met.

It was long ingrained in our psyche, that Jesus had outlined reconciliation patterns, and that if Christians followed them, disputes could be solved. On that occasion, however, I saw that a 50/50 compromise would not bring reconciliation. I finally broke the logjam and offered an unconditional forgiveness on my part. It worked. The problem was solved. I paid the price and was forever blessed!

Small-Groups Facilitate Change

In my third pastorate, as my associates and I began discipling people in groups of 8 to 12 (100 women and 200 men), it became apparent that the small-group format, with powerful group dynamics, offered great potential for affecting reconciliations. Lesson four of the Golden Stairway Discipleship Course covered issues like anger, animosity, thought control and clearing conscience.

One day, in one of my early groups, a fellow in his thirties requested prayer regarding his conflict with a business associate over the use of a vehicle they owned together. So we prayed, especially the week he decided to talk to the associate. What a joy it was, the following week, for our group to place a PTL after that request! The reconciliation had gone well and all friction was gone. Fortunate are the men (and I single out the men intentionally and specifically), who have support groups to help them as they climb that stairway of discipleship toward maturity!

Across Canada and the USA, there is a dearth of programs designed to build the spiritual lives of men. Women have opportunities galore: a club, a class, or a coffee klatsch. But men, that is another matter. Men need much help in building wholesome relationships, whether at work, at church or with their own sons and daughters. The findings of Search Institute are shocking. Of 20 million members in five mainline denominations, over 50 percent of the males (age 20-59) have an "undeveloped" faith. Or put another way, those having an "integrated" faith (age 40-59), represent 40 percent of the females and a mere 15 percent of males![7]

Light on the Pathway (Matthew 18:18)

"I tell you the truth, whatever you bind on earth will be bound in heaven, and whatever you loose on earth will be loosed in heaven."

This verse follows on the heels of verses 16 and 17. They are inseparably linked. In the three-step reconciling process taught by Jesus, an authority is given to the obedient united church. Standing on the Word of Christ, ministering in the Name of

Christ, blessing in the Spirit of Christ, churches have a binding and loosing power. This is awesome! Disobedient saints are judged by the Word; repentant sinners are marvelously liberated by the Gospel of grace. It is probably more accurate to say that the church on earth complies with the policies of heaven than that heaven verifies the deliberations of the church on earth.

A contemporary theologian portrays the Church of Jesus Christ in its loving potential: "...binding and loosing gives more authority to the church than does Rome. It trusts more to the Holy Spirit than does Pentecostalism. It has more respect for the individual than does humanism. It makes moral standards more binding than Puritanism. It is more open to a given situation than the 'new morality.' If practiced it would change the life of the churches more fundamentally than has yet been suggested by current, popular discussions of changing church structures."[8] What food for thought!

Church-centered evangelism which lacks church-discipline makes mockery of God's grace. "Loosing and binding" needs to be recaptured in our faith heritage—with reconciliation as the goal and gentle love, prayer and tears as the means. This is the plea of Paul M. Lederach. "There is fear that discipline leads to legalism. It does if it is not grounded in the gospel. But laxity...is not the answer to legalism. The gospel releases from sin—whether legalism or indulgence....Discipline is an effort to reclaim persons from sin. As such it is not...a disgrace" to be corrected.[9] Discipline dare never spring from revenge. It must spring only from redemptive caring loving concern.

In my Anabaptist tradition, the discipline of Matthew 18 has long been accented, though forever difficult to administer. Nationwide, fifty years ago, things were often handled too strictly, but today too leniently—if at all. I have seen churches with congregational polity suffer from a kind of paralysis that was unable to exercise church discipline. On the other hand, I have seen Elder-run churches discipline members for insubordination or cantankerous attitudes, and a ground swell of sympathizers caused the body to split in half. Always, church discipline needs to be grounded in genuine love.

The Promise and The Presence
Light on the Pathway (Matthew 18:19-20)

"Again, I tell you that if two of you on earth agree about anything you ask for, it will be done for you by my father in heaven. For where two or three come together in my name, there am I with them."

Here is the Promise and the Presence! When brothers and sisters in Christ forsake their bickering and strife and unite their hearts in the love of Jesus, God promises them special answers to prayer. Joyful togetherness becomes the spiritual atmosphere that moves the hand of God's blessing. His blessed presence hovers over every cell of believers who meet to bring praise and glory to Jesus Christ. Christian friends—never forget the Promise and the Presence.

"In those words," writes Richard Foster, "Jesus gave his disciples both assurance and authority. There was the assurance that when a people genuinely gathered in his name his will could be discerned. The superintending Spirit would utilize the checks and balances of the different believers to ensure that when their hearts were in unity they were in rhythm with the heartbeat of the Father. Assured that they had heard the voice of the true Shepherd, they were able to pray and act with authority. His will plus their unity equaled authority."[10] Those who pray most in the will of God, will have the most answers!

45. the RELATIONSHIP-TRANSFORMATION factor

The teachings of Jesus are clear—as disciples we are responsible to maintain a healthy rapport with others. While all of our relationships are important, few are as intense as our family bonds: child to parent, spouse to spouse, and parent to child. In these closest of all relationships, the potential for happiness (or hurt) is the profoundest. The areas of our most intimate connectedness, are also the areas of the greatest vulnerability. In essence, the ones closest to us can provide our deepest joy, or for that matter, our most distressing pain!

In the spirit of Jesus, courageous control-taking is necessary. People tend to give up or give in, when actually, a small dose of determined effort can bring change. This chapter ends with four real-life situations that hopefully will inspire each of us to work harder at mending torn relationships.

The Case of the Child's Punishment

As a missionary and anthropologist, I. M. Friedmann noticed his own violent behavior whenever he was falsely accused. Perplexed about this knee-jerk reaction to certain happenings, he sought counsel. The therapist thought that, perchance, some childhood event could still be affecting him.

One day he quizzed his mother. Tearfully, she recalled an experience back in Russia when he was a mere lad of three. She was baking those double-decker zwieback buns and left them on a baking sheet to rise. Returning, she found them all pressed flat. "Who did it?" she exclaimed. The children accused him; but he vehemently denied it. Mother spanked him until he admitted to it, only to learn later that another child had actually done it.[11] This whole event was still fresh in Mother's memory after all these years.

The chat between Mr. Friedmann and his elderly mother had a twofold benefit. It gave her another opportunity to make peace with her son. And, he was delighted to assure her of forgiveness. At the same time, he gained new insight to help him cope more effectively with certain stressful experiences.

Since parents are fallible and prone to mistakes, even the best of them need to be forgiven. Yes—children need to learn to forgive their parents. Carrying grievances forward from year to year violates the command of Jesus to forgive. On top of that, a bitter unforgiving spirit is hazardous to health. Whether parents are alive anymore or not, it is important that we release them with forgiveness.

The Case of the Father's Denial

A lady came to a counselor, seething with anger. Her father, a noted pastor, had sexually abused her from ages nine to fourteen. When memories of the abuse surfaced some years later, she confronted him; but his response was total denial. Some family members recalled highly inappropriate sexual comments and gestures; however, Father admitted to nothing. If only he had responded warmly, humbly, repentantly! If only he had asked forgiveness, the daughter's hurt and guilt would have healed, and the relationship been normalized.

To the contrary, the father retaliated viciously, and attempted to have her declared mentally incompetent! He schemed to discredit her. In the eye of the public he was exonerated on the basis of his spiritual ministry: "How could God use him to lead countless people to Christ, if he really sexually abused his daughter?"[12] So the lady was left with scars, and memories, and anger, while her father arrogantly denied wrong and disowned any need for repentance. A final disposition will ultimately lie in the hands of our sovereign God Almighty. In the meantime, a broken life needs mending and restoring, with potential help lying in a sphere outside of her own family.

Case of the Mother's Anguish

When Helen Hostetler penned, *A Time To Love,* she unveiled a heartrending saga of courageous love. One winter in central Kansas (1978) their mail carrier left a letter postmarked San Jose, California. Roger, the 28-year-old son, was proud of his weight loss, and his booming printing work. Then timidly he told a secret: "...I'm gay...I have a relationship with a really wonderful man...by far the most natural satisfying romantic relationship I've ever had..."[13] Helen stood numb, then convulsed with sobs. Later husband, Marvin, shared the shock.

One summer their Christian convictions were tested—in uncharted waters. Roger's Gay Men's Chorus was planning a concert in Lincoln, Nebraska. He invited his parents—months in advance. Mother agonized for two days, then sent a letter declining the invitation. Roger's response cut deep, "Your letter hurt me deeply...I have never been so totally put down...or had my self-esteem so damaged..." Helen's anguish was unbearable; tears drenched her pillow countless nights.[14]

That decision, to boycott the concert, has haunted the Hostetlers ever since. In retrospect, what felt so right, later felt so wrong. For one, it took months and even years to renew relationships with Roger. Secondly, when Roger told them in 1985 that he suffered from AIDS, they had to beg and plead before he allowed them to come and visit him. Even then he asked why they had come. That was the beginning of ten months of Christian love and care, agony and ceaseless prayer, and many miles of travel. Roger died at the age of 36 on May 21, 1986.

The Case of the Family's Healing

Jesus insisted that we claim ownership to our own rapport with others. The story of Psychiatrist Harold Bloomfield is a case in point. As a skilled therapist, he took possession of his own dysfunctional family and saw a radical change! We share a small glimpse.

This West Coast doctor rarely got to New York to see his parents. His once-a-week phone call veiled the fact that he harbored deep conflicting feelings. As a teenager, he couldn't leave home quickly enough! Father had a martyr complex, forever getting raw deals. The parents typically argued or maintained a hostile silence. When Father hit sixty-five he was trapped with a "can't win" choice: to work until he dropped dead, or spend twenty-four hours a day with Mother!

Then came the bombshell: Mother phoned that Father had cancer of the pancreas with three to six months to live. Dr. Bloomfield caught the next plane to New York—determined to show love to his father and to take care of unfinished business. As a therapist, he decided to practice what he taught: to seek change.

He assured his father of love and embraced him time and

again. He asked his father to do the same. It took until the 200th hug before Father finally said, "Son, I love you." Next, he helped his parents work through some of the "buried resentments and emotional distance" between them. His older sister joined in on the family consultations. Relationships blossomed beautifully, the family was reconciled and Father lived another four high-quality years.

"If I would have never found out what it is like to really feel my parent's love," writes Dr. Bloomfield, "I would have missed a tremendous opportunity. I decided to write, *Making Peace with Your Parents,* because I understood the harmful price we each pay by having an incomplete and strained relationship with our parents. No matter how we try to rationalize our distance and resentments, or think that we have the relationship 'handled,' there are emotional wounds and even health burdens that we suffer from the unfinished business..."[15] His chapter "From Resentments to Forgiveness" is warm, potent, and moving!

Summary. These four cases challenge us to harness our relationships. The anthropologist learned to cope better through new insights. The victim of sexual abuse, fortunately, went public and found a counselor to help. Relating to a gay lifestyle can be frustrating. At times, what feels like a compromise, is not. Redemptive love keeps relationships intact for the greater good of God's kingdom. And finally, families can be transformed—when someone cares and takes charge.

Conclusion

It's our choice. We can be helpless, hopeless victims of circumstances, always wallowing in self-pity; or we can be helpful, hopeful agents of change where we prayerfully, graciously and effectively strive for improvement. The need of the hour is for more of God's people to assume responsibility for their own rapport with others. Far too soon we write people off as "beyond hope" when really—patient prayer and deliberate love can change many of our relationships. At age 30, I had an appendectomy at the St. Francis Hospital of Lynwood, California. Each night they played the beautiful prayer of St. Francis of Assisi.

> Lord, make me an instrument of Your peace
> Where there is hatred, let me sow love
> Where there is injury, pardon;
> Where there is doubt, faith;
> Where there is despair, hope;
> Where there is darkness, light;
> And where there is sadness, joy.
> O divine Master, grant that I may not
> So much seek to be consoled as to console;
> To be understood as to understand;
> To be loved as to love;
> For it is in giving that we receive;
> It is in pardoning that we are pardoned;
> And it is in dying that we are born to eternal life.

Relationships are always fragile, sensitive and tender. When harnessed for the Kingdom of God and permeated with love, they become vehicles for in-depth communications, for building trust, for showing care, and for exhibiting our faith. When violated and abused, these relationships become tools of fear, hatred and selfishness. This in turn fosters insecurity, alienation and distrust. Our rapport with others is a sacred trust, a trust to be guarded.

Questions for Discussion:

1. Discuss Dr. Peale's handling of his rapport with the irate motorist.
2. Can churches treat all sinners with equal regard, while upholding right?
3. Compare fair-fighting & foul-fighting methods in building relationships.
4. Was the church wrong in "making good" Jimmy's $2000 check writing spree?
5. Why does the church seldom succeed in affecting personal reconciliations?
6. Under Relationship-Transformation which of the four stories rang a bell?

PRACTICING HIS PRESENCE: DEVOTIONAL PAUSE FOR BUSY DISCIPLES
Theme of the week — Building Reconciling Relationships

	Monday	**Tuesday**	**Wednesday**	**Thursday**	**Friday**
Light on the pathway	Matthew 7:1-6, 12	Matthew 12:9-21	Matthew 5:21-26	Matthew 18:15-20	Luke 6:27-36
Lesson for this day	Factor #41 Golden Rule	Factor #42 Christlike	Factor #43 Overcoming	Factor #44 Reconcile	Factor #45 Our Rapport
Life in Jesus' way	Take time to pray	Take time to pray	Take time to pray	Take time to pray	Take time to pray

PRACTICE HIS PRESENCE IN CHURCH ON SUNDAY

Chapter

11

The Healthy Church

46. Accountability
47. Strategy
48. Educational
49. Hands-On Training
50. Liberation

Introduction

One day Alexis and Brittany (ages 6 and 4), helped Grandpa set out vinca plants. Grandpa came prepared with kneeling pads, string, a spade, and a camera. We carefully stretched a 10-foot line, dug holes, and placed plants in straight rows, along the sidewalk and by the fence. While we worked on hands and knees, Brittany used her toy pouring can, to water each plant. In essence, Grandpa was laying out the basic plan to fill the yard with beautiful flowers.

As a gardener shapes the landscape, the Church of Christ must line up its disciplines in proper order as it pursues the goals of God's kingdom. In Chapters Two, Three and Four we laid out foundational aspects: a discipleship that mirrors Christlikeness, clothed in a "new birth" theology that does not shy away from self-denial, cross-bearing and a full surrender to Jesus. The central chapters covered functional aspects: evangelizing, serving, praying, forgiving, giving and reconciling. Churches wander aimlessly when they ignore basic planning.

As Grandpa laid out the plan for Alexis and Brittany to follow, Jesus laid out his kingdom blueprint for his disciples, "...I will build my church, and the gates of hades (or, hell) will not overcome it..." (Matthew 16:18). The disciples were hardly more qualified than little children. They were weak, uncertain and fickle. Notwithstanding, Jesus proposed to build his church squarely on the shoulders, lives and confession of Peter and his cohorts.

The church is not a building, an institution, or an ethnic group; it is peoplehood. First, it is a converted church. Persons, redeemed from sin, touched and transformed, minister the same grace to others. Next, it is a confessing church. Believers still confess Christ as Lord. Thirdly, it is a committed church. Disciples voluntarily unite their hearts in the common cause of Christ's work. One cannot be a true member of Christ's church, without being a servant of Christ and of others. And finally, the church is a covenant community. In both Matthew 16 and 18, the church-idea is linked to "loosing and binding," where people live in mutual accountability. A church both obligates and liberates.

The Church embodies God's paramount program for today's world. This chapter highlights five marks of a healthy church: accountability, mission strategy, education, hands-on training, and a liberation-ministry. The Jesus-Way of discipling can teach us much; and I'll illustrate from my recent discipleship groups. The church is not called to successfulness, but to faithfulness and fruitfulness.

46. the ACCOUNTABILITY factor

God needs healthy and vigorous disciples in his kingdom. In many churches the vast majority of laypersons are spiritually unemployed—they don't "lift a finger" or can't find their niche. All the while, the harried minority suffers from stress and burnout. This is precisely at a time when the church enjoys religious freedom and unparalleled resources. Never has the urgency been greater for reevaluating programs and organizing for ministry. It is imperative that churches allow pastors to adopt truly biblical and fruitful patterns of ministry.

Light on the Pathway (Matthew 21:33-46)

"...There was a landowner who planted a vineyard....Then he rented the vineyard to some farmers and went away on a journey. When the harvest time approached, he sent his servants to the tenants to collect his

fruit. The tenants seized his servants; they beat one, killed another, and stoned a third....Last of all, he sent his son....But when the tenants saw the son...they took him and threw him out of the vineyard and killed him. Therefore when the owner of the vineyard comes, what will he do to those tenants? 'He will bring those wretches to a wretched end,' they replied, 'and he will rent the vineyard to other tenants, who will give him his share of the crop at harvest time'....Therefore I tell you that the kingdom of God will be taken away from you and given to a people who will produce its fruit..."

This powerful parable is linked to Isaiah (5:1-7) where Israel is called "the vineyard of the Lord Almighty." God expected luscious grapes (justice and righteousness), but got a crop of sour grapes (bloodshed and distress). In disappointment, God predicted drought and abandonment.[1] In Jesus' story, God is the landlord and Israel is the tenant. The Pharisees and chief priests understood this and were furious. When the landowner finally retrieved the vineyard from "those wretches," he gave it to "others" who are none other than the circle of Jesus' disciples.[2] God's kingdom is entrusted to those who produce fruit for the owner, to stewards who exhibit accountability.

The history of the Christian church shines with the stars of accountability: Paul, the dogged church-planter; St. Ignatius Loyola, the founder of the Jesuits; Martin Luther, the spark plug of the Protestant Reformation; Michael Sattler, the mastermind of the Schleitheim Confession; John Calvin, the framer of Reformed theology; Count Nikolaus von Zinzendorf, the firebrand of Moravian missions; John Wesley, the flaming revivalist. And hundreds more. Each had a moment in history, to produce fruit for Christ, and after that, to give account.

You and I, in our 350,000 plus churches of the USA and Canada, are shaping destiny. Be assured, if we fail the landlord of the universe, he will raise up fruitful tenants elsewhere. Charles Wesley's "A Charge to Keep I Have" strikes a responsive cord in my heart: "To serve the present age, My calling to fulfill, O may it all my powers engage, To do my master's will."

Evaluating Denominations Today

Whole denominations are accountable to God. Tom Sine sympathetically yet courageously, assesses the influence of contemporary churches: mainline Protestants, evangelicals, charismatics, Catholics and the Mennonites. It is with a heavy heart that I share his appraisal of my own people, and with a prayer that God's grace will yet bring a renewal and a turnabout.

"For many years," writes Sine, "Mennonites have quietly worked with those in need all over the world, maintaining their witness for peace and justice often at a very high price. While Mennonites haven't yet joined the mainline decline, their membership is static and...graying. And not even Mennonites are immune to encroaching secularization. There are signs that they are beginning to relinquish their historical concerns for peace, justice, and social responsibility to embrace a more popular and privatized brand of Christianity and a more comfortable way of life. Unless present trends change, they are likely to be less, not more, responsive to the challenges of the twenty-first century."[3]

No doubt, Tom Sine is correct in assuming that certain tough issues like peace and social justice will be overlooked, if Mennonites, Catholics and mainline churches don't address them. Evangelical and charismatic churches may not assume this agenda. Still, history may surprise us. God often raises up other fruitful vineyards and faithful tenants in times of need. Let me illustrate.

The mainline denominations' heavy emphasis on peace, justice and social concerns, says Eugene C. Roehlkepartian, has not motivated people as expected. In their churches "78 percent of adults never spend time promoting social justice. Seventy-two percent have never marched, met, or gathered with others to promote social change."[4] By contrast, an awareness of social concern is rising among evangelical people. Take World Vision USA—a California based humanitarian agency. Only a few decades old, it collected $215,500,000 in 1990, of which 82 percent went to social service needs around the world. In the same year Church World

Service (the outlet for mainline churches) collected 43 million dollars of which 80 percent went to programs.[5] So, some evangelicals are moving beyond a narrow soul-saving stance.

Accountable in The Local Church

Finally, the spotlight shifts from denominations to local churches. How are parishioners best motivated and involved? In my third parish, both the worship hour and the Sunday School hour still played vital roles in spiritual formation—the growth and nurture process. Inspiration and instruction flowed from both. However, I sensed one element missing, that of holding people accountable. With this in mind we added a small-group component and saw marvelous change.

While congregations in America grapple with the proper role of women in the church, men are often forgotten. Very few have opportunity for peer group encounters like their female counterparts. Men need a setting where they find both accountability and confidentiality. Churches can provide this.

Our women had a zeal for Christ, doing a fantastic job with teaching, praying, serving and providing occasions for fellowship. As is generally the case, our men excelled in undertaking regional disaster projects, canning meat for relief, and giving money for church planting. Yet the idea of men ministering to men on a spiritual level was lacking. Their conversation in coffee shops seldom included in-depth Christ-centered subjects. Absent was the concept of a covenant community, where even MEN pray and share!

The outcome was—I as senior pastor (helped by men we trained) discipled 200 men in eight years. For three months we met weekly in a covenant relationship of learning, sharing and praying. After that each group met monthly for several more years. Clearly, it was the most significant action in my 35 years of ministry.[6]

One day one of our denominational leaders quizzed me about our men's discipleship groups. I listed the three facets:

prayer/sharing, biblical growth lessons, and the sharing of our spiritual autobiographies. For home work, I said, we read up-to-date relevant Christian books, one per week. "I know it sounds childish," I added, "but I go around the circle each week and record the number of pages read by each man. And do they read!" He lit up with enthusiasm, "Brother, you are on to something. That is exactly what our churches lack. There is nothing juvenile about that. That is top-notch accountability, and I like it."

The small-group format is conducive towards accountability: (1) the pledge to pray for each other, (2) the keeping of a prayer page, marking answers with a PTL, (3) the commitment to confidentiality, (4) the sharing of our spiritual life stories, and (5) the discerning of our "spiritual gifts." The latter occupied three lesson periods and required that each disciple identify his spiritual gifts. The group then processed his evaluation, and affirmed his gifts or added others. This was strenuous; but it required the highest form of accountability. Each disciple was urged to develop his gifts (whether serving, teaching, leading, mercy, encouraging or exhorting) and to use them in the life of our congregation.

47. the STRATEGY factor

A church's faithfulness in fruit-bearing also requires a biblical strategy. The prime force that shapes a church's strategy should not be fads, current trends or even "felt needs." It should be the Great Commission spoken from the lips of the Risen Christ. The commission appears in each gospel, in some form, as well as in the book of Acts. The Great Commandment (love) is included in the commission's mandate: to teach all that Christ commanded. The Great Commission is binding on all believers everywhere. It should be central to all church strategy.

Light on the Pathway

"All authority in heaven and on earth is given to me. Therefore go and make disciples of all nations, baptizing them in the name of the Father, and of the Son and of the Holy Spirit, and teaching them to obey everything I have commanded you. And surely I am with you always, to

the very end of the age." (Matthew 28:18-20)

"Go into all the world and preach the good news to all creation."
(Mark 16:15)

"...The Christ will suffer and rise from the dead on the third day
and repentance and forgiveness of sins will be preached in his name to all
nations, beginning at Jerusalem. You are witnesses of these things."
(Luke 24:46-48)

"Peace be with you! As the Father has sent me, I am sending you."
(John 20:21)

"But you will receive power when the Holy Spirit comes on you;
and you will be my witnesses in Jerusalem, and in all Judea and
Samaria, and to the ends of the earth." (Acts 1:8)

Our Kingdom Directives

There they are: kingdom-directives from our Risen Lord. He
is Lord of the Church. These orders hold each church and its
denomination accountable. The philosophy of every church body
(and each of its educational institutions, social/relief agencies,
publishing houses and mission boards) must be shaped by these
parting words of Christ. They must foster Christ's overall purpose.[7]

These five scriptures contain dynamic components: (1)
Authority. The Risen and Exalted Christ has triumphed via his
death and resurrection and so has earned the right to issue
authoritative orders, (2) *Mobility.* The sending-motif is clear and
reminds us that the church is ever a mobile unit, with an on-the-
go posture, (3) *Strategy.* Disciple-Making is the crux of the
church's task: winning people, baptizing them in a public profession, and instructing them intensely—so the disciple becomes like
his or her teacher, and (4) *Capability.* Enablement comes by the
power of the Holy Spirit (which the church is to seek), and the
presence of Christ (which the church is to enjoy).

These Commission teachings, plus the caring patterns
embodied in Jesus' ministry, comprise a strategy for church work.
Intrinsically, the need is to upgrade our circles of friendship,

evangelism, and caring activities. It speaks of assimilating new people, offering belongingness and "goal-ownership." It implies the diligent teaching of the principles of the Christ. At the core, it necessitates hands-on training in discipleship, with attention given to commitment, Holy Spirit-empowering, growth, "gift" discernment and the commissioning of people.

Grasping a biblical principle is one thing, but implementing it in a church is quite another. This is especially so when a new pastor comes to a 100-year-old church and wants to introduce Great Commission methods. At the outset, the pastor needs to learn the views, values and virtues of that congregation. Only after adopting their dreams, and celebrating their successes, can the pastor hope to place before them new stepping stones—the Jesus-Way of discipleship.

My Pastoral Pilgrimage

In my pastoral pilgrimage, the first charge was a big-city church. Its membership grew from 140 to 240. What a delight: pastor and people blending vision and ministry. One August, four came for baptism. One I had led to Christ, the other three were won by laypersons—one in the baby nursery, one in the neighborhood, and one at a businessman's luncheon. What a celebration! My discipling approach was one-on-one. I had not yet learned the way of small-group discipling.

My next church—900 members—was in a Kansas town of 17,000. Attendance grew and we expanded to two worship hours. One issue surfaced—why accept more members when the present membership feels they are not adequately served? A high-point came one Sunday morning; we dedicated 37 Shepherding couples, each to care for a cluster of families. This network of caring blessed the church long after my decade of service, yet it still wasn't a full-orbed discipleship method.

Finally, in my third pastorate, I stumbled into a Jesus-style strategy of discipleship. The church (1100 members + 500 children) was in a small Nebraska town. My special burden was the young men (age 25-45) who appeared spiritually dysfunctional. Some had married wives from Catholic, Methodist or Lutheran backgrounds—wives who took instruction and then affiliated. Yet often wives complained, "My husband never discusses religion, nor does he train our children."

One day my wife put fire to the fuse. Susan Joann has gifts of service and hospitality. I was talking again about discipling. "Al," she exclaimed, "I'm sick and tired of this, you continue to brainstorm about discipling men by 12s. I'll make breakfast for next Thursday (2-25-82) and you'll have twelve men there to eat it!" I was trapped. I phoned 12 men—the most mature—ages 30 to 40. All came to breakfast and eleven enrolled. We met two hours per week for three months and climaxed with a banquet, including our wives. After this we became a monthly support group. For many, this was their only place for prayer or sharing.

Each year I recruited a new group. I avoided publicity, not wanting my early disciples to feel "watched" or unduly self-conscious. The Deacon/Elder Board gave strong support. After three years it made two requests: (1) go public with sign up sheets, and (2) start discipling women. As to the first, I was glad to affirm that anyone was welcome, yet of the 128 men that I myself discipled, less than five walked into the office to sign up! In men's work, personal recruitment is essential. (Note: Jesus never chose his disciples via synagogue sign up sheets.) Our Deacons soon hosted the men's support groups at their own homes, thus accepting responsibility for them. This was strategic—it offered goal-ownership. For this I was most grateful.

The second idea was feasible—after we published the Golden Stairway Discipleship Course. So we trained a gifted lady. Four woman, after taking the course, also discipled groups. Our strategy was for each lady-discipler to lead several groups and after that, to care for them for some years, like a mother hen watches her chicks. The strategy worked. Soon 100 enthusiastic women were discipled. The women confirmed an insight—sharing is deepest, man-to-man or woman-to-woman.

A Pastor's Job Description

Once a disgruntled parishioner questioned my use of time. "You know those meetings at your house," he remarked, "they have never been in any previous pastor's schedule! You should be out visiting." I was stunned. I listened for a while and then replied, "I consider our discipleship work as very significant. Even in the groups I lead, laymen minister to each other and save a pastor many hours of counseling. People are greatly helped. They are growing spiritually. It appears to be an efficient use of time." He wasn't convinced; discipleship-stuff looked suspect.

He raised a crucial point on the strategy of pastoral care. If a pastoral staff could visit 500 homes every 60 days, those visits would be mostly social plus a little Bible and prayer. (Frankly, I would enjoy a job like that!) In a casual brief visit people feel uneasy when you probe into deeper spiritual issues. You just don't barge in.

How different in discipleship work. Dealing with spiritual issues is automatic. A covenant-group starts with a "contract," an agreement to learn and to grow together. The prayer requests, Bible lessons, life-stories, and book reading move persons to deeper levels quickly. And everyone expects it. (It is like growing up with brothers and sisters. They provide some fast gratuitous learning!) Discipleship via "group dynamics" educates forcefully. In terms of shaping lives for Christ, it far outweighs the benefits of one-on-one visitation. So, Jesus' training of the Twelve modeled strategy for fruitful discipling today, and his commission gives us guidelines.

48. the EDUCATIONAL factor

One hallmark of a healthy fruit-bearing church is a solid educational program. Christ's commission calls for it: "...teaching them to obey everything I have commanded you..." (Matthew 28:20). But alas, this tends to be the weakest area in most churches. A shortcut fast-food microwave generation simply lacks the will, patience and the "stick-to-itiveness" that this spiritual task requires.

If I were a cartoonist hoping to touch the sensitive nerve of a relevant issue, I would draw four frames. They would carry a caption like, "The Church's Worst Nightmare" or better yet, "A Sunday School Superintendent—the Grand Champion of Arm-twisters!" The frames would depict a Saturday night phone call.

Cartoon Scene 1: "Hi, is this Mary? We've got a small crisis at First Church. We need a teacher; of course, no big deal. I've phoned 37 folks and all are busy. The young couple's class—that's the one I'm talking about. The enrollment is 65; but don't worry, last month the attendance averaged 17. The job is easy!" *Scene 2:* "Ohhhhh, you don't think you can? Yoooour schedule is tight? Yoooour summer is planned?" *Scene 3:* "Say, Mary, last week I taught the class with no preparation. No sweat. All went great. They're big talkers. Mary, how about 60 days? Last week we bare-ly looked at the lesson and we were off into a grand discussion of whatever the class wanted to talk about. I just let the conversation rise spontaneously out of the class." *Scene 4* "Did I hear, YES! Oh, thanks, Mary. That's 8 Sundays, Wow, a big load off my shoul-ders. One more thing, Mary. I hardly know how to ask this—butah—ah—ah, Mary, can you start tomorrow morning at ten?"

A Tired Enterprise

In most churches, Christian education is a "tired enterprise," out of touch with youth or adult needs, often using outdated pro-cedures. That's the conclusion of Carolyn Eklin and Peter Benson in *Effective Christian Education: A National Study of Protestant Congregations* (a report on faith, loyalty and congregational life). This monumental 3-year study compared The Southern Baptist Convention (leaders in education) with five mainline churches: Christian Church (Disciples of Christ), Evangelical Lutheran Church in America, Presbyterian Church in the USA, United Church of Christ, and United Methodist Church. These bodies total 35,015,000 members; and the survey tested 11,122 persons (as I stated earlier).

Benson's research team unveiled its findings in March of

1990. Christian education, they insisted, is clouded with myths: *Myth 1.* It is for children. Proof is in the percentage of people participating: children 60, junior high 52, senior high 35, and adults 28. *Myth 2.* Good teaching only transfers information. No, it also aids decision making and learning in the crucible of experience. *Myth 3.* Teaching does not require training. Sadly, only half of the churches offer annual classes in effective teaching methods. *Myth 4.* Christian education is peripheral and not really at the hub-of-energy for all that the church does.[8]

With the help of experts, 38 indicators were chosen to measure maturity of faith.[9] As we stated earlier, "family religiousness" impacts these indicators more profoundly than anything else (e.g. a child and mom conversing about God, a teen with dad, or a friend, talking about faith, family devotions, and a home project like making a meal for the sick, or a Christmas package for the poor).

However, at church, nothing equaled the value of good Christian education. "One of the most important findings in this study is that congregations in promoting faith maturity reap the benefit of greater loyalty. By concentration on their ultimate purpose of nurturing an ongoing growth in faith, congregations appear to gain the kind of commitment that thwarts dropout, switching and inactivity."[10] It is obvious the potential of Christian education is profound.

The State of Health

In essence, this study serves as a window to the spiritual health of much of American Christianity. Typically, youth and adults had a strong bias against Christian education and most dropped out after grade nine. While Southern Baptists excelled, having 49 percent showing a mature "integrated faith," the mainline church adults had only 30 percent. And women always excelled the men. In mainline denominations, 38 percent of the women, overall, were rated as having a mature faith, compared to 21 percent of the men. The greatest disparity came among adults in their 40s and 50s. Women rated 40 and men only 15 percent.[11]

What lessons can we glean from the Search Institute report? Churches need clear mission statements about youth and adult education. It is essential for pastors to be interested and well versed in Christian education principles. The teachers need enthusiasm, teaching skills, a mature faith, and knowledge of educational theory and practice. The curriculum needs to be upbeat, up-to-date, relevant, and useful both in biblical content and in moral decision making. Peer involvement is also necessary—with men deserving extraordinary attention. And finally, the church needs homes that reflect a deep religious commitment.[12]

Education is a Pastor's Friend

In 35 years of pastoral work, I have found Christian education to be pivotal to outreach, nurture, and ministry. Aside from the church doctrine class for baptismal candidates, at each church I also tackled a special job of teaching a class with no registered pupils. It was exciting.

In my first big-city charge, I advertised a Life of Christ class to meet in the Social Hall kitchen for three months. We recruited community adults—parents of Sunday School kids—to study Bible, with no strings attached. Average attendance was 16. When we disbanded some called it failure. "Not for a minute," I responded. "We had one grand 3-month-chance to befriend people and share faith."

At the second church, I taught a 6-month elective (the book of Romans). I visited 40 couples, not regular in Sunday School, age 20-39. Sixteen couples enrolled in that "Sunshine Class." Meeting in a superb classroom, and enjoying a social time with refreshments, we raised the S.S. attendance by 28 per week. Six persons even joined church during this period. The Director of Christian Education took over the class and provided continuity. The experience was memorable.

Our chapter "Counting the Cost" under "Planning Factor" details the starting of a new class in my third church. We mailed invitations to 400 people who had dropped out in recent years. In a 15-year decline Sunday School attendance dipped into the 500s. By strengthening classes and creating a new one, attendance jumped back to 650 and stayed there for four years. The new class enrolled in excess of 100 people. (After ten years, this class was still vigorous.)

Proof is in The Pudding

How did a small-group ministry, in my third parish, fit in with the church's program of education? A small-group strategy cannot function as an appendage unrelated to the other learning experiences, such as Sunday School and worship hour. I began my discipling approach quietly and experimentally. First off, prodded by my wife, I invested my own energy to implement my own ideas! Soon I reported regularly to the Deacon/Elder Board, the body responsible for Church Doctrine and Membership Orientation. I was elated when they agreed to host the ongoing support groups in their homes. Some pastors may wish to approach their education board first, if they have printed material to show, at first I did not.

In our case, the Board of Education supervised Sunday School, Youth work and Music. So as we neared the 300-mark of persons trained in our discipleship groups we researched a crucial concern: are we producing idle super-spiritual saints or good sound healthy workers? To my joy I discovered that 61 disciples were teaching Sunday School and 45 were serving as leaders or sponsors in the youth and children's programs (Sunday/ Wednesday). On top of that 53 were singing in the Chancel Choir or the Male Chorus. So at every turn our discipleship was training servants for our Board of Education. (Note: our discipleship course accented gift-discernment and the need of finding one's Christ-appointed niche in church.)

49. the HANDS-ON TRAINING factor

Being the church speaks of who we are; and this determines what we do. Out of essence flows action. This chapter, "The Healthy Church," holds members in a covenant community accountable to each other. Secondly, the Great Commission provides a strategy for ministry, if not also setting some perimeters. Thirdly, the Commission mandates educational activity. Now, our fourth principle, one modeled openly in the life of Jesus. With the three, the Twelve, and the Seventy, Jesus demonstrated "hands-on training." It's like learning to swim by jumping into a pool, watched by trainers. It's like "the plunge" in Chicago's Urban Training as persons are sent to skid row with one dollar—to share and to beg for two days.

In Mark's gospel, Jesus singled out Peter, James and John three times for a special hands-on lesson: at the house of Jairus (5:37), on the Mount of Transfiguration (9:2), and in the Garden of Gathsemane (14:33). Three specific lessons: on healing, on prophesy, on praying. Such selectivity is not playing favorites; it is the training technique of giving high-potential people hands-on help.

Many churches reflect an urgent need for hands-on equipping, sense of divine calling, gift-discerning and leadership-monitoring. The all-too-common practice of elevating persons to top church leadership positions because of their business acumen, family prominence, apparent wealth or social status, does the church a disservice. While it gives goal-ownership, it overlooks spiritual qualifications.

Church of Our Dreams

I can dream of an ideal church where people at the top have all proven themselves: where each pastor, each deacon/elder, the Sunday School superintendent, each youth sponsor and each board chairperson has passed a fourfold screen test: 1. *Test of Spiritual Disciplines* (e.g. praying, Bible reading, forgiving, and tithing); 2. *Test of Character* (do peers and business associates perceive a caring-Christlike spirit?) 3. *Test of Hands-On Training* (e.g. a 1-year supervised stint in teaching Sunday School, leading a small-group, or winning a family to Christ and assimilating them into the church), and 4. *Test on Servanthood:* a one year stint of service (helping in a soup kitchen, tutoring children, counseling at a pregnancy-crisis center, or going overseas in voluntary service).

But the real world—that's a different matter. Sometimes we fly on wings of vision, dreams and prayer. So in my third parish, our discipling was innovative and experimental—really a supplement to Christian education programs already in place for decades. On the tenth anniversary of the first discipleship breakfast (by now 300 men and women had been discipled in support groups), I consulted our yearbook and surveyed the leadership. I was pleased. Five of our six deacon/elders were "disciples," as were eight of the ten Church Board members, as well as the Sunday School superintendent and assistant. My co-workers and I provided the small-group discipling and the church, time and again, affirmed the "disciples." With no coaching from me, the Nominating Committee, knowingly or unknowingly, placed person after person into positions of service. It was a dream come true.

Research on Hands-On Training

Leadership education, the hands-on kind alone, can liberate a faltering laity. Pastors often bemoan the fact that few people are willing to lead. But Barna's research disagrees. There are plenty of capable willing people. The crux of the problem is that churches press people into immediate service with no regard for their spiritual gifts or ministry calling. The net result—frustration.[13] So abilities go unused, as persons are given jobs foreign to their gifting.

The hands-on process of serving others, doing deeds of mercy, or promoting social justice, has a deepening affect on our faith. That's the conclusion reached by Peter Benson. "Some of the best religious education occurs in these moments of giving, of connection, of bonding to others. Service needs to be the cornerstone of educational programming, partly because it is educationally-rich, and ultimately because, as people of faith, we are called to serve."[14]

Frankly, two groups in the church seem most susceptible to discouragement and burnout: the under-trained and the over-worked. Many zealous church workers suffer from both ailments—haphazard training and then being "worked to death."

...When he saw the crowds, he had compassion on them, because they were harassed and helpless, like sheep without a shepherd....He called his twelve disciples to him and gave them authority to drive out evil spirits and to heal every disease and sickness....These twelve Jesus sent out with the following instructions: "....Go rather to the lost sheep of Israel. As you go, preach this message: 'The kingdom of heaven is near.' Heal the sick, raise the dead, cleanse those who have leprosy, drive out demons. Freely you have received, freely give..."

On the timeline of Jesus' three years of ministry, it was near midpoint when he sent his Twelve, in six pairs, to serve residents in the villages of Galilee. The assignment was awesome and scary. They were on their own. A degree of success was assured. Many people would welcome them with open arms since they had authority to target some basic needs of the countryside, needs which had frustrated their most capable rulers, teachers and doctors.

People craved instruction. The disciples declared that the kingdom of heaven had come in the person of Jesus. People suffered from undiagnosed illnesses; the disciples healed them. People were plagued by evil spirits. The disciples offered deliverance. Having freely received kingdom blessings, the disciples freely gave.

Some of Jesus' instructions were for the immediate tour, like avoiding the Samaritans and Gentiles (10:5). Other teachings were for all times. The extended account is full of hands-on training. Two lessons emerge: don't aggravate the hostile Jews. Rather, intentionally help and heal the hurting Jews, the receptive ones, the potential givers of hospitality. Be shrewd as snakes and harmless as doves (10:16). Clearly, Jesus was shielding novice workers from needless trouble.

Building on Biblical Principles

No one in church life today illustrates hands-on preparation better than Bill Hull. Leaving an established church in 1984, Hull

244 • Discipleship Therapy

planted the Green Valley Church of San Diego with this goal: "My motivation was to see if installing disciple-making at the heart of the church would work." Within a few years he wrote the book, *The Disciple Making Pastor,* to show pastors how the Great Commission, coupled with the methods of Jesus, can be implemented. The design is not "bigger" faster-growing churches, but rather, obedient, dynamic, healthier churches.[15]

The chapter, "Making it Work in the Local Church," credits the seed thought to the classic by A. B. Bruce, *The Training of the Twelve,* where three calls are pinpointed: (1) "Come and See" (John 1:39), (2) "Come and Follow Me" (Mark 1:17), and (3) "Come and Be With Me" (Mark 3:14).[16] Superimposed on these triple calls is a six-step training method proposed by Howard Hendricks. Interwoven in these principles, Hull offers creative hands-on, church-operational instructions.

"If I were starting a ministry from scratch," asserts Hull, "I would begin by inviting all who like to 'come and see' to a small-group Bible study. Then, in that context, I would allow the cream to rise to the top and select those who respond to the 'come and follow Me' call into another small-group for training. From those who finished that basic training, I would select a few more to 'come and be with Me.' These I would train to replace me, and I would work through them" (to multiply, decentralize, and add group-effectiveness).[17]

Later, Hull went from "Christocentric" to "churchocentric" thought, reflecting the transition from the gospels to epistles. Eight discipling keys are basic to the New Testament: intentional strategy, Great Commission at the core, multiplication as a method, accountability, the small-group as a vehicle, apprenticeship for leaders, leadership selection by gifts/character, and decentralizing.[18] Few writers have as clearly demonstrated a biblical hands-on method, with the Great Commission as the determinate factor. It is excellently done.

Churches tend to resemble hospitals with maternity wards, but with inadequate facility for all the subsequent stages of life (pediatrics to geriatrics). Mainline churches gear children for confirmation; then comes a big drop-off. The "Believers Churches" ready children and youth for baptism. After that, again, comes a fairly big drop-off. Among the Southern Baptists (who excel in education) half of their membership is not in church on a typical Sunday. "We dip them and drop them," said one pastor. All churches need to educate and deploy adolescents and adults—in evangelism and service—or they simulate hospitals who deliver babies but give no after-care.

50. the LIBERATION factor

Beyond accountability and strategy, education and hands-on training, we move to the fifth mark of a healthy fruitful church: a liberation-posture. This idea incorporates both compassion and capability. Do we feel compelled to respond to need? Do we have the spiritual power to deliver a broken, hurting world?

Light on the Pathway (Luke 4:14-21)

Jesus returned to Galilee in the power of the Spirit....He went to Nazareth, where he had been brought up, and on the Sabbath day he went into the synagogue, as was his custom. And he stood up to read. The scroll of the prophet Isaiah was handed to him. Unrolling it, he found the place where it is written: "The Spirit of the Lord is on me, because he has anointed me to preach good news to the poor. He has sent me to proclaim freedom for the prisoners and recovery of sight for the blind, to release the oppressed, to proclaim the year of the Lord's favor." Then he rolled up the scroll, gave it back to the attendant and sat down....

Luke seems to place this synagogue-event (at Nazareth) earlier than in the other gospels; but it fits his theme of writing—God's love for the non-Jew as well. He does not claim that this event launched Jesus' Galilean ministry; he refers to Jesus' previous work at Capernaum (4:23). As guest rabbi, Jesus stood to read the scripture, probably first in Hebrew, then translating into Aramaic. After this he sat down to expound it, as was the custom. At any rate, Jesus told his hometown worshipers that his own life fulfilled the scripture he had read (Isaiah 61:1-2), thus linking himself to Jubilee teachings from Leviticus 25.[19]

Year of Jubilee

The Jubilee Year, every fiftieth, was the year of "the Lord's favor"—to fallow ground, remit debts, free slaves, and restore land back to its ancestral owners. The Prophet Isaiah picked up this Jubilee theme, and portrayed the coming Messiah as helping the broken hearted (good news for the poor, and release for captives and prisoners) while proclaiming the favor of God.

Luke also gives the "Holy Spirit" special recognition in the life of Jesus—his Conception (1:35), his Baptism (3:22), his Temptation (4:1), his Ministry (4:14). And he quotes Jesus' parting instructions: "...stay in the city until you have been clothed with power from on high" (24:49), a clear reference to the Baptism of the Holy Spirit at Pentecost (Acts 1:5, 2:1-4). According to Luke, a liberation ministry grows out of a mighty moving of the Holy Spirit.

A Spirit-Anointed Deliverance

If the church is to offer deliverance in Jesus' name, less reliance on self and more on the Holy Spirit is imperative. It was in July of 1948, on a Sunday night that I left my balcony seat, in my jam-packed home church, to dedicate my life to God for service. And in that act of obedience I was so filled with the Spirit, so flooded with joy, so overwhelmed with God's presence that my usual youthful run-of-the-mill temptations never touched me for weeks. So it seems: the more we are yielded, the more we are filled. And secondly, in the doing, in the commitment to service comes God's special enablement. It appears that God doesn't empower the spiritually unemployed. Our suffering world of addiction, oppression, alcohol, and abuse, needs a church that cares, that comes in Jesus' name, and above all, a church that ministers in the mighty power of the Holy Spirit! Let me share seven vignettes out of today's world.

* *Heartaches.* The Bear Valley Church (Denver) targets some twenty-five areas of need outside the church. Examples are:

unwed mothers, abused children, jail inmates, singles, international students, juvenile offenders, members of cults, and others. Members already skilled in these areas don't need much training. Bear Valley requires that "the idea-person" must always implement the program![20]

* *Incest.* Debra Wall joined a Kansas church. She felt a nurturing support and the warmth of God's love. Basking in that "acceptance," she unveiled a secret that had haunted her for 30 years: she had been raped by her adoptive brother. She first "purged" herself by talking and praying with her pastors. The "turning point" came when her congregation held a public healing service for her. She allowed the church to enter her pain; they laid hands upon her and prayed for her deliverance. For Debra, this act of love restored her self-worth.[21]

* *Murder.* In 1988, my birthday dinner was cut short by the horrible news that a 12-year-old girl in my parish was shot to death. The distraught parents cried, "Why, oh God, Why?" The dad, Daniel, was in my Men's Discipleship Group of 1987. At the funeral other men from that group and their families sat at the front, next to the grieving family. This small-group of 12 met often after that—to love, to pray, to support him—just to let Daniel talk out his grief. I learned, firsthand, the therapeutic value of a support group in life's toughest hour.

* *Divorce.* Myron and Esther Augsburger were "torn inside" when one of their children went through a divorce. At his church Myron prayed for strength to preach, as tears flowed down his cheeks. The congregation understood. One evening three members came to pray, "You are carrying all of this burden by yourself. We would like you to disengage emotionally....We don't want you even to talk, think or pray about it for several weeks. We promise you we will do the praying in your place."[22] The Augsburgers found the strength of love in the prayers of others.

* *Promiscuity.* In a hotel lobby, Dick Innes was approached by an attractive lady. "Why are you in this business?" he asked. "For money," she replied. "Tell me about your home, family and dad,"

Dick insisted. She began talking. "Wait, Dick," she paused, "No one ever quizzed me before, who are you?" Sheepishly he grinned, "a minister of religion." "You mean you believe in the Lord? So do I. I often pray in the shower and ask God to forgive my sins." Toni shared how she despised her work. Her parents had divorced; Dad moved away—deserting them. She showed anger. "Dick," she said tearfully, "I have never felt that anyone loved me. I am terribly lonely." Dick wept too: "My parents also divorced; I also hated my father." Toni's superior moved in—tears hurt business! Quickly, Dick embraced Toni, "Remember, God loves you; so do I." Promptly, Toni was whisked away.[23]

* *Occultism.* Laurel's home is traditional. Her mom is regularly in church, Dad isn't. Laurel stopped praying at eleven and dropped out of Sunday School. A typical teen, she worries over acne, a new car, and "big things" like earth-pollution or world-terrorism. Mom is busy with the kids, and Dad is tired; so Laurel talks with her English teacher, Miss Grant. In Laurel's eyes, she's awesome! Actually, she is a witch in the "goddess movement." Laurel suffers "destructive spells" and gets hooked on her boyfriend's music of Slayer and King Diamond. She ends up in a locked hospital ward—accidental overdose or a botched suicide try? Her parents are frantic, "Who failed?" Laurel refuses to talk.[24]

* *Demonism.* Our nephew, Pastor Jim, served a small-town Mennonite church in Kansas. In his 30s, a graduate of Dallas Seminary, he was discipling a young man who had a wife and child. One day this convert was found hanging in the garage. Pastor Jim preached the funeral; then all hell broke loose. Physically, Jim collapsed on the floor. Spiritually, he lost salvation-assurance. Emotionally, he was paralyzed. For some weeks he retreated to Iowa to his mentor, Mark Bubeck. Later, at Grandma's funeral in South Dakota, four of us uncles met with Jim. Using scripture, praying in Jesus' name, claiming the blood of the Lamb (Revelation 12:11) we asked for his deliverance and a restoring to ministry. God heard!

A healthy church incorporates accountability. It plans and

strategizes. It prioritizes education. It provides hands-on training. It seeks an empowering of the Holy Spirit that brings to hurting people comfort, healing, and deliverance.

Conclusion

The Christians's symbol is not a glint of superiority in the eye, but a cloak of humility, an apron of service—deeds done in Jesus' name. To follow Christ is to love the last, the lowest and the least (Matthew 25:31-40). A newsman observed Mother Teresa's daily routine among sores, sickness, and suffering. "I wouldn't accept your job for a million dollars," he concluded. "I wouldn't either," said Mother Teresa, founder of the "Missionaries of Charity."

At age 20, Agnes Bojaxhiu of Yugoslavia left an Irish convent to join the "Loreta Sisters" in Calcutta. For sixteen years "Mother Teresa" taught geography to well-to-do girls. In 1946, on a train ride in the Himalayas, she heard God calling her to serve the poorest of the poor. This started an incredible venture!

In 1952, as monsoon rains drenched Calcutta, Mother Teresa stumbled over an old lady lying in a pool of water. Her toes were chewed off by rats. She was scarcely breathing. Mother Teresa carried the lady to a hospital. They refused her. So she started for the next hospital; but the victim died in her arms. The next day she stormed the Municipal offices regarding the dying. They offered a house and Mother Teresa founded the Nirmal Hriday—a home for dying destitutes. Soon a hundred indigent folk, cot by cot, lined the rooms. (By 1985, Mother Teresa had 285 such homes worldwide).[25]

A man photographed workers on the day Sadhana, a high caste girl, started working at Nirmal Hriday. Her first task was to clean up a man reeking with gangrened maggot-filled sores. Suddenly she fled. "You've lost a worker," quipped the reporter. Mother Teresa went to chat with Sadhana. Soon Sadhana returned to her task. When completed, the reporter quizzed her, "What did Mother Teresa tell you?" "She told me to do it for Jesus," said

Sadhana, "I have been touching Christ's body for the last three hours!"[26]

How do we become the faithful church? Believers today want to make a "spiritual commitment," and walk away scot-free; but alas, we are forever obligated. Jesus is Lord! He modeled leadership and humble service. The aimless church, like leached-out salt, is useless! The would-be dynamic church integrates worship, family religious life, Christian education and pastoral discipleship techniques. Its goal is not cookie-cutter Christian look-alikes, but creative disciples who very consciously live first and foremost for the Kingdom of God.

Questions for Discussion:

1. If Jesus requires accountability, is your church faithful and fruitful?
2. Does the Great Commission need to shape the ministry of every church?
3. Why is church education a tired enterprise, and Sunday School declining?
4. Do "men" need peer groups? Do teachers/workers need hands-on training?
5. Does your church have a deliverance-posture of helping the hurting?

PRACTICING HIS PRESENCE: DEVOTIONAL PAUSE FOR BUSY DISCIPLES
Theme of the week — The Healthy Church

	Monday	Tuesday	Wednesday	Thursday	Friday
LIGHT on the pathway	Matthew 21:33-46	Luke 24:36-53	John 13:1-17	Matthew 10:1-16	Luke 4:14-30
LESSON for this day	Factor #46 Accountable	Factor #47 Planning	Factor #48 Educating	Factor #49 Hands-on Help	Factor #50 Liberating
LIFE in Jesus' way	Take time to Pray	Take time to Pray	Take time to Pray	Take time to Pray	Take time to Pray

PRACTICE HIS PRESENCE IN CHURCH THIS SUNDAY

Chapter

12

The Committed Christian

This book pulsates with one passion—salvation not only denotes forgiveness, it implies walking in newness. No Christians go scot-free. We block out the old; we lock in the new. As Christ sacrificed himself to pardon us; we offer ourselves in service to please him. Our daily lives become ongoing expressions of praise.

I also pursued a second theme: the church's place in a Christian's life. Weak, aged or decrepit as the church may appear, it is God's only model. God counts on His Church to do his work (Matthew 16:18). Healthy Christianity at all levels is church-related. Moreover, our despair-filled world is in constant flux. The church must continually update and upgrade ministries to meet current needs.

Normal life illustrates the need for adjusting to change. Take my wife and me, for example. As my 60th birthday neared, Susan Joann invited a few couples—of our age group. Jokingly we watched one fellow who already was 60 to see what faculties he had lost. He appeared brilliant! Some months later my wife helped me fix a fence. Using a new drill and bit, the wood seemed hard as iron. Nearing despair, I noticed the lever was on "Reverse!" "Oh, well," I sighed, "I'm 60."

After my wife turned 60, our preschool granddaughters came

for the weekend. We drove quite a distance to eat breakfast and catch a church service. Halfway, my wife gasped, "I forgot my shoes." Luckily, the cafeteria had no "No shirt-No shoe" sign! We ate, and drove straight home—laughing all the way. "If I go to church," Susan Joann quipped, "the pastor might take an offering 'for the destitute woman in our midst!' Well, what can you expect, I'm 60."

Seriously, as a couple we realize that what we want to do in life, must be done while we still have energy, health and a good memory. I suppose the predicament is akin to what each denomination, each church and each parishioner faces. Our separate worlds change so rapidly. Life is fluid. It is incumbent on all Christians to refocus priorities and to make mid-course corrections in ministry.

One consultant in futures' research is dismayed at how few denominations, churches and Christian organizations anticipate change. "I am even more concerned," Tom Sine avers, "at how few take seriously the importance of vision....I firmly believe the number-one crisis in the church today is a crisis of vision."[1] Vision is that dream that moves and motivates us.

Unfortunately, often Christians have a vision, so small, they need no divine help to fulfill it! That limited vision is my burning concern. Actually, the ethic of Jesus is so demanding, no human can perform it; and the needs of the world so pressing, no church can meet them. Only a vision—bigger than ourselves—will be adequate. I'm reminded of the story Robert Schuller loves to tell pastors. A man threw back all the large fish he caught—his frying pan was only 9 inches across! Any miniature-sized vision is self-limiting and robs God of honor!

We each need a vision of our potential in Christ. We need 5, 10 or 15-year plans. We need spiritual dreams. As a starter, this chapter will feature seven personal goals for Christians. They are sample ideas and can be applied to other areas as well. The community of faith is your support, your accountability group. Why not take control of your schedule and courageously shape the next ten years.

First — My "Following" Goal

The Anglican Bishop, Michael Marshall, observes "The problem with contemporary Christianity is that many people have settled for a facsimile of Christian freedom: running their own lives while at the same time, saying they believe in Christ....Believers have accepted a decaffeinated Christianity—it promises not to keep you awake at night."[2] They bypass the whole idea of Lordship.

Christianity, at the core, is following Christ—in loyalty, in obedience, in self-denial. Jesus warned that genuine discipleship may arouse opposition, often from the nearest relatives. In our faith commitment we count the cost, seek carefully our niche in the church and commit ourselves unreservedly to God's kingdom. That commitment calls for an unconditional allegiance to Jesus Christ. To be like Jesus is our passion. The purpose of our living is linked to the purpose of his dying. That is our cross-bearing task.

In our heart of hearts, the inner core of our being, the depth of commitment is tested. There it is visualized, verified and validated. There its genuineness is affirmed by the assuring work of the Holy Spirit (John 7:17, cf. Romans 8:16). My reader friend, if assurance of salvation escapes you, please seek out a Christian friend: a pastor, counselor or acquaintance. Help is available!

Recently I was moved as I read the frank and open statement of commitment by one of my contemporaries. On the fifteenth anniversary of Focus on the Family, an admirer asked founder James Dobson: "What could sink this ministry?" He answered: "...I would rather never have been born than to have this ministry ultimately wound Christian people, disillusion them and weaken their faith. My great passion is to serve out my years on this earth without stepping on one of the familiar land mines, such as pride, sexual sin, financial misdealings or internal conflict. May God help us to remain faithful!"[3] What an example for all visionary goal-setting disciples. That is "following" the Lord.

Second — My "Fishing" Goal

During our years in central Kansas, we spent an occasional holiday fishing at Marion Reservoir. The boys were teenagers and enjoyed our family-fun outings. My wife came from a "fishing" family and gladly went the second mile with food preparations, hook-baiting, and fish-cleaning. When bypassers queried, "How is luck?" our favorite reply was, "Great, we haven't fallen in yet!"

Imagine—for a moment—that we forgot our fishing gear and decided to fish by "presence." How long would we sit on shore before a fish jumped into our bucket? Remember, Jesus promised to turn his disciples into fishers of people (Matthew 4:19). Yet countless believers, expect by some streak of luck, to land a fish, as though their magical "presence" is enough. Generally, a full-orbed witness also includes "performance," like deeds of kindness, and "proclamation" like words of explanation.

Joe Aldrich, college president, is a champion of lifestyle evangelism. In a chapter, "Cashing In On Your Networks" he states a marvelous-measurable goal in his personal life. "My wife and I are praying that God will allow us to see six people from our networks trust Christ this year. Having identified those whom we believe to be most responsive, we anticipate that the Lord, our co-laborer, will work with, in, and through us to bring insight, conviction, and new-birth to our as-yet-unsaved friends."[4] That is faith. That is vision. That is goal-setting!

For my wife and myself, the pivotal points of our witness have been in the churches we pastored—via counseling, nursery work, preaching, teaching and leading discipleship covenant-groups. However, in the business world we have given countless gift-subscriptions of *Guideposts* magazine, as a gentle nonthreatening witness. We have been thrilled at open doors! One of our apartment renters asked me, her landlord, to preach her funeral. She even willed her fish aquarium to our boys. The funeral became a neighborhood opportunity to share the Christian faith.

Third — My "Working" Goal

Jesus depicted his disciples as salt, as light, as loving neighbors—serving with childlike spontaneity and servile humility. It is heartening to see current authors of evangelism/ministry books, like Keith Phillips, Tom Sine, Donald Posterski, Alan Kreider, Tony Campolo, Ray Bakke, and Joe Aldrich, to name a few, all emphasize creative hands-on methods of deeds of mercy, education and social action. Always, the word-deed combination is powerful, effective and Christlike.

Each Christian needs 10/15-year long-range goals, as well as 1-year short-range goals. While a handful in each church suffers from burnout fatigue, the majority drift along, devoid of goals and weak on commitment. Churches tend to overwork their willing workers, while the bulk are "spiritually" unemployed. This has to change. I urge parishioners not to spread themselves too thinly. That implies saying, "No" to a lot of phone calls; so they can excel in the few things they accept. Churches pay too little attention to gifting, calling, and training. As a result, leaders burn out trying to fill slots! (And many Christian Education departments have not been updated in 25 years.)

Driving with lights "blazing" (Matthew 5:16) means we use our respective spiritual gifts—whether serving or showing mercy, teaching or leading, giving or exercising hospitality, evangelizing or encouraging, pastoring or prophesying. Our community of faith can help discern gifts and affirm us. Well-planned small-groups are excellent avenues for gift-discernment, if good leadership is present. Al and Nadine Peters work with Prison Fellowship. They were motivated when their Bible Study group asked: "What can we each be doing for Jesus in our community?"

Habitat for Humanity got high visibility when a famous volunteer, Jimmy Carter, joined ranks. The founders, Millard and Linda Fuller, became millionaires while still in their twenties. But an affluent high-stepping lifestyle left them empty and unfulfilled. In a crisis period, on their knees, they covenanted to give their wealth away—to serve poor people. Today, Habitat for

Humanity works in 450 communities worldwide, offering afford-
able low-cost housing (with no interest, or down payment) to
deserving families. The monthly payments on the long-term loans
are much lower than prevailing rents, and the new owners agree
to donate hundreds of hours to help build a house for the next
family. Beautiful!

I am delighted to be part of a people that majors in humanitarian efforts like: disaster help, relief sales for world hunger,
meat canning for the displaced, emergency refugee aid, and self-
help thrift shops to assist artisans overseas. Mobilizing millions of
Christians in "joyful witness" through programs of charity could
impact our society and our world immeasurably. What a goal!

Fourth — My "Praying" Goal

Timothy M. Warner insists that the most powerful praying is
the positive kind: full of praise to God for his unending love, for
his sovereign ruling and reigning, and for his victory at Calvary
over all the enemies of God.[5]

In our day, a refreshing prayer movement is crumbling the
denominational, racial, and ethnic barriers among some 600
churches in New York City. David Bryant, National Director of the
Minneapolis-based "Concerts of Prayer" asserts that pastors are
meeting, networking and pooling resources. "We sense," he
claims, "God is doing something here that he is not doing in any
other urban center." In the Flushing/Queens area, the network
includes many Korean churches. About 1000 persons pray each
week at the predominantly black Brooklyn Tabernacle. And
recently, a bilingual meeting was held in the Bronx. Some 125
church leaders (Spanish/English) "wept openly as they prayed
for the city of 18 million."[6]

Each family needs to reevaluate its prayer patterns on a year-
ly basis. Goals must be tailor-made. During the writing of this
book, Susan Joann and I enjoy the freedom of the "empty nest."
Our devotional times are separate in the morning, but on a normal evening we have a joint hour of prayer (after a 2-mile walk,

supper and the evening TV-news). We begin with a newly memorized hymn (our first was: "Sweet Hour of Prayer"). We alternate with verbal praying in five-minute segments, and use prayer lists. Two things always amaze us: (1) the number of concerns and/or persons we actually uphold (about 200) in an hour, and (2) how fast the hour slips by. It becomes a high-point for our day.

Prayer is no quick-as-a-flash gimmick; it is an exacting discipline. It is a relationship. Many Christians lack the patience and persistence that spiritual warfare requires. We need a vision of our Heavenly Father who waits for us to pray unselfishly for ourselves, our families, our churches, our communities and our world! Why not set a goal to increase your prayer time by a specified number of minutes per day, and secondly, decide to network with others (Matthew 18:19-20). In this way, you will learn to enjoy his "Promise" and his "Presence."

Fifth — My "Forgiving" Goal

Forgiveness is the genius of Christianity. It grows out of love, and shows itself in "turned-cheek" attitudes and "second-mile" activities. As disciples of our Lord, we contradict our faith, the teachings of Jesus, and the very will of God, when we refuse to extend forgiveness to fellow travelers on the upward way. This is not negotiable. Why? Because God, the Heavenly Father, has forgiven us through repentance of sins, and through faith in Jesus Christ. He requires that the subjects of his kingdom forgive as he forgives.

As stated earlier, forgiveness is first and foremost anchored in mature love and becomes a full-blown expression of it. It gets tested to the extreme when Jesus suggests an endless repetition of its performance (70 X 7), even extending it to one's enemies. Once again, a supernatural ethic of radical discipleship mandates a supernatural enabling by the Holy Spirit.

My friend—practice forgiveness, release vindictiveness, leave all vengeance to God. In 35 years of pastoral work, God has taught me the absolute necessity of forgiving offenses on a daily basis—with no anger slopping over to poison my tomorrows! The reward is an inner peace—a wholesome therapy for bodily health and mental well-being. Don't overlook this goal. Its reward is awesome!

Sixth — My "Giving" Goal

The most sensitive nerve may not be the one in the tooth, or for that matter the one that connects the spine to the foot, but the one that runs to the pocketbook! Pastors have noticed that money topics often are delicate areas and tend to trigger quick responses. After all, money affects everything—it gets very personal. However, nowhere is goal-setting more needful. If we do not give the Lord a share right off the top, the high cost of living will consume our incomes.

Years ago, Sunday School teachers taught me that we were entrusted with the triad of time, of talents, and of treasures—for careful use in God's kingdom. If God is indeed the owner-lender and we are user-managers, the issue of accountability is real. Some writers downplay tithing and emphasize that "all" belongs to God. While true, in a sense, this approach hasn't adequately motivated giving.

In a recent survey of Anabaptist denominations, the median household income stood between $30,000 and $40,000. Of all households, 46% earned between $20,000 and $40,000 while 27% earned between $40,000 and $75,000. Of the six percent earning more than $75,000, one half earned over $100,000.[7]

Nevertheless, in my denomination, parishioners consume 95% of their wealth on themselves! (And few denominations do better!) What a travesty of stewardship! God gets 5% of our American/Canadian church riches. The rest we spend, invest or hoard. When people take discipleship seriously, they give right off the top, based on how God prospers. God deserves more than our measly-meager leftovers.

The old adage, "Do your giving while you're living, so you're knowing where it's going" carries some real wisdom. As Christians put their money to work and watch it, they are inspired. In fact, in my denomination, if each member gave his or her first tithe to the local church for its worldwide ministry, denominational giving would double. Beyond this, members with more maturity and added prosperity, could pick any needy project in the world for their second and third tithe, and God's work would be advanced. I recommend you start with a tithe (a tenth). I believe God will honor that (Luke 6:38); but if that seems too much, start somewhere. Few people, catching the joy of giving, want to downgrade later!

Our giving needs to rise out of our covenant with God. Giving is an act of faith. As we give God a portion—right off the top, we earn the right to ask God for wisdom in our money matters, and for the means to meet financial obligations.

Seventh — My "Relating" Goal

While relationships tend to be fragile, Jesus taught us to claim ownership to our rapport with others, and not to shift blame on them. When we live by the Golden Rule and exhibit a true Christlike spirit (one that refuses to damage bruised plants, or snuff out flickering lights—Matthew 12:20), we will have opportunities galore to build rapport redemptively.

Too quickly we label people hopeless, when in reality, fervent prayer and decisive-deliberate love can do miracles. We must take charge; Christ demands it. Here, precisely, goal-setting comes into play. Rather than seeing ourselves as hopeless victims in a chain of events, we need to see ourselves as key players on the stage of life—with every contact arranged providentially by our loving Heavenly Father. So all relationships become a sacred trust. Each has a divine purpose, which we are destined to bless, nurture and strengthen.

As a start, consider making a list of five or ten relationships that irritate you. Pray over them. Plan an action, or two, that will reflect a loving, caring attitude in each case. Of course, if you have wronged someone, ask forgiveness. A word of caution—do not let failure spoil your day. Don't allow others to control your feelings.

Draw your inspiration from prayer, scripture and affirmation from Christian brothers and sisters. Settle in for the long haul, and watch God transform relationships. God answers prayer.

Conclusion

All Christians, congregations and denominations need purpose, vision and goals. Haphazard aimless procedures will never make a dent in the astronomical needs of today's world. On the other hand, churches and individual disciples, intensely fired with vision, and freshly filled by the Holy Spirit, will make a powerful impact on their society (Luke 24:49).

These goals are not intended to encumber an already heavily-loaded schedule, nor to add guilt to an overloaded circuit of frustrations. Not for a minute! Our hope is to free, to inspire, to encourage. The process of taking charge—and actually controlling the accomplishments of any given month—is truly liberating. We are not helpless, hopeless victims; we are disciples who have a big say in what we really do to advance God's kingdom. Living by Christ-honoring goals brings pleasure to the heart of God, and joyful satisfaction to each of us.

Christians continually need renewal—a kind of shot in the arm. Concepts like "coasting downhill," "floating with stream," or "following the crowd," are not consistent with the principles of sound Christian discipleship. The Christian life, to put it plainly, is a climb. It is striving to stay on the "straight and narrow." It is following Christ in newness of life.[8]

When our youngest son, Nathan, was in junior high, I sometimes played basketball with him, on the drive in front of our house. One day we played "horse," and later took turns driving to the basket. I smugly viewed myself as adequately fulfilling my proper father-role. Suddenly he startled me, "Dad, pay attention!" True, I had watched the cars go by on First Street, I had waved a neighbor in her yard, and I had talked with a couple who sauntered by on their daily stroll. But Nathan wanted my total concentration! Christian friends, I can visualize our Heavenly Father saying to each of us, "My child, pay attention. I want your undivid-ed..." There you have it. That's the message of this book!

Questions for Discussion:

1. Tom Sine says the No. 1 church crisis is "lacking vision." Do you agree?
2. Do denominations, churches and individual disciples need 10 year goals?
3. What work could you do for Christ—if someone encouraged you?
4. Why is the prayer-level so low in most churches? What is the solution?
5. Do your goals with relationships and forgiveness need strengthening?

PRACTICING HIS PRESENCE: DEVOTIONAL PAUSE FOR BUSY DISCIPLES
Theme of the week — The Committed Christian

	Monday	Tuesday	Wednesday	Thursday	Friday
Light on the pathway	Luke 5:1-11	John 6:26-37	Matthew 9:35-38	Luke 16:1-15	John 15:9-13
Lesson for this day	Goal # 1 Follow	Goal # 2/3 Fish/Work	Goal # 4/5 Pray/Forgive	Goal # 6 Give	Goal # 7 Relate
Life in Jesus' way	Take time to pray	Take time to pray	Take time to pray	Take time to pray	Take time to pray

PRACTICE HIS PRESENCE IN CHURCH ON SUNDAY

DISCUSSION GUIDE FOR LEADERS

Teaching the Bible is a grand privilege—and awesome task. Persons highly gifted in teaching, lead classes or groups with amazing ease. Others may teach out of a sense of duty. They see an urgent need and volunteer to help. The weekly preparation can be a stressful chore; but we can have a deep sense of satisfaction if we have done our best for Christ. We appreciate the input or participation of each class member. We like Bible study materials that are designed to build up the ordinary church member.

The format of this book. Chapter 1 deals with crippling sicknesses in the typical church. Class discussion can be vigorous as it centers on the questions at the end of the chapter. The next chapters are foundational: Chapter 2 sees Christianity as following Christ in discipleship, Chapter 3 deals with costs in following, and Chapter 4 clarifies basic salvation truths—God's great rescue operation. Here is the heart of the Gospel.

Chapters 5 to 11 discuss the functional aspects of healthy churches—aspects that foster true faithfulness and fruitfulness: Chapter 5: Evangelizing. "Fishing" with Christlike sensitivity. Chapter 6: Serving. We serve the last, the lowest and the least. Chapter 7: Praying. Christians live in utter dependence on God. Chapter 8: Forgiving. Practicing cheek-turning/second-mile living. Chapter 9: Sharing. We manage money with Christlike generosity. Chapter 10: Relating. We reconcile and build rapport with others. Chapter 11: Strategizing. The Great Commission dictates strategy.

Chapter 12 urges all churches and Christians to set goals and aim toward higher ground. Rather than drifting aimlessly, the faithful fruitful community of faith determines its own destiny by following the mandates of Christ as Lord.

FOR EXPERIENCED TEACHERS.

You will find this material easy to teach. Apart from the opening and closing chapters, each chapter is centered on the life and teachings of Jesus—based on the Gospels. Each chapter also has multiple illustrations from daily life; so your problem will be—how to cover everything. You will have to be selective.

Remember—good teaching goes beyond the dissemination of information, facts, or doctrines. It helps pupils grapple with decision-making. It helps persons sort through key options in life and subsequently make wiser choices. Secondly, good teaching motivates and changes people. A wise teacher will have a goal in mind for each session: helping students understand some aspect of the gospel, relating it to daily life, and hoping to move people to a new or deeper walk with Christ.

FOR TEACHERS WITH LITTLE OR NO EXPERIENCE.

1. Be well-prepared. That's half the battle.
2. Start preparing a week before your class/group meeting.
3. Make an outline of your teaching plan:
   a. Use a relevant story to introduce your lesson.
   b. Look at each scripture passage highlighted in this chapter. Plan to touch on each; but select one or more to emphasize deeply.
   c. Look at the illustrations in the chapter and see if any strike you as especially important for confronting issues in today's world. Your group can evaluate these and suggest other options as well.
   d. Never forget to pray. The Holy Spirit loves to guide us in our difficult assignments. Pray that all persons will be touched and helped.
4. Normally, you teach one discipleship chapter per week. Make certain that each group member has access to the book—so each can prepare for the class.
5. Attempt to get good participation. Encourage some to talk more, and others less—so all have a chance to express themselves. Treat everyone with equal regard. Affirm the quiet hesitant pupil; challenge the talkative.

Conclusion. In your Bible study preparations, a good Bible commentary or Bible dictionary can be helpful. Your pastor will be delighted to assist you at any point. As author, I am praying that this book will be a help to your group.

Endnotes

Chapter One — The Crippled Church

1. C. Peter Wagner, *Your Church Can Be Healthy*. Creative Leadership Series, Lyle E. Schaller, Editor (Nashville: Abingdon, 1979), 9.
2. C. Peter Wagner, 29-120.
3. George Barna, *What Americans Believe* (Ventura, CA: Regal, 1991), 297.
4. George Barna, *The Frog in the Kettle* (Ventura, CA: Regal, 1990), 132.
5. Peter L. Benson & Carolyn H. Eklin, *Effective Christian Education: A National Study of Protestant Congregations* (Minneapolis: Search Institute, 1990), 2.
6. Benson & Eklin, 2.
7. Lyle E. Schaller, *It's a Different World* (Nashville: Abingdon, 1987), 62.
8. Ron Blue, *Master Your Money* (Nashville: Thomas Nelson, 1986), 13/flyleaf.
9. J. Howard Kauffman and Leo Driedger, *The Mennonite Mosaic* (Scottdale, PA: Herald, 1991), 145.
10. Bill Hull, *Jesus Christ, Disciplemaker*. The Foreword by Joe Aldrich, (Colorado Springs: NavPress, 1984), 7-8.
11. Dallas Willard, *The Spirit of the Disciplines* (San Francisco: Harper, 1988), 264-265 (Taken from *Christianity Today*, October 10, 1980).
12. Dallas Willard, 258.

Chapter Two — Following the Master

1. Bill Hull, *The Disciple Making Pastor* (Old Tappan, NJ: Revell, 1988), 15.
2. John R. Martin, *Ventures in Discipleship* (Scottdale, PA: Herald, 1984), 276.
3. *Effective Christian Education: A National Study of Protestant Congregations* (Minneapolis, MN: Search Institute, 1990), 66.
4. Charles Colson, *Against the Night* (Ann Arbor, MI: Servant, 1989), 10.
5. E. Calvin Beisner, *Prosperity and Poverty* (Westchester, IL: Crossway, 1988), 19f.
6. Robert E. Coleman, *The Master Plan of Discipleship* (Old Tappan, NJ: Revell, 1987), 117.
7. John Bunyon, *The Holy War*. Wycliffe Christian Classics (Chicago: Moody Press, 1956), 41-145.
8. John Bunyon, 327-336.
9. F. Franklin Wise, "Some Implications of Wesleyan." *Self Esteem*, Ed. Craig W. Ellison (Oklahoma City: Southwestern Press, 1976), 47.
10. F. F. Bruce, *The Hard Sayings of Jesus* (Downers Grove, IL: InterVarsity, 1983), 162.
11. Rolf Zettersten, *Dr. Dobson: Turning Hearts Toward Home* (Dallas: Word, 1989), 24.
12. Donald B. Kraybill, *The Upside-Down Kingdom*. Revised (Scottdale, PA: Herald, 1990), 122.

13. John C. Wenger, *Even Unto Death* (Richmond, VA: John Knox, 1961), flyleaf.
14. John F. MacArthur, *The Gospel According to Jesus* (Grand Rapids, MI: Academie Books, 1988), XIV.
15. John Howard Yoder, *The Priestly Kingdom* (Notre Dame, IN: University of Notre Dame Press, 1984), 194.
16. John Howard Yoder, 195.
17. Myron Augsburger, *Matthew,* The Communicator's Commentary (Waco, TX: Word, 1982), 231.
18. George E. Ladd, *A Theology of the New Testament* (Grand Rapids: Eerdmans, 1974), 64.
19. Walter A. Elwell, *Revelation,* Evangelical Commentary of the Bible (Grand Rapids: Baker Book, 1989), 1207.

Chapter Three — Counting the Cost

1. Donald McGavran, *How Churches Grow* (New York: Friendship, 1957), 97.
2. George Ladd, *A Theology of the New Testament,* 67.
3. Ladd, 626.
4. Ladd, 69.
5. F. F. Bruce, *The Hard Sayings of Jesus,* 119.
6. Walter C. Kaiser Jr., *Hard Sayings of the Old Testament* (Downers Grove, IL: InterVarsity, 1988), 245.
7. David Swartz, *The Magnificent Obsession* (Colorado Springs: NavPress, 1990), 199f.
8. Albert H. Epp, *The Golden Stairway Discipleship Course.* Revised (Henderson, NE: Stairway Discipleship Inc., 1990), 2.
9. John A. Martin, *Luke,* The Bible Knowledge Commentary (Wheaton, IL: Victor, 1983), 243.
10. Quoted in John C. Wenger, *Even Unto Death,* 51.
11. Wenger, 52f.
12. Eugene C. Roehlkepartain, "What Makes Faith Mature?" *Christian Century* (9 May 1990), 496.
13. Peter L. Benson & Carolyn H. Eklin, *Effective Christian Education,* 38.
14. John F. MacArthur, *The Gospel According to Jesus,* 179f.
15. John F. MacArthur, Foreword by James Montgomery Boice, XI-XII.
16. Jim Petersen, *Living Proof* (Colorado Springs: NavPress, 1989), 84.
17. Peter Benson & Carolyn Eklin, 9.
18. Benson & Eklin, 57.
19. Penelope J. Stokes, *Grace Under Pressure* (Colorado Springs: NavPress, 1990), 62.
20. Benson & Eklin, 58.
21. On CBS News (6 May 1992) Charles Osgood announced that Desert Storm had cost a total of 61 billion dollars with the USA paying 7.4 billion.
22. Myron Augsburger, *Mastering Outreach and Evangelism.* Co-authors, Calvin Ratz, Frank Tillapaugh (Portland, OR: Multnomah, 1990), 94.
23. Myron Augsburger, *Mastering Outreach,* 17-24.
24. George E. Ladd, *A Theology of the New Testament,* 132.
25. Archibald D. Hart, *15 Principles For Achieving Happiness* (Dallas: Word, 1988), 16.

26. Taken from *My Heart—Christ's Home* by Robert Boyd Munger. ©1954 by InterVarsity Christian Fellowship of the USA. Used by permission of InterVarsity Press, P.O. Box 1400, Downers Grove, IL 60515.
27. David Mains, "Prophet Amos" and Interview with Leonard Ravenhill (Chapel of the Air Radio, ca 1985), Cassette # 600.
28. Corrie ten Boom (with John/Elizabeth Sherill) *The Hiding Place* (Minneapolis: Chosen Books, 1971), 146.

Chapter Four — Born For Eternity

1. George E. Ladd, *A Theology of the New Testament*, 87.
2. Simon Kistemaker, *The Parables of Jesus* (Grand Rapids: Baker, 1980), 221.
3. Myron Augsburger, *Matthew,* The Communicator's Commentary, 216.
4. Harold Lindsell, *Missionary Principles and Practice* (Westwood, NJ: Revell, 1955), 69.
5. George Barna, *What Americans Believe*, 191-199.
6. J. Howard Kauffman and Leo Driedger, *The Mennonite Mosaic*, 70.
7. Clark H. Pinnock, *A Wideness in God's Mercy* (Grand Rapids, MI: Zondervan, 1992), 156-157. (A provocative book on current soteriology & Christology.)
8. Ray Charles Jarman (with Russell Bixler), *Sunrise at Evening* (Monroeville, PA: Whitaker, 1975), 122. (Used by permission.)
9. Jarman, 129.
10. T. M. Dorman, "The Virgin Birth of Jesus Christ," *The International Standard Bible Encyclopedia*, Vol. 4 (Grand Rapids, MI: Eerdmans, 1988), 990. This is an excellent up-to-date treatment.
11. Myron Augsburger, *The Christ-Shaped Conscience* (Wheaton, IL: Victor, 1990), 13.
12. J. Gresham Machen, *The Virgin Birth of Jesus Christ*. Reprint (Grand Rapids, MI: Baker, 1985), 334-339.
13. John R. Martin, *Ventures in Discipleship*, 67.
14. Dallas Willard, *The Spirit of the Disciplines*, 32-38.
15. John C. Wenger, *Introduction to Theology* (Scottdale, PA: Herald, 1954), 273-275.
16. Philip Mason, *Niagara and the Daredevils* (Niagara Gallery, 1969), 6.
17. John R. Martin, *Ventures in Discipleship*, 287.
18. E. J. Tinsley quoted in Michael Griffiths, *The Example of Jesus* (Downers Grove, IL: InterVarsity, 1985), 73.
19. John C. Wenger, *Even Unto Death*, 95.
20. Franz Agricola in 1582; quoted in Harold S. Bender, *The Anabaptist Vision* (Scottdale, PA: Herald, 1944), 24.
21. Howard A. Snyder, *The Radical Wesley and Patterns For Church Renewal* (Downers Grove, IL: InterVarsity, 1980), 45-47.
22. John F. MacArthur, Jr., *The Gospel According to Jesus*, 183.
23. George R. Brunk III, "Conversion," *The Mennonite Encyclopedia*, Vol. 5 (Scottdale, PA: Herald, 1990), 205.
24. John C. Wenger, *Introduction to Theology*, 272-273.
25. E. Stanley Jones, *Conversion* (Nashville, TN: Abingdon, 1959), 185.
26. Donald B. Kraybill, *The Upside-Down Kingdom*. Revised, 266.

27. Richard B. Gardner, *Matthew,* Believers Church Bible Commentary (Scottdale, PA: Herald, 1991), 86.

Chapter Five — Fishing for People

1. Arnell Motz, Editor, *Reclaiming a Nation* (Richmond, BC: Church Leadership Library, 1990), 5, 135.
2. Motz, 7.
3. A. B. Bruce, *The Training of the Twelve* (Grand Rapids: Kregel, 1971), 11.
4. *NIV Study Bible,* Ed. Kenneth Barker (Grand Rapids: Zondervan, 1985), 1480.
5. Arthur McPhee, *Friendship Evangelism* (Grand Rapids: Zondervan, 1978), 44-48.
6. George Barna, *How to Find Your Church* (Minneapolis, MN: World Wide, 1989), 88.
7. Donald C. Posterski, *Reinventing Evangelism* (Downers Grove, IL: InterVarsity, 1989), 153.
8. Posterski, 144.
9. Donald Mc Gavran, *Understanding Church Growth* (Grand Rapids: Eerdmans, 1970), 198.
10. C. Wayne Zunkel, *Church Growth Under Fire* (Scottdale, PA: Herald, 1987), 105ff.
11. Joseph Aldrich, *Gentle Persuasion* (Portland, OR: Multnomah, 1988), 98f.
12. Gerhard Kittel, *Theological Dictionary of the New Testament,* Vol. IV, Ed. Geoffrey Bromiley, (Grand Rapids: Eerdmans, 1967), 441.
13. Richard B. Gardner, *Matthew,* Believers Church Bible Commentary, 405.
14. Kenneth Scott Latourette, *Three Centuries of Advance,* A History of the Expansion of Christianity, Vol. 3 (New York: Harper & Brothers, 1939), 25.
15. Franklin H. Littell, *The Anabaptist View of the Church,* Revised (Boston: Starr King, 1958), 112.
16. David A. Shank, "Anabaptists and Mission," in *Anabaptism and Mission,* ed. Wilbert R. Shenk (Scottdale, PA: Herald, 1984), 213.
17. Wolfgang Schaeufele, "The Missionary Vision and Activity of the Anabaptist Laity," in *Anabaptism and Mission,* 79.
18. Nanne van der Zijpp, "From Anabaptist Missionary Congregation to Mennonite Seclusion," in *Anabaptism and Mission,* 126.
19. Donald R. Jacobs, *Pilgrimage in Mission* (Scottdale, PA: Herald, 1983), 15.
20. John H. Yoder/Alan Kreider, "The Anabaptists," *Eerdmans' Handbook to the History of Christianity* (Grand Rapids: Eerdmans, 1977), 403.
21. Donald R. Jacobs, *Pilgrimage in Mission,* 16.
22. Wilbert R. Shenk, "Highlights...1945-1990," *Mennonite World Handbook,* ed. Diether Gotz Lichdi (Carol Stream, IL: Mennonite World Conf., 1990), 129.
23. Wilbert Shenk, "Mission Boards," *The Mennonite Encyclopedia,* Vol. 5, 593.
24. Estimate based on study by Andrew R. Shelly. Definitive research needed.
25. *Living in Faithful Evangelism,* Introductory Material, 4th ed.(Newton, KS: General Conference Mennonite & Mennonite Church, 1991), 3-23.
26. Compiled by Andrew R. Shelly, Associate pastor (1986-1992).
27. Centennial Committee, *History of the Emmaus Mennonite Church* (Hillsboro, KS: Kindred Press, 1978), 90-91.
28. From letter to participants of a Seminar at Richmond, BC (April, 1991).

29. Taken from *Out of the Saltshaker & Into the World* by Rebecca Manley Pippert. ©1979 by InterVarsity Christian Fellowship of the USA. Used by permission of InterVarsity Press, P.O. Box 1400, Downers Grove, IL 60515.
30. Posterski, *Reinventing Evangelism*, 146f.
31. Posterski, 147.
32. Wilbert R. Shenk, Editor, *Exploring Church Growth* (Grand Rapids: Eerdmans, 1983), Preface, vii.
33. Ray Bakke, *The Urban Christian* (Downers Grove, IL: InterVarsity, 1987), 14.
34. Ray Bakke, 159.
35. Keith Phillips, *No Quick Fix* (Ventura, CA: Regal, 1985), 144-148.
36. George Barna, *The Frog in the Kettle*, 129-130.
37. Joe Aldrich, *Gentle Persuasion*, 186.

Chapter Six — Showing Good Works

1. F. F. Bruce, *The Hard Sayings of Jesus*, 38.
2. Jim Wallis, *The Call To Conversion* (San Francisco: Harper & Row, 1981), 13.
3. John C. Wenger, Ed., *The Complete Writings of Menno Simons*, 307.
4. Alan Kreider, *Journey Toward Holiness* (Scottdale, PA: Herald, 1987), 242.
5. Charles Colson, *Transforming Society* (Colo. Springs: NavPress, 1988), 8.
6. Minutes of Mennonite Disaster Service (August, 1980), per August Franz.
7. Morris E. Sider, "Christian Neff Hostetter, Jr.," in *Something Beautiful For God*, Editor, C. J. Dyck (Scottdale, PA: Herald, 1981), 184f.
8. C. S. Lewis, *Mere Christianity* (London: Collins, 1971), 172.
9. Raelene Phillips, *The One Year Book of Family Devotions* by the Children's Bible Hour (Wheaton, IL: Tyndale, 1988), 117.
10. Lawrence O. Richards, *Teacher's Commentary* (Wheaton, IL: Victor, 1987), 673.
11. Lawrence O. Richards, 674.
12. Paul Welter, *Learning From Children* (Wheaton, IL: Tyndale, 1984), 21.
13. Paul Welter, 168.
14. Paul Welter, 111.
15. Paul Welter, 95.
16. John Haggai, *Be Careful What You Call Impossible* (Eugene, OR: Harvest, 1989), 191.
17. John Drescher, *Seven Things Children Need*. Second Edition (Scottdale, PA: Herald, 1988), 46.
18. Edward J. Carnell, *The Case For Orthodox Theology* (Philadelphia: Westminster, 1959), 123.
19. Donald C. Posterski, *Reinventing Evangelism*, 157.
20. Elmer Neufeld, "The Mennonite Central Committee," *The Mennonite Encyclopedia*, Vol. 5, 561.
21. Atlee Beechy, "Relief Work," *Mennonite Encyclopedia*, Vol. 5, 763.
22. Peter J. Dyck, "A Theology of Service," *Mennonite Quarterly Review*, XLIV (Goshen, IN: Mennonite Historical Society, July, 1970), 273.
23. Quoted by Peter J. Dyck, 265.
24. Myron S. Augsburger, *The Christ-Shaped Conscience*, 168.

Chapter Seven — Living by Prayer

1. Earl O. Roe, Editor, *Dream Big: The Henrietta Mears Story* (Ventura, CA: Regal Books, 1990), 3.
2. Earl Roe, 336.
3. Earl Roe, 21.
4. Earl Roe, 330-357.
5. D. A. Carson, *Matthew,* The Expositor's Bible Commentary (Grand Rapids, MI: Zondervan, 1984), 170.
6. George Barna, *The Frog in the Kettle,* 211 (based on 1988 Population Survey, Census Bureau).
7. George Ladd, *A Theology of the New Testament,* 115.
8. John Howard Yoder, *The Politics of Jesus* (Grand Rapids: Eerdmans, 1972), 66-74.
9. David Augsburger, *When Caring is Not Enough,* 76.
10. Jerry Bridges, *The Pursuit of Holiness* (Colo. Springs, CO: NavPress, 1978), 96.
11. Kurt Koch's books have been reprinted in America, one example is still very relevant: *The Occult ABC's* (Grand Rapids, MI: Kregel Pub., 1981).
12. Oswald J. Smith, *The Revival We Need* (London: Marshall, Morgan, Scott, 1933), 35.
13. William Barclay, *The Gospel of John.* Revised, Vol. 2 (Philadelphia, PA: Westminster Press, 1975), 204-207.
14. Peter Benson & Carolyn Eklin, *Effective Christian Education,* 51.
15. Search Institute, *Effective Christian Education,* 26.
16. Abram G. Conrad, "Religious Beliefs and Participation." *Gospel Herald* (7 August 1990), 542.
17. See overview: Leon Morris, *NIV Study Bible* (Grand Rapids, MI: Zondervan, 1985), 1630.
18. Quoted by E. M. Bounds, *The Possibility of Prayer,* Reprint (Grand Rapids, MI: Baker, 1979), 52.
19. Mark I. Bubeck, *The Satanic Revival* (San Bernardino, CA: Here's Life Publishers, 1991), 64-66.
20. Kenneth Scott Latourette, *A History of The Expansion of Christianity,* Vol. 3, 47.
21. Howard A. Snyder, *The Radical Wesley...,* 3 and 26.
22. Quoted by J. I. Packer, *A Quest For Godliness* (Wheaton, IL: Crossway, 1990), 325f.
23. J. Edwin Orr, *The Second Great Evangelical Awakening* (London: Marshall, Morgan & Scott, 1955), 35.
24. Peter J. Dyck, "Refugees." *The Mennonite Encyclopedia,* Vol. 5, 754.
25. Frank H. Epp, *Mennonite Exodus* (Altona, MB: Friesen & Sons, 1962), 366.
26. Peter J. Dyck, *Up From the Rubble* (Scottdale, PA: Herald, 1991), 152-205.
27. D. A. Carson, *Matthew,* The Expositor's Bible Commentary, Vol. 8, 187.
28. Bruce Larson, *Luke,* The Communicator's Commentary, Vol. 3, 189.
29. Fred W. Hoffman, *Revival Times in America* (Boston: W.A.Wilde, 1956), 86f.
30. Archibald Hart, *15 Principles For Achieving Happiness,* 174.
31. Rosalind Rinker, *Prayer—Conversing With God* (Grand Rapids, MI: Zondervan, 1959), 7.
32. Earl Roe, *Dream Big, The Henrietta Mears Story,* 59-69.

33. See Mark 1:35, 6:46; Luke 5:16, 6:12, 9:18, 11:1 and 22:41.
34. Levi Keidel, "Can Prayers Change the Course of History?" The editorial of *The Mennonite Weekly Review* (17 January 1991).
35. Myron Augsburger, *The Christ-Shaped Conscience*, 83.

Chapter Eight — Forgiving Without Limits

1. Paul Welter, *Learning From Children*, 99.
2. George Barna, *The Frog in The Kettle*, 137-138.
3. George E. Ladd, *A Theology of The New Testament*, 115.
4. Myron Augsburger, *The Christ-Shaped Conscience*, 41.
5. D. A. Carson, *Matthew*, The Expositor's Bible Commentary, 407.
6. George Ladd, 115.
7. John Howard Yoder, *The Politics of Jesus*, 134.
8. David Augsburger, "Forgiveness." *The Mennonite Encyclopedia*. Vol. 5, 308.
9. David Augsburger, *Pastoral Counseling Across Cultures* (Philadelphia, PA: Westminster, 1986), 111-143.
10. Archibald D. Hart, *15 Principles For Achieving Happiness*, 60-61.
11. D. A. Carson, *Matthew*, 158-160.
12. David Jacobsen, "Remember Them." *Guideposts* (Carmel, NY: March, 1991), 2f.
13. Marian Hostetler, *They Loved Their Enemies* (Scottdale, PA: Herald, 1988), 79f.
14. Quoted by David Swartz in *The Magnificent Obsession*, 125.
15. Marian Hostetler, *They Loved Their Enemies*, 86.
16. Alan Loy McGinnis, *The Friendship Factor* (Minneapolis, MN: Augsburg, 1979), 159f.
17. Archibald Hart, *15 Principles For Achieving Happiness*, 65.
18. David Augsburger, *Caring Enough To Forgive* (Ventura, CA: Regal, 1981), 30.
19. David Augsburger, 31.
20. David Augsburger, 6 (In the Prologue of the second half).
21. David Augsburger, 9-75 (The Second Half). This book I highly recommend.
22. Archibald Hart, 3.
23. Quoted by Archibald Hart, 62.

Chapter Nine — Giving With Generosity

1. Centennial Committee, *History of the Emmaus Mennonite Church* (Hillsboro, KS: Kindred Press, 1978), 79.
2. John M. Drescher, "The Price of Wealth," *Christian Leader* (11-6-90), 6.
3. Daniel Kauffman, *Managers With God* (Scottdale, PA: Herald, 1990), 152f.
4. E. Earle Ellis, *The Gospel of Luke*, The Century Bible (London: Thomas Nelson and Sons, 1966), 200f.
5. Ron Blue, *Master Your Money* (1986), 13.
6. Tony Campolo, *Wake Up America* (San Francisco: Harper/Zondervan, 1991), XII.
7. Larry Burkett, *The Coming Economic Earthquake* (Chicago: Moody, 1991), 214.
8. Tom Sine, *Wild Hope* (Dallas, TX: Word, 1991), 202.
9. Paul Levertoff, "First Fruits," *The International Standard Bible Encyclopedia*, Vol. II (Grand Rapids, MI: Eerdmans, 1982), 307.
10. Daniel Kauffman, *Managers of God*, 75.

11. Donald B. Kraybill, *The Upside-Down Kingdom*, 139. (See Ronald J. Sider, *Rich Christians in an Age of Hunger* (Dallas: Word, 1990), 154-157.
12. Daniel Kauffman, *Managers of God*, 78.
13. Waldo J. Werning, *Supply-Side Stewardship* (St. Louis, MO: Concordia, 1986), 45f.
14. George Barna, *The Frog in the Kettle*, 213.
15. Tom Sine, *Wild Hope*, 273f.
16. George Barna, *The Frog in the Kettle*, 211, 213.
17. Dallas Willard, *The Spirit of the Disciplines*, 175f.
18. Betty Munson, "His Two Strips of Wheat," *Guideposts*. (Dec. 1991), 24-27.
19. Bruce Larson, *Luke*, The Communicator's Commentary, Vol. 3, 185.

Chapter Ten — Building Reconciling Relationships

1. David Augsburger, *When Caring Is Not Enough*, 17.
2. David Augsburger, 75.
3. David Augsburger, 77-78.
4. Myron Augsburger, *The Christ-Shaped Conscience*, 123.
5. F. F. Bruce, *The Hard Sayings of Jesus*, 50.
6. D. A. Carson, *Matthew*, The Expositor's Bible Commentary, 150.
7. Peter L. Benson & Carolyn H. Eklin, *Effective Christian Education...*, 18.
8. Quote in Paul M. Lederach, *A Third Way* (Scottdale, PA: Herald, 1980), 46.
9. Paul M. Lederach, 47.
10. Richard J. Foster, *Celebration of Discipline*. Revised Edition (San Francisco, CA: Harper & Row, 1988), 177.
11. I.M.Friedmann, *Helping Resolve Conflict* (Scottdale, PA: Herald, 1990), 82.
12. Dan B. Allender and Tremper Longman III, *Bold Love* (Colorado Springs, CO: NavPress, 1992), 188.
13. Helen Hostetler, *A Time To Love* (Scottdale, PA: Herald, 1989), 16-17.
14. Helen Hostetler, 31.
15. Harold H. Bloomfield, *Making Peace With Your Parents* (New York: Random House—Ballantine Books, 1985), 8.

Chapter Eleven — The Healthy Church

1. In the Hebrew—a striking poetic play on words (cf. Isaiah 5:2 and 5:7).
2. George E. Ladd, *New Testament Theology*, 199. The disciples are a faithful remnant. Another view is that "others" refers to Gentiles (Acts 13:46).
3. Tom Sine, *Wild Hope*, 197.
4. Eugene C. Roehlkepartian, "What makes faith mature?" *Christian Century* (9 May 1990), 496.
5. "Rating the Charities," *Christianity Today* (10 February 1992), 54.
6. Albert H. Epp, *Golden Stairway Discipleship Course*, 46 (8-year project).
7. The Risen Christ, Lord of history, evaluates his church (Revelation 1-3).
8. Roehlkepartian, *Christian Century* (9 May 1990), 498.
9. Peter Benson and Carolyn Eklin, *Effective Christian Education*, 72.
10. Benson and Eklin, 9.
11. Benson and Eklin, 15-18.
12. Benson and Eklin, 53-58.

13. George Barna, *The Frog in the Kettle*, 149.
14. Benson and Eklin, 66.
15. Bill Hull, *The Disciple Making Pastor*, 25-27.
16. Bill Hull, 212-250.
17. Bill Hull, 199-200.
18. Bill Hull, *The Disciple Making Church* (Old Tappan, NJ: Fleming H. Revell, 1990), 205-220. (Bill Hull is the Executive Director of Church Ministries for the Evangelical Free Church of America.)
19. The Jubilee theme is prominent in the writings of John Howard Yoder, Ronald J. Sider, Donald B. Kraybill and Daniel Kauffman.
20. Augsburger, Ratz, Tillapaugh, *Mastering Outreach & Evangelism*, 52-54.
21. Debra Wall, "A Different Kind of Healing," *The Mennonite* (10 March 1992), 106.
22. Augsburger, Ratz, Tillapaugh, 95.
23. Dick Innes, *I Hate Witnessing* (Ventura, CA: Regal, 1983), 179-182.
24. Bob and Gretchen Passantino, *When the Devil Dares Your Kids* (Ann Arbor, MI: Servant, 1991), 15-16. The case of Laurel is a true-to-life vignette.
25. Dominique Lapierre, *The City of Joy* (New York, NY: Warner, 1985), 247-256.
26. D. Jeanene Watson, *Teresa of Calcutta: Serving the Poorest of the Poor* (Milford, MI: Mott Media, 1984), 71-74.

Chapter Twelve — The Committed Christian

1. Tom Sine, *Wild Hope*, 298-312.
2. Arnell Motz, Editor, *Reclaiming a Nation*, 149.
3. Interviewed by the editors of *Focus on the Family* magazine, Colorado Springs, CO (March, 1992), 13.
4. Joe Aldrich, *Gentle Persuasion*, 142.
5. Timothy M. Warner, *Spiritual Warfare* (Wheaton, IL: Crossway, 1991), 139.
6. Edward E. Plowman, Editor, *National and International Religion Report*, Publisher: Stephen Wike (Roanoke, VA: May, 1992), 4.
7. Kauffman and Driedger, *The Mennonite Mosaic*, 39-40.
8. Quote from Albert H. Epp, *Golden Stairway Discipleship Course*, 2.

NAME INDEX

Agee, Joe 214-215
Agricola, Franz 74
Aldrich, Joe 6, 92, 104, 256-257
Aldrich, Ruthe 104, 256-257
Allender, Dan B. 221
Amin, Idi 171
Augsburger, Clarence 161
Augsburger, David 135, 166, 167, 173, 174, 175, 205, 206, 207
Augsburger, Esther 50, 127, 247
Augsburger, Myron 28, 50-51, 63, 68, 126-127, 152, 161, 208, 247

Bakke, Ray 85, 103, 257
Barclay, William 136
Barna, George 4, 63, 90, 104, 123, 134, 158-159, 193, 195, 242
Beechy, Atlee 125
Beisner, E. Calvin 19
Bender, Harold S. 7, 12, 74
Benson, Peter 4-5, 17, 46-47, 49, 113, 137, 217, 237-239, 242
Benson, Carmen 66-67
Bibby, Reginald 84, 101
Blaurock, George 45
Blinco, Joe 148
Blondin-the Great 72-73
Bloomfield, Harold 222-223
Blue, Ron 5, 181-182
Boehler, Peter 141
Boice, M. James 47
Bonhoeffer, Dietrich 7
Bontrager, G. Edwin 96
Boom, Corrie ten 55-56, 122
Bounds, E. M. 138
Bouwens, Leenaert 46
Bridges, Jerry 135
Bright, Bill 131
Brown, R. R. 148
Bruce, A. B. 85, 244
Bruce, F. F. 22, 41, 108, 212
Brunk, George III 76
Bryant, David 258
Bubeck, Mark I. 140, 248
Bunyon, John 18-19
Burkett, Larry 183
Bush, George (ex-President) 50

Calvin, John 229
Campolo, Tony 183, 257

Carnell, Edward J. 124
Carson, D. A. 133, 145, 165, 168, 214
Carter, Jimmy (ex-President) 257
Catherine II 95
Chadwick, Samuel 138
Chafer, Lewis Sperry 75
Chafin, Kenneth 21
Clay, General Lucius 143
Coleman, Robert E. 19
Colson, Charles 15, 18, 111
Conrad, Abram C. 137

Delitzsch, F. 184
Denck, Hans 12
Detweiler, Bill & Ruth 96
Dobson, James 23-24, 255
Dobson, James, Sr. 23
Dorman, T. M. 67
Drescher, John 123, 179
Driedger, Leo 5-6, 63, 260
Duerksen, John 11
Dyck, Elfrieda 142-144
Dyck Peter J. 126, 142-144

Earl, Ralph 30
Edwards, Jonathan 135, 141
Eklin, Carolyn 4-5, 17, 46-47, 49, 137, 217, 237-239, 242
Elliot, Elizabeth 103
Ellis, E. Earle 181
Elwell, Walter A. 32
Enz, Jacob 127
Epp, Alexis & Brittany 227, 253-254
Epp, Frank H. 142
Epp, J. Gregory 48, 157, 191
Epp, John E. 115
Epp, John Jr. 37, 180, 189, 191
Epp, John Sr. 116, 188-189
Epp, Marie Harder 189
Epp, Nathan 157, 262
Epp, Ruth 92
Epp, Steven W. 157, 190
Epp, Sylvia 176
Epp, Vernelle 16
Evans, Coleen & Louis Jr. 131

Father Jenko 169
Finney, Charles 146
Foster, Richard 219
Franz, August 113-114

Frederick, the Great 95
Friedmann, I. M. 220
Fuller, Linda & Millard 257-258

Gardner, Richard B. 79, 93
Gesswein, Armin 148
Graham, Billy 15, 83
Graham, James 170-171
Gravelet, Jean Francois,
  "the Great Blondin" 72-73
Grebel, Conrad 45
Griffiths, Michael 74

Haggai, John 102-103, 122
Halverson, Richard 131
Hart, Archibald D. 52, 146-147, 168,
  173, 176
Harvey, Paul 59
Hendricks, Howard 244
Hodges, Zane 26, 75
Hostetler, Helen 221-222
Hostetler, John 125
Hostetler, Marian 169, 171
Hostetter, C. N. Jr. 114-115
Hull, Bill 16, 243-244
Hus, Jan 109
Hut, Hans 94

Innes, Dick 247-248
Ironsides, Harry 133

Jacobs, Anna Ruth 96
Jacobs, Donald R. 95, 96, 171
Jacobsen, David 169
Jarman, Ray Charles 64-67
Jenko, Father 169
Jensen, Hal 15
Johnston, Don 88
Jones, E. Stanley 7, 77
Judson, Adoniram 63

Kaiser, Walter C. Jr. 41
Kauffman, Daniel 180, 185, 192
Kauffman, J. Howard 5-6, 63, 260
Kauffman, Milo 180, 185-186
Keidel, Levi 152
Kistemaker, Simon 62
Kittel, Gerhard 93
Kivengere, Festo 171
Klassen, C. F. 143-144
Koch, Kurt 136, 148
Kraemer, Henrik 15
Kraybill, Donald B. 25, 78-79, 187

Kreider, Alan 95, 110-111, 257

Ladd, George E. 30, 39-40, 52, 62, 134,
  160, 166, 229
Lapierre, Dominique 249
Larson, Bruce 146, 199-200
Latourette, Kenneth Scott 93, 141
Lederach, Paul M. 218
Levertoff, Paul 185
Lewis, C. S. 116, 135-136
Lindsell, Harold 63
Littell, Franklin 12, 94, 109-110
Longman, Tremper III 221
Luther, Martin 15, 74, 93, 109, 229
Luwum, Archbishop 171

MacArthur, John Jr. 26, 47, 75
Machen, J. Gresham 68
Mains, David 54-55
Mains, Karen, 54, 176
Marshall, Michael 255
Martin, John A. 45
Martin, John R. 17, 71, 73
Mason, Philip 72-73
McCluskey, George 23
McGavran, Donald 15, 38, 85, 91, 102
McGinnis, Alan Loy 172
McNeill, John 22
McPhee, Arthur 86-87
Mears, Henrietta 131-132, 147-148, 152
Melanchton, Philipp 93
Miller, Marilyn 96
Moley, Joshua 117
Moody, Dwight L. 142
Morken, David 43, 148
Morris, Leon 138
Mother Teresa 15, 249-250
Motz, Arnell 84-85, 255
Mouw, J. Arthur 6, 140
Munger, Robert B. 52-53, 148-149
Munson, Betty & Cliff 198
Murphy, Robert 144
Mylander, Charles 11

Neufeld, Elmer 125

Orr, J. Edwin 142, 148
Ortiz, Juan Carlos 85
Osgood, Charles 265

Packer, J. I. 141, 271
Paul I 95
Paul, the Apostle 229

Passantino, Gretchen & Bob 248
Peale, Norman Vincent 203-204
Peters, Nadine & Al 257
Petersen, Jim 48
Phillips, Keith 85, 103, 257
Phillips, Raelene 117
Pinnock, Clark 64
Pippert, Rebecca 15, 99-100
Plowman, Edward 258
Pope John Paul 176
Posterski, Donald 85, 90, 101, 124, 125, 257

Ravenhill, Leonard 54-55
Ray, Bishop Chandu 103
Richards, Lawrence O. 118-119
Rinker, Rosalind 147
Rodeheaver, Homer 199
Roe, Earl O. 147-148, 131-132
Roehlkepartain, Eugene C. 46, 230, 238
Rudy, John 180

Sattler, Michael 229
Sawatzky, Jack 156
Schaeufele, Wolfgang 95
Schaller, Lyle 3, 5, 131
Schmidt, Henry J. 96-97
Schuller, Robert 254
Sedelmair, Elizabeth, 95
Shank, David A. 94
Sheen, Bishop Fulton 7
Shelly, Andrew R. 96
Shenk, Wilbert R. 94-96, 102, 269
Shoemaker, Samuel 6
Sider, Morris 115
Sider, Ronald J. 187
Simons, Menno 15, 45-46, 109-110
Sine, Tom 183, 193, 230, 254, 257
Smith, Oswald J. 136
Snyder, Howard A. 75, 141
Sokolovsky, Marshal 144
St. Francis of Assisi 224
St. Ignatius Loyola 229
Stokes, Penelope J. 49
Sullivan, Harry Stack 116, 158

Swartz, David 42, 170

Taylor, Kenneth 165
Thiessen, Mary 103
Tillapaugh, Frank 246-247
Toews, J. B. 27
Tozer, A. W. 7
Trueblood, Elton 7

Unrau, Hilda 209
Udubre, Lazaro 167-170

Veldcamp, Ruth 140
Voth, John 214-215

Wagner, C. Peter 3, 13, 102
Wall, Debra 247
Wall, Donald 51
Wallis, Jim 108
Walter, Joseph and Janette 134
Walter, Joe M. 31
Walter, Susie Hofer 31, 139, 197
Warner, Timothy M. 258
Watson, D. Jeanene 249-250
Weir, Benjamin 169
Welter, Paul 120, 121, 155
Wenger, John C. 25-26, 72, 74, 76, 110
Werning, Waldo J. 193
Wesley, Charles 229
Wesley, John 74-75, 141, 149, 229
Willard, Dallas 7, 71, 197-198
Wingert, Eunice & Norman 115
Winter, Roberta 102
Wise, F. Franklin 20
Wright, H. Norman 176
Wyclif, John 109

Yoder, John Howard 26, 86, 95, 134, 166, 218

Zettersten, Rolf 23
Zijpp, Nann Van der 95
Zinzendorf, Count Nicolaus 140-141, 229
Zunkel, C. Wayne 91